THE BOOK OF WI-FI
Install, Configure, and Use
802.11b Wireless Networking

THE BOOK

of

WI - FI

INSTALL, CONFIGURE, AND USE *802.11B* WIRELESS NETWORKING

John Ross

**NO STARCH
PRESS**

San Francisco

Publisher: William Pollock
Managing Editor: Karol Jurado
Cover and Interior Design: Octopod Studios
Technical Reviewer: Mike Kershaw
Composition: Octopod Studios
Proofreader: Stephanie Provines
Indexer: Broccoli Information Management

Distributed to the book trade in the United States by Publishers Group West, 1700 Fourth Street, Berkeley, CA 94710; phone: 800-788-3123; fax: 510-658-1834.

Distributed to the book trade in Canada by Jacqueline Gross & Associates, Inc., One Atlantic Avenue, Suite 105, Toronto, Ontario M6K 3E7 Canada; phone: 416-531-6737; fax 416-531-4259.

For information on translations or book distributors outside the United States, please see our distributors list in the back of this book or contact No Starch Press, Inc. directly:

No Starch Press, Inc.
555 De Haro Street, Suite 250, San Francisco, CA 94107
phone: 415-863-9900; fax: 415-863-9950; info@nostarch.com; http://www.nostarch.com

Library of Congress Cataloging-in-Publication Data
Ross, John, 1947-
   The book of Wi-Fi: install, configure, and use 802.11b wireless networking / John Ross.
            p. cm.
   ISBN 1-886411-45-X
1. Wireless LANs--Installation. 2. Wireless LANs--Standards. I. Title.

TK5105.78.R67 2003
004.6'8--dc21
                      2003000711

You see, wire telegraph is a kind of a very, very long cat. You pull his tail in New York and his head is meowing in Los Angeles. Do you understand this? And radio operates exactly the same way: you send signals here, they receive them there. The only difference is there is no cat.

—Albert Einstein

ACKNOWLEDGMENTS

Everything in this book has been improved by the attention of the editorial and production folks at No Starch Press, including Karol Jurado, Andy Carroll, Octopod Studios, and Stephanie Provines. And I'm particularly grateful to Bill Pollock for suggesting the book in the first place.

Thanks also to the nice people at Orinoco, Zoom, and D-Link, who provided wireless equipment that allowed me to compare and contrast an assortment of network adapters, access points, and software; to Karen Anderson, for allowing me to play with her AirPort network; and to Dave Pinion and Tom Eckels at Hatfield & Dawson, for their technical guidance and advice.

Wireless networking has been subjected to a rapidly-changing business environment over the last couple of years, as service providers have come and gone, and the technical standards have evolved. Glenn Fleishman's *802.11b Networking News* (80211b.weblogger.com) has been a hugely valuable resource in keeping up with it all.

BRIEF CONTENTS

CONTENTS IN DETAIL

1
HOW WI-FI WORKS

2
WHAT YOU NEED FOR WIRELESS

3

INSTALLING AND CONFIGURING ACCESS POINTS

4

INSTALLING AND CONFIGURING NETWORK INTERFACES

5

WI-FI FOR WINDOWS

6

WI-FI FOR MACINTOSH

7

WI-FI FOR LINUX

8

WI-FI FOR UNIX

9

WI-FI FOR PDAS AND OTHER HANDHELD DEVICES

10

EXTENDING THE NETWORK BEYOND YOUR OWN WALLS

11

POINT-TO-POINT LINKS AND REPEATERS

12

PUBLIC AND COMMUNITY NETWORKS

13

GUERILLA NETWORKING

14

WIRELESS NETWORK SECURITY

15

VIRTUAL PRIVATE NETWORKS

16

TIPS AND TROUBLESHOOTING

INDEX

245

INTRODUCTION

Wireless links between local computers and wireless access to the Internet are two more steps toward the Internet's ultimate domination of everything in the known universe. Live connections from anywhere in a building, or even an entire college campus or office park without the need to find a place to plug in a wire can make the network and the tools connected to the network much more flexible. And quick access to the Internet from a coffee shop, an airport concourse or a conference center can change the way you work and play online when you're away from home base.

This book will help you understand the most popular wireless Ethernet system, known as 802.11b, or Wi-Fi, and help you select and install the network adapters, base stations and antennas that you will need to install and use a wireless network at home, at work, and in public spaces. It includes information about using Wi-Fi networks with computers running Microsoft Windows, Macintosh, Linux and Unix, and explains how to connect computers running different operating systems to a single network. It should also give you some ideas about how to make the best use of your wireless network after you have installed it and how to deal with the security issues related to operating a wireless network.

As you read the book, I hope you will keep a couple of important things in mind: first, an ideal wireless network should be absolutely invisible — once it's up and running, you should never have to think about it; the real point of the exercise ought to be exchanging messages or viewing the contents of a Web site rather than tweaking the antenna or changing your encryption key. A wireless network, and for that matter, any kind of computer or network is supposed to be a tool rather than a final product. Remember that your original goal was to find out if the Red Sox won, or to invite your friends to a dinner party, or read your class notes, or listen to a radio station in Scotland (as I'm doing while I write this). The wireless link to the Internet is a means to an end, and not the ultimate objective.

Don't install a wireless network if some other type of connection will do the job better. It doesn't matter if the connection is wired, wireless or via carrier pigeons, just as long as it lets you do what you want to do.

And equally important, you are in control. The computer and the network should do things the way you want them to, and they shouldn't force you to adjust your own life or work to meet the needs of the machine. If you have trouble making your Wi-Fi network (or any other computer-related function) work "properly," it's almost always the computer's fault, or the fault of the people who designed the hardware and software. You should be the master, and not the servant.

Wireless networking is still an evolving technology, so the information in this book represents a snapshot of a moving target — within another year, some of the hardware manufacturers and some wireless network service suppliers will certainly have merged or suspended operation, and others will open hundreds of new hot spots. Faster 802.11a base stations and network adapters will move data through the network at higher speed, and new security standards will make your wireless network more difficult to crack. But the general principles described in this book won't change; you'll still need to understand how to configure your computer to send and receive data through a wireless network, and how to move your wireless-enabled computer from one network to another. The best places to learn about new wireless networking features and functions include network hardware manufacturers' marketing literature and Web sites, and third-party Web sites such as the 802.11b Networking News site (http://802.11b.weblogger.com/).

It would be nice to think that this book will become a constant reference for people who use Wi-Fi networks, but if that happens, I've probably failed to give you the information you will need to set up and use your network. I have tried to include all the information necessary to install and use a network, but once it's up and running, you shouldn't have to think about it. You'll just fire up the computer and start exchanging data and messages with your network. After reading this book (even if you skip the chapters that don't interest you), you'll have a better idea of how Wi-Fi works and how to use it to your own best advantage than most people who use wireless networks. And that ought to be worth a lot more than the time and money you've invested in the book.

John Ross
Seattle, WA

1

HOW WI-FI WORKS

Up to a point, it's quite possible to treat your wireless network as a set of black boxes that you can turn on and use without knowing much about the way they work. That's the way most people relate to all of the technology that surrounds them—you shouldn't have to worry about the 802.11b specification to connect your laptop computer to a network. In an ideal world (ha!), it would work just as soon as you turn on the power switch.

But wireless Ethernet today is about where broadcast radio was in 1923. The technology was out there, but people spent a lot of time tweaking their equipment. And the people who understood what was happening behind that Bakelite-Dilecto panel were able to get better performance from their radios than the ones who expected to just turn on the power switch and listen.

In order to make the most effective use of wireless networking technology, it's still important to understand what's going on inside the box (or in this case, inside each of the boxes that makes up the network). This chapter describes the standards and specifications that control wireless networks, and it explains how data moves through the network from one computer to another.

Figure 1.1: Every new technology goes through the tweak-and-fiddle stage

When the network is working properly, you should be able to use it without thinking about all of this internal plumbing—just click a few icons on your computer's screen, and you're connected. But when you're designing and building a new network, or when you want to tweak the performance of an existing network, it can be essential to know how all that data is supposed to move from one place to another. And when the network does something you aren't expecting it to do, you will need a basic knowledge of the technology to do any kind of useful troubleshooting.

Moving data through a wireless network involves three separate elements: the radio signals, the data format, and the network structure. Each of these elements is independent of the other two, so it's necessary to define all three when you invent a new network. In terms of the familiar OSI (Open Systems Interconnection) reference model, the radio signal operates at the Physical layer, and the data format controls several of the higher layers. The network structure includes the interface adapters and base stations that send and receive the radio signals.

In a wireless network, the network adapters in each computer convert digital data to radio signals, which they transmit to other devices on the network, and they convert incoming radio signals from other network elements back to digital data. The IEEE (Institute of Electrical and Electronics Engineers) has produced a set of standards and specifications for wireless networks under the title "IEEE 802.11" that defines the format and structure of those signals.

The original 802.11 standard (without the "b" at the end) was released in 1997. It covers several different types of wireless media: two kinds of radio transmissions (which we'll explain later in this chapter) and networks that use infrared light. The more recent 802.11b standard provides additional specifications for wireless Ethernet networks. A related document, IEEE 802.11a, describes wireless networks that operate at higher speeds on different radio frequencies. Still other 802.11 radio networking standards with other letters are also moving toward public release.

The specification in widest use today is 802.11b. That's the *de facto* standard used by just about every wireless Ethernet LAN that you are likely to encounter in offices and public spaces and in most home networks. It's worth the trouble to keep an eye on the progress of those other standards, but for the moment, 802.11b is the one to use, especially if you're expecting to connect to networks where you don't control all the hardware yourself.

NOTE *The wireless networks described in this book follow the 802.11b standard, but much of the same information also applies to other kinds of 802.11 networks.*

You ought to know about two more names in the alphabet soup of wireless LAN standards: WECA and Wi-Fi. WECA (Wireless Ethernet Compatibility Alliance) is an industry group that includes all of the major manufacturers of 802.11b equipment. Their twin missions are to test and certify that wireless network devices from all of their member companies can operate together in the same network and to promote 802.11 networks as the worldwide standard for wireless LANs. WECA's marketing geniuses adopted the more "friendly" name of Wi-Fi (short for Wireless Fidelity) for the 802.11 specifications and changed their own name to the Wi-Fi Alliance.

Once or twice a year, the Alliance conducts an "interoperability bake-off" where engineers from many hardware manufacturers confirm that their hardware will communicate correctly with equipment from other suppliers. Network equipment that carries the Wi-Fi logo has been certified to meet the relevant standards, and to pass those interoperability tests. Figure 1.2 shows the Wi-Fi logos on network adapters from two different manufacturers.

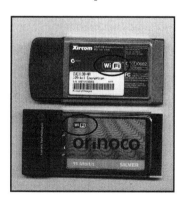

Figure 1.2: Network adapters with the Wi-Fi logo

Radio Signals

802.11b networks operate in a special band of radio frequencies around 2.4 GHz that have been reserved in most parts of the world for unlicensed point-to-point spread-spectrum radio services.

The *unlicensed* part means that anybody using equipment that complies with the technical requirements can send and receive radio signals on these frequencies, without the need for a radio station license. Unlike most radio services, which require licenses that grant exclusive use of a frequency to a single user or group of users, and which restrict the use of that frequency to a specific type of service, an unlicensed service is a free-for-all, where everybody has an equal claim on the same piece of the spectrum. In theory, the technology of spread-spectrum radio makes it possible to coexist with other users (up to a point) without significant interference.

A *point-to-point* radio service operates a communication channel that carries information from a transmitter to a single receiver. The opposite of point-to-point is a *broadcast* service (such as a radio or television station) that sends the same signal to many receivers at the same time.

Spread spectrum is a family of methods for transmitting a single radio signal using a relatively wide segment of the radio spectrum. Wireless Ethernet networks use two different spread-spectrum radio transmission systems, called FHSS (frequency-hopping spread spectrum) and DSSS (direct-sequence spread spectrum). Some older 802.11 networks use the slower FHSS system, but the current generation of 802.11b and 802.11a wireless Ethernet networks use DSSS.

Spread-spectrum radio offers some important advantages over other types of radio signals that use a single narrow channel. Spread spectrum is extremely efficient, so the radio transmitters can operate with very low power. Because they operate on a relatively wide band of frequencies, they are less sensitive to interference from other radio signals and electrical noise, which means that the signals are often able to get through in environments where a conventional narrow-band signal would be impossible to receive and understand, and because a frequency-hopping spread-spectrum signal shifts among multiple channels, it can be extremely difficult for an unauthorized listener to intercept and decode the contents of a signal.

Spread-spectrum technology has an interesting history. It was invented by the actress Hedy Lamarr and the American avant-garde composer George Antheil as a "Secret Communication System" for directing radio-controlled torpedoes that would not be subject to enemy jamming. Before she came to Hollywood, Lamarr had been married to an arms merchant in Austria, where she learned about the problems of torpedo guidance at dinner parties with her husband's customers. Years later, during World War II, she came up with the concept of changing radio frequencies to cut through interference.

Antheil turned out to be the ideal person to make this idea work. His most famous composition was something called *Ballet Mechanique,* which was scored for 16 player pianos, two airplane propellers, four xylophones, four bass drums, and a siren. He used the same kind of mechanism that he had previously used to synchronize the player pianos to change radio frequencies in a spread-spectrum transmission. The original slotted paper-tape system had 88 different radio channels—one for each of the 88 keys on a piano.

In theory, the same method could be used for voice and data communication as well as guiding torpedoes, but in the days of vacuum tubes, paper tape, and mechanical synchronization, the whole process was too complicated to actually build and use. By 1962, solid-state electronics had replaced the vacuum tubes and piano rolls, and the technology was used aboard U.S. Navy ships for secure communications during the Cuban Missile Crisis. Today, spread-spectrum radios are used in the U.S. Air Force Space Command's Milstar satellite communications system, in digital cellular telephones, and in wireless data networks.

Frequency-Hopping Spread Spectrum (FHSS)

Lamarr and Antheil's original design for spread-spectrum radio used a frequency-hopping system. As the name suggests, FHSS technology divides a radio signal into small segments and "hops" from one frequency to another many times per second as it transmits those segments. The transmitter and the receiver establish a synchronized hopping pattern that sets the sequence order in which they will use different subchannels.

FHSS systems overcome interference from other users by using a narrow carrier signal that changes frequency many times every second. Additional transmitter and receiver pairs can use different hopping patterns on the same set of subchannels at the same time. At any given point in time, each transmission is probably using a different subchannel, so there's no interference between signals. When a conflict does occur, the system resends the same packet until the receiver gets a clean copy and sends a confirmation back to the transmitting station.

For wireless data services, the unlicensed 2.4 GHz band is split into 75 subchannels, each of them 1 MHz wide. Because each frequency hop adds overhead to the data stream, FHSS transmissions are relatively slow.

Direct-Sequence Spread Spectrum (DSSS)

DSSS technology uses a method called an 11-chip Barker sequence to spread the radio signal through a single 22 MHz–wide channel without changing frequencies. Each DSSS link uses just one channel, without any hopping between frequencies. As Figure 1.3 shows, a DSSS transmission uses more bandwidth but less power than a conventional signal. The digital signal on the left is a conventional transmission, in which the power is concentrated within a tight bandwidth. The DSSS signal on the right uses the same amount of power, but it spreads that power across a wider band of radio frequencies. Obviously, the 22 MHz DSSS channel is a lot wider than the 1 MHz channels used in FHSS systems.

A DSSS transmitter breaks each bit in the original data stream into a series of redundant bit patterns called *chips* and transmits them to a receiver that reassembles the chips back into a data stream that is identical to the original. Because most interference is likely to occupy a narrower bandwidth than a DSSS signal, and because each bit is divided into several chips, the receiver can usually identify noise and reject it before it decodes the signal.

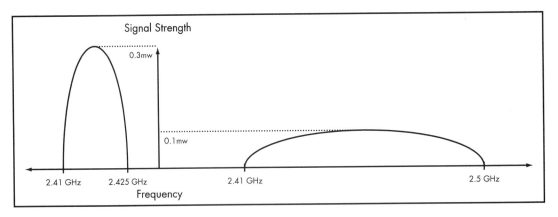

Figure 1.3: Conventional and DSSS radio signals

Like other networking protocols, a DSSS wireless link exchanges *handshaking* messages within each data packet to confirm that the receiver can understand each packet. The standard data transmission rate in an 802.11b DSSS network is 11 Mbps, but when the signal quality won't support that speed, the transmitter and receiver use a process called *dynamic rate shifting* to drop the speed down to 5.5 Mbps. The speed might drop because there's a source of electrical noise near the receiver or because the transmitter and receiver are too far apart to support full-speed operation. If 5.5 Mbps is still too fast for the link to handle, it drops again, down to 2 Mbps, or even 1 Mbps.

Frequency Allocations

By international agreement, a window of the radio spectrum near 2.4 GHz is supposed to be reserved for unlicensed industrial, scientific, and medical services, including spread-spectrum wireless data networks. However, the exact frequency allocations are slightly different from one part of the world to another; the authorities in different countries have assigned slightly different frequency bands. Table 1.1 lists the frequency assignments in several locations.

Table 1.1: Unlicensed 2.4 GHz Spread-Spectrum Frequency Assignments

Region	Frequency Band
North America	2.4000 to 2.4835 GHz
Europe	2.4000 to 2.4835 GHz
France	2.4465 to 2.4835 GHz
Spain	2.445 to 2.475 GHz
Japan	2.471 to 2.497 GHz

Just about every other country in the world also uses one of these bands. Those minor differences in frequency allocations are not particularly important (unless you plan to transmit across the border between France and Spain, or something equally unlikely), because most networks operate entirely within a single country or region, and the normal signal range is usually just a few hundred feet. There's also enough overlap among the various national standards to allow the same equipment to operate legally anywhere in the world. You might have to set your network adapter to a different channel number when you take it abroad, but there's almost always a way to connect, assuming there's a network within range of your adapter.

In North America, Wi-Fi devices use 11 channels. Many other countries have authorized 13 channels, but Japan uses 14 channels, and only 4 are available in France. Fortunately, the entire world uses the same set of channel numbers, so Channel 9 in New York uses exactly the same frequency as Channel 9 in Tokyo or Paris. Table 1.2 lists the channels used in different countries and regions. Canada and some other countries use the same channel assignments as the United States.

Table 1.2: Wireless Ethernet Channel Assignments

Channel	Frequency (MHz) and Location
1	2412 (U.S., Europe, and Japan)
2	2417 (U.S., Europe, and Japan)
3	2422 (U.S., Europe, and Japan)
4	2427 (U.S., Europe, and Japan)
5	2432 (U.S., Europe, and Japan)
6	2437 (U.S., Europe, and Japan)
7	2442 (U.S., Europe, and Japan)
8	2447 (U.S., Europe, and Japan)
9	2452 (U.S., Europe, and Japan)
10	2457 (U.S., Europe, France, and Japan)
11	2462 (U.S., Europe, France, and Japan)
12	2467 (Europe, France, and Japan)
13	2472 (Europe, France, and Japan)
14	2484 (Japan only)

If you're not sure which channels to use in some other country, consult the local regulatory authority for specific information. Or use Channels 10 and 11, which are legal everywhere.

Note that the frequency specified for each of those channels is actually the center frequency of a 22 MHz channel. Therefore, each channel overlaps several other channels that are above and below it. The whole 2.4 GHz band has space for only three completely separate channels, so if your network runs on, say, Channel 4, and your neighbor is using Channel 5 or Channel 6, each network will detect the other network's signals as interference. Both networks will work, but the performance (as reflected in the data transfer speed) will not be as good as it would be when the channels are more widely separated from one another.

To minimize this kind of interference, you should try to coordinate channel use with nearby network managers. If possible, each network should use channels that are at least 25 MHz, or six channel numbers, apart. If you're trying to eliminate interference between two networks, use one high channel number and one low number. For three channels, your best choices are Channels 1, 6, and 11, as shown in Figure 1.4. For more than three networks, you'll have to put up with some amount of interference, but you can keep it to a minimum by assigning a new channel in the middle of an existing pair.

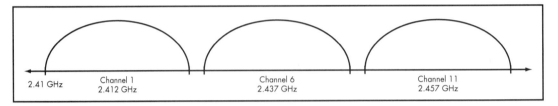

| 2.41 GHz | Channel 1 2.412 GHz | Channel 6 2.437 GHz | Channel 11 2.457 GHz |

Figure 1.4: Channels 1, 6, and 11 do not interfere with one another

This all sounds like a more serious problem than it is likely to be on the ground. In practice, you can optimize the performance of your network by staying away from a channel that somebody else is using, but even if you and your neighbor are on adjacent channels, your networks will probably work just fine. You're more likely to have problems with interference from other devices using the 2.4 GHz band, such as cordless telephones and microwave ovens.

The 802.11 specifications and various national regulatory agencies (such as the Federal Communications Commission in the United States) have also set limits on the amount of transmitter power and antenna gain that a wireless Ethernet device can use. This restriction is intended to limit the distance that a network link can travel, and therefore to allow more networks to operate on the same channels without interference. We'll talk about methods for working around those power limits and extending the range of your wireless network without violating the law later in this book.

Moving Data Around

So now we have a bunch of radio transmitters and receivers that all operate on the same frequencies and all use the same kind of modulation (*modulation* is the method a radio uses to add some kind of content, such as voice or digital data, to a radio wave). The next step is to send some network data through those radios.

To begin, let's quickly recap the general structure of computer data and the methods networks use to move that data from one place to another. This is very basic stuff that might already be familiar to you, but bear with me for a couple of pages. This really will help you to understand how a wireless network operates.

Bits and Bytes

As you probably know, the processing unit of a computer can recognize only two information states: either a signal is present at the input to the processor, or there is no signal there. These two conditions are usually described as 1 and 0, or on and off, or mark and space. Each instance of a 1 or a 0 is a *bit*.

Individual bits are not particularly useful, but when you string eight of them together (into a *byte*), you can have 256 different combinations. That's enough to assign different sequences to all the letters in the alphabet (both uppercase and lowercase), the ten digits from 0 to 9, spaces between words, and other symbols, such as punctuation marks and some letters used in foreign alphabets. A modern computer recognizes and processes several 8-bit bytes at the same time. When processing is complete, the computer uses the same bit code at its output. The output might be connected to a printer, a video display, or a data communications channel. Or it might be something else entirely, such as a series of flashing lights.

The inputs and outputs that we're concerned about here are the ones that form a communications circuit. Like the computer processor, a data channel can recognize only one bit at a time. Either there's a signal on the line or there isn't.

Over short distances, it's possible to send the data through a cable that carries eight (or some multiple of eight) signals *in parallel* through separate wires. Obviously, a parallel connection can be eight times faster than sending one bit through a single wire, but those eight wires cost eight times as much as a single wire. When you're trying to send the data over a long distance, that additional cost can be prohibitive. And when you're using existing circuits, such as telephone lines, you don't have any choice; you must find a way to send all eight bits through the same wire (or other media).

The solution is to transmit one bit at a time, with some additional bits and pauses that identify the beginning of each new byte. This is a *serial* data communications channel, because you're sending bits one after another. At this stage, it doesn't matter what medium you use to transmit those bits — it could be electrical impulses on a wire, or two different audio tones, or a series of flashing lights, or even a lot of notes attached to the legs of carrier pigeons — but you must have a method for converting the output of the computer to the signals used by the transmission medium, and converting it back again at the other end.

Error Checking

In a perfect transmission circuit, the signal that goes in at one end will be absolutely identical to the one that comes out at the other end. But in the real world, there's almost always some kind of noise that can interfere with the original pure signal. *Noise* is defined as anything that is added to the original signal; it can be caused by a lightning strike, interference from another communications channel, or dirt on an electrical contact someplace in the circuit (or in the case of those carrier pigeons, an attack by a marauding hawk). Whatever the source, noise in the channel can interrupt the flow of data. In a modern communications system, those bits are pouring through the circuit extremely quickly — millions of them every second — so even a noise hit for a fraction of a second can obliterate enough bits to turn your data into digital gibberish.

Therefore, you must include a process called *error checking* in your data stream. Error checking is accomplished by adding some kind of standard information called a *checksum* to each byte; if the receiving device discovers that the checksum is not what it expected, it instructs the transmitter to send the same byte again.

Handshaking

Of course, the computer that originates a message or a stream of data can't just jump online and start sending bytes. First it has to warn the device at the other end that it is ready to send and make sure the intended recipient is ready to accept data. To accomplish this, a series of *handshaking* requests and answers must surround the actual data.

The sequence of requests goes something like this:

Origin: "Hey destination! I have some data for you."

Destination: "Okay, origin, go ahead. I'm ready."

Origin: "Here comes the data."

Origin: Data data data data . . .

Origin: "That's the message. Did you get it?"

Destination: "I got something, but it appears to be damaged."

Origin: "Here it is again."

Origin: Data data data data . . .

Origin: "Did you get it that time?"

Destination: "Yup, I got it. I'm ready for more data."

Finding the Destination

A communication over a direct physical connection between the origin and destination doesn't need to include any kind of address or routing information as part of the message. You might have to set up the connection first (by placing a telephone call or plugging cables into a switchboard), but after you're connected, the link remains in place until you instruct the system to disconnect. This kind of connection is great for voice and for simple data links, but it's not particularly efficient for digital data on a complex network that serves many origins and destinations because it ties up the circuit all the time, even when no data is moving through the channel.

The alternative is to send your message to a switching center that will hold it until a link to the destination becomes available. This is known as a *store and forward* system. If the network has been properly designed for the type of data and the amount of traffic in the system, the waiting time will be insignificant. If the communications network covers a lot of territory, you can forward the message to one or more intermediate switching centers before it reaches the ultimate destination. The great advantage of this approach is that many messages can share the same circuits on an as-available basis.

To make the network even more efficient, you can divide messages that are longer than some arbitrary limit into separate pieces, called *packets*. Packets from more than one message can travel together on the same circuit, combine with packets containing other messages as they travel between switching centers, and reassemble themselves into the original messages at the destination. Each data packet must contain yet another set of information: the address of the packet's destination, the sequence order of this packet relative to other packets in the original transmission, and so forth. Some of this information instructs the switching centers where to forward each packet, and other information tells the destination device how to reassemble the data in the packet back into the original message.

That same pattern is repeated every time you add another layer of activity to a communications system. Each layer may attach additional information to the original message and strip off that information after it has done whatever the added information instructed it to do. By the time a message travels from a laptop computer on a wireless network through an office LAN and an Internet gateway to a distant computer connected to another LAN, a dozen or more information attachments might be added and removed before the recipient reads the original text. A package of data that includes address and control information ahead of the bits that contain the content of the message, followed by an error-checking sequence, is called a *frame*. Both wired and wireless networks divide the data stream into frames that contain various forms of handshaking information along with the original data.

It might be helpful to think of these bits, bytes, packets, and frames as the digital version of a letter that you send through a complicated delivery system:

1. You write a letter and put it into an envelope. The address of the letter's recipient is on the outside of the envelope.

2. You take the letter to the mailroom, where a clerk puts your envelope into a bigger Express Mail envelope. The big envelope has the name and address of the office where the recipient works.

3. The mailroom clerk takes the big envelope to the post office, where another clerk puts it into a mail sack. The post office attaches a tag to the sack, marked with the location of the post office that serves the recipient's office.

4. The mail sack goes onto a truck to the airport, where it gets loaded into a shipping container along with other sacks going to the same destination city. The shipping container has a label that tells the freight handlers there's mail inside.

5. The freight handlers place the container inside an airplane.

6. At this point, your letter is inside your envelope, which is inside the Express Mail envelope, which is inside a mail sack, inside a container, inside an airplane. The airplane flies to another airport, near the destination city.

7. At the destination airport, the ground crew unloads the container from the airplane.

8. The freight handlers remove the sack from the shipping container and put it on another truck.

9. The truck takes the sack to a post office near the recipient's office.

10. At the post office, another mail clerk takes the big envelope out of the sack and gives it to a letter carrier.

11. The letter carrier delivers the big Express Mail envelope to the recipient's office.

12. The receptionist in the office takes your envelope out of the Express Mail envelope and gives it to the final recipient.

13. The recipient opens your envelope and reads the letter.

At each level, the information on the outside of the package tells somebody how to handle it, but that person doesn't much care what's inside. Neither you nor the person who ultimately reads your letter ever sees the big Express Mail envelope, the mail sack, the truck, the container, or the airplane, but every one of those packages plays an important part in moving your letter from here to there.

Instead of envelopes, sacks, and containers, an electronic message uses strings of data to tell the system how and where to handle your message, but the end result is just about the same. In the OSI network model, each mode of transportation would be a separate layer.

Fortunately, the network software automatically adds and removes all of the preambles, addresses, checksums, and other information, so you and the person receiving your message should never see them. However, each item added to the original data increases the size of the packet, frame, or other package, and therefore it increases the amount of time necessary to transmit the data through the network. Because the nominal data transfer speed includes all the overhead information along with the "real" data, the actual data transfer speed through a wireless network is a lot slower. In other words, even if your network connects at 11 Mbps, your actual file transfer speed might only be about 6 or 7 Mbps.

802.11b Wireless Network Controls

The 802.11b specification controls the way data moves through the Physical layer (the radio link), and it defines a Media Access Control (MAC) layer that handles the interface between the Physical layer and the rest of the network structure.

The Physical Layer

In an 802.11 network, the radio transmitter adds a 144-bit preamble to each packet, including 128 bits that the receiver uses to synchronize the receiver with the transmitter and a 16-bit start-of-frame field. This is followed by a 48-bit header that contains information about the data transfer speed, the length of the data contained in the packet, and an error-checking sequence. This header is called the *PHY preamble* because it controls the Physical layer of the communications link.

Because the header specifies the speed of the data that follows it, the preamble and the header are always transmitted at 1 Mbps. Therefore, even if a network link is operating at the full 11 Mbps, the effective data transfer speed is considerably slower. In practice, the best you can expect is about 85 percent of the nominal speed. And, of course, the other types of overhead in the data packets reduce the actual speed even more.

That 144-bit preamble is a holdover from the older and slower DSSS systems, and it has stayed in the specification to ensure that 802.11b devices will still be compatible with the older standards, but it really doesn't accomplish anything useful. So there's an optional alternative that uses a shorter, 72-bit preamble. In a short preamble, the synchronization field has 56 bits combined with the same 16-bit start-of-frame field used in long preambles. The 72-bit preamble is not compatible with old 802.11 hardware, but that doesn't matter as long as all the nodes in a network can recognize the short preamble format. In all other respects, a short preamble works just as well as a long one.

It takes the network a maximum of 192 milliseconds to handle a long preamble, compared to 96 milliseconds for a short preamble. In other words, the short preamble cuts the overhead on each packet in half. This makes a significant difference to the actual data throughput, especially for things like streaming audio and video and voice-over-Internet services.

Some manufacturers use the long preamble as the default, and others use the short preamble. It's usually possible to change the preamble length in the configuration software for network adapters and access points.

For most users, preamble length is one of those technical details that you don't have to understand, just as long as it's the same for all the devices in the network. Ten years ago, when telephone modems were the most common way to connect one computer to another, we all had to worry about setting the "data bits" and "stop bits" every time we placed a call through the modem. You probably never knew exactly what a stop bit was (it's the amount of time an old mechanical Teletype printer needed to return to the idle state after sending or receiving each byte), but you knew that it had to be the same at both ends. Preamble length is the same kind of obscure setting: it has to be the same on every node in a network, but most people neither know nor care what it means.

The MAC Layer

The MAC layer controls the traffic that moves through the radio network. It prevents data collisions and conflicts by using a set of rules called Carrier Sense Multiple Access with Collision Avoidance (CSMA/CA), and it supports the security functions specified in the 802.11b standard. When the network includes more than one access point, the MAC layer associates each network client with the access point that provides the best signal quality.

When more than one node in the network tries to transmit data at the same time, CSMA/CA instructs all but one of the conflicting nodes to back off and try again later, and it allows the surviving node to send its packet. CSMA/CA works like this: when a network node is ready to send a packet, it listens for other signals first. If it doesn't hear anything, it waits for a random (but short) period of time and then listens again. If it still doesn't sense a signal, it transmits a packet. The device that receives the packet evaluates it, and if it's intact, the receiving mode returns an acknowledgement. But if the sending node does not receive the acknowledgement, it assumes that there has been a collision with another packet, so it waits for another random interval and then tries again.

CSMA/CA also has an optional feature that sets an access point (the bridge between the wireless LAN and the backbone network) as a point coordinator that can grant priority to a network node that is trying to send time-critical data types, such as voice or streaming media.

The MAC layer can support two kinds of authentication to confirm that a network device is authorized to join the network: *open authentication* and *shared key authentication*. When you configure your network, all the nodes in the network must use the same kind of authentication.

The network supports all of these housekeeping functions in the MAC layer by exchanging (or trying to exchange) a series of control frames before it allows the higher layers to send data. It also sets several options on the network adapter:

- **Power mode**   The network adapter supports two power modes: Continuous Aware Mode and Power Save Polling Mode. In Continuous Aware Mode, the radio receiver is always on and consuming power. In Power Save Polling Mode, the radio is idle much of the time, but it periodically polls the access point for new messages. As the name suggests, Power Save Polling Mode reduces the battery drain on portable devices such as laptop computers and PDAs.

- **Access control**   The network adapter contains the access control that keeps unauthorized users out of the network. An 802.11b network can use two forms of access control: the SSID (the name of the network), and the MAC address (a unique string of characters that identifies each network node). Each network node must have the SSID programmed into it, or the access point will not associate with that node. An optional table of MAC addresses can restrict access to radios whose addresses are on the list.

- **WEP encryption**   The network adapter controls the Wired Equivalent Privacy (WEP) encryption function. The network can use a 64-bit or a 128-bit encryption key to encode and decode data as it passes through the radio link.

Other Control Layers

All of the activity specified in the 802.11 standards takes place at the Physical and MAC layers. The higher layers control things like addressing and routing, data integrity, syntax, and the format of the data contained inside each packet. It doesn't make any difference to these higher layers whether they're moving packets through wires, fiber optic lines, or radio links. Therefore, you can use an 802.11b network with any kind of LAN or other network protocol. The same radios can handle TCP/IP, Novell NetWare, and all the other network protocols built into Windows, Unix, Mac OS, and other operating systems equally well.

Network Devices

Once we have defined the radio links and the data format, the next step is to set up a network structure. How do computers use the radios and the data format to actually exchange data?

802.11b networks include two categories of radios: *stations* and *access points*. A station is a computer, or some other device such as a printer, connected to a wireless network through an internal or external wireless network interface adapter.

An access point is the base station for a wireless network and a bridge between the wireless network and a traditional wired network.

Network Adapters

Network adapters for stations can take several physical forms:

- *Plug-in PC Cards that fit the PCMCIA sockets in most laptop computers*
  To bypass the internal shielding in most computers, the antennas and status lights in most wireless PC Card adapters extend about an inch beyond the opening of the card socket. Other PC Card adapters have sockets for external antennas.

- *Internal network adapters on PCI cards that fit inside a desktop computer*
  Most PCI adapters are actually PCMCIA sockets that allow a user to plug a PC Card into the back of the computer, but a few are built directly on the PCI expansion cards. As an alternative to a rear-panel socket, separate PCMCIA sockets that fit a computer's external front-panel drive bays are available from Actiontec and several other manufacturers.

- *External USB adapters*
  USB adapters are often a better choice than PC Cards, because it's almost always easier to move an adapter at the end of a cable to a position with the best possible signal path to the nearest access point.

- *Internal wireless adapters built into laptop computers*
  Internal adapters are modules that plug into the computer's motherboard. They present the same appearance to the operating system as an external PC Card. The antennas for built-in radios are usually hidden inside the computer's fold-over screen.

- *Plug-in adapters for PDAs and other handheld devices*

- *Internal network interfaces built into other devices, such as Internet-capable telephone sets and office or household appliances*

A network adapter should work with any operating system, as long as a driver for that adapter is available. In practice, that means you can find Windows drivers for just about everything, but you will have fewer choices if you're using a computer running Mac OS, Linux, or Unix. You can find pointers to sources for Linux and Unix drivers in the chapters devoted to those operating systems later in this book.

Access Points

Access points are often combined with other network functions. It's quite possible to find a stand-alone access point that just plugs into a wired LAN through a data cable, but there are plenty of other options. Common access-point configurations include the following:

- Simple base stations with a bridge to an Ethernet port for connection to a LAN
- Base stations that include a switch, hub, or router with one or more wired Ethernet ports along with the wireless access point

- Broadband routers that provide a bridge between a cable modem or DSL port and the wireless access point
- Software access points that use one of the wireless network interface adapters as the base station
- Residential gateways that support a limited number of operating channels

As Figure 1.5 shows, the physical design of access points varies from one manufacturer to another. Some look like industrial devices that were intended to be placed out of sight on the floor or mounted on an inconspicuous wall, but others have swooshy "aerodynamic" shapes that appear to have been designed for the top of a coffee table. Some have internal antennas, others have short vertical whips permanently attached, and still others have connectors for external antennas (which may or may not be supplied with the access point). Regardless of its size and shape, every access point includes a radio that sends and receives messages and data between network stations and an Ethernet port that connects to a wired network.

Figure 1.5: Access points from Zoom and D-Link

Operating Modes

802.11b networks operate in two modes: *ad hoc* networks and *infrastructure* networks. As the name suggests, an ad hoc network is usually temporary. An ad hoc network is a self-contained group of stations with no connection to a larger LAN or the Internet. It includes two or more wireless stations with no access point or connection to the rest of the world. Ad hoc networks are also called peer-to-peer networks and Independent Basic Service Sets (IBSS). Figure 1.6 shows a simple ad hoc network.

Infrastructure networks have one or more access points, almost always connected to a wired network. Each wireless station exchanges messages and data with the access point, which relays them to other nodes on the wireless network or the wired LAN. Any network that requires a wired connection through an access point to a printer, a file server or an Internet gateway is an infrastructure network. Figure 1.7 shows an infrastructure network.

An infrastructure network with just one base station is also called a Basic Service Set (BSS). When the wireless network uses two or more access points, the network structure is an Extended Service Set (ESS). Remember from a few pages back that the technical name for a network ID is the SSID? You might also see it called a BSSID if the network has just one access point, or an ESSID when it has two or more access points.

A network with more than one access point (an Extended Service Set) creates several new complications. First, the network must include a way for only one base station to handle data from a particular station, even if the station is within range of more than one base station. And if the station is moving during a network session,

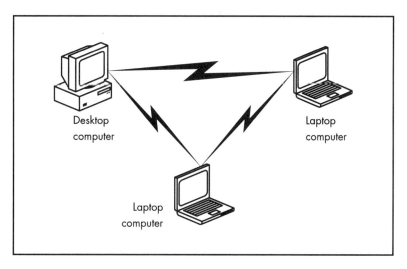

Figure 1.6: An ad hoc wireless network with three stations

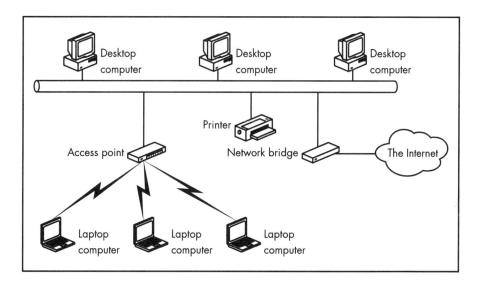

Figure 1.7: A simple infrastructure network

or if some kind of local interference crops up near the first access point, the network might have to hand off the connection from one access point to another. An 802.11b network handles this problem by associating a station with only one access point at a time and ignoring the signals from stations that are not associated. When the signal fades at one access point and improves at another, or the amount of traffic forces the network to rebalance the load, the network will reassociate the station with a new access point that can provide acceptable service. If you think this sounds a lot like the way a cellular telephone system handles roaming, you're absolutely correct; even the terminology is the same — it's called *roaming*.

Putting It All Together

The radio link, the data structure, and the network architecture are the three essential elements that form the internal plumbing of an 802.11b wireless Ethernet network. Like the components of most other networks (and most plumbing systems, for that matter), these elements should be entirely transparent to the people using the network — if users can send and receive messages, read files, and perform other activities on the network, they should never have to worry about the low-level details.

Of course, this assumes that it always works exactly as it's supposed to work, and no users ever have to call a network help desk to ask why they can't read their email. Now that you have read this chapter, you probably know more about the way your wireless LAN moves messages from here to there than 95 percent of the people who use Wi-Fi networks, and you have a good chance of understanding the support person who tells you to make sure you're using Channel 11 or you need to change your preamble length, or your adapter is operating in infrastructure mode.

2

WHAT YOU NEED FOR WIRELESS

A wireless local area network (LAN) requires a somewhat different set of hardware components from a traditional wired network. Obviously, the biggest difference is the absence of wires between the network server and the wireless client computers and other devices that form the network, but that's not the only difference. A Wi-Fi network must also use radio transmitters and receivers as the interface to and from the network and between the wired and wireless portions of the network.

This chapter identifies the components that form a wireless network, and it offers advice about deciding which components will best meet your particular requirements. As you read the descriptions of various features and functions in access points, network adapters, and antennas, remember that the marketplace for wireless networking equipment is extremely competitive, and it's changing rapidly. If one manufacturer offers an access point or network adapter with a hot new feature, you can expect that same feature to show up in competing products within a few months. Therefore, this chapter does not talk about specific brands or models; by the time you read this, any such recommendations would be wildly out-of-date.

Everybody Speaks the Same Language (More or Less)

Before we talk about specific features and functions, it may be useful to review the rules—and the realities—about using 802.11b equipment made by more than one manufacturer in the same wireless network. It can be done, but it's not quite as simple as the people at the Wi-Fi Alliance would have you believe.

Several dozen companies make equipment that qualifies for Wi-Fi certification. In order to receive that certification, each device must undergo interoperability testing by the Wi-Fi Alliance's independent testing lab. If an access point or network adapter carries a Wi-Fi logo, it has passed an extensive series of tests with previously certified hardware from several other vendors.

Access points and network adapters from different manufacturers may look different on the outside, and each maker provides its own configuration software, but the radio circuits inside are all pretty similar. Adapters that carry many brand names are actually made under contract by other companies, and just about everybody uses one of just a few standard chip sets.

In other words, it's possible to use any combination of Wi-Fi–certified adapters and access points together in the same network. The critical word in that last sentence is *possible*. In a carefully run series of tests, under tightly controlled laboratory conditions, a group of technicians who are intimately familiar with the internal workings of 802.11b networks can get a mixed-vendor network to operate properly.

Does that mean that a homeowner or the IT person in a small business who has never installed a wireless network can get that same combination of products to work? Oh, probably, but maybe not on the first attempt. It may take a lot of time and aggravation to set all the configuration options to the correct values. It's almost always a safe bet that devices from different makers will have different default settings. For example, some systems use short preambles as the default, and others use long preambles; some configurations request WEP keys as ASCII characters, but others want them in hexadecimal. You can make all this stuff work together, but it might be a somewhat painful experience.

As a general rule, it's almost always a lot easier to equip your entire network with hardware from a single manufacturer, but that's not always possible, or even the best choice. You can control the brands of access points in your network, and you can buy the same brand of network adapters for your desktop computers, but eventually, one of the users in your office network (and you can probably predict who it will be, can't you?) will come to you with a Wi-Fi adapter made by somebody you've never heard of, and they'll expect it to connect to your network. Maybe the adapter showed up at a garage sale or a swap meet, or it came with a shiny new laptop computer. Or it's the one your daughter's school recommended for its on-campus network. For one reason or another, you'll eventually have to integrate hardware and software from more than one maker into the same network.

The information in this book will help you to understand exactly what you need to do to make everything work together. When you're assembling the first batch of hardware, though, you can reduce the number of headaches by using equipment from a single source.

Network Adapters

A *network adapter* is the interface between a computer and a network. In a wireless network, the adapter contains a radio transmitter that sends data from the computer to the network, and a receiver that detects incoming radio signals that contain data from the network and passes it along to the computer. A wireless adapter presents the same appearance to the computer's operating system as any other network interface.

You should consider several things when you select an interface adapter: the physical package, the type of antenna (captive or external?), compatibility with the network's access points and other nodes in the network, and compatibility with the computer's operating system. And of course, you should also consider all the standard issues that apply to any piece of computer hardware or software: ease of use, quality of technical support, and other users' experiences with the product and the company.

Form Factor

In most cases, the wireless adapter plugs into one of the computer's high-speed I/O ports—either an internal expansion card slot, a PCMCIA socket, or a USB port. The exceptions are late-model laptop computers that include optional internal 802.11b interfaces that use internal expansion slots such as mini-PCI or Apple AirPort, or are mounted on the computers' motherboards. Network adapters for PDAs usually fit into CompactFlash sockets.

Each type of adapter has its own set of advantages and drawbacks. The choice of a particular package depends on the computer you will use with the adapter and the way you expect to use it. For example, if you want to connect a laptop computer to the network, a PC Card is usually the best option because it's easy to install, it doesn't take up much space, and it doesn't force you to carry a special cable. But in a desktop system, an interface adapter on an internal expansion card or a USB adapter is often a better choice.

PC Cards

Network adapters on PC Cards are the most popular type, because the most common use of a wireless Ethernet network is to add laptop computers to existing LANs. Just about every maker of 802.11b devices has at least one PC Card adapter in its product line.

Wireless adapters on PC Cards are compact and don't add much weight to a portable computer, which are both important features. However, it's important to remove the adapter from the computer when you don't need a network link. Otherwise the adapter will continue to radiate unwanted signals and possibly allow an intruder to connect to your computer without your knowledge. Most PC Card adapters have power-saving features, but even when they are inactive they also place a small but unnecessary drain on the computer's battery.

It's particularly important to remove the wireless adapter from your laptop when you carry the computer aboard a commercial airliner. Like cellular telephones and all other radios, the airlines do not permit wireless networks on their aircraft because they might interfere with on-board navigation systems.

PC Card adapters all look pretty much the same because they all have to fit into a computer's PCMCIA socket. As Figure 2.1 shows, they're about the size of a credit card, with a connector at one end and a plastic cover for the internal antenna, or a connector for an external antenna, at the other end.

Figure 2.1: A Xircom Wireless Ethernet Adapter with an internal antenna

Most PC Card adapters include one or two indicator lights on the section of the adapter that extends beyond the end of the PCMCIA slot. One of these indicators lights up when the adapter is receiving power from the computer, and the other lights up when the adapter detects an active radio link from an access point or another node in an ad hoc network.

Many PC Card adapters contain two internal antennas with a diversity system that constantly compares the quality of the incoming signals from each antenna and automatically selects the stronger one. Even though the two antennas inside a PC Card are only an inch or two apart, the improvement over a single antenna can be substantial.

Network adapters on PC Cards usually have built-in omnidirectional diversity antennas, but some manufacturers also offer versions with connectors for external antennas. The choice of internal versus external antenna is always a trade-off. In most cases, the internal antenna is a lot easier to use with a portable computer because it doesn't force you to carry a separate antenna and cable. But it's much easier to adjust the exact location of an antenna at the end of a cable instead of trying to place the side or back of a computer in a position where reception is good and you can comfortably see the screen and reach the keyboard. If you want to link to an access point from the extreme edges of a network's coverage area, or if you're operating in a location with a lot of interference, a separate high-gain directional antenna can give you better and more reliable network performance than the antennas built into most PC Cards.

USB Adapters

If your computer has a USB (universal serial bus) port, as most desktop and laptop computers built since about 1999 do, a wireless USB adapter might be the best way to connect that computer to your 802.11b network. The adapter connects to the computer through a cable, so it's never a problem to move the whole adapter (with its built-in antenna) to the position that provides the best network performance. Even if the optimal location is on top of a bookcase or filing cabinet, or on the floor under your computer table, the location of the adapter won't interfere with your ability to use the computer. It's easier to install a USB adapter than an adapter on an internal expansion card because you don't have to take apart the computer to install a USB device.

USB adapters come in many shapes and sizes, reflecting the design philosophies of the manufacturers. Most USB adapters have captive antennas, often mounted on hinges or swivels that allow a user to make fine adjustments to their positions. Because the antennas on USB adapters are usually larger and easier to manipulate than the antennas in PC Card adapters, you can expect somewhat better signal quality through a USB device (but remember that you won't notice any improvement over the threshold of a full-speed connection).

Figure 2.2 shows a wireless USB adapter from D-Link. Like the adapters on PC Cards, most USB adapters take their power from the computer, so they don't require a separate battery or an external power supply.

Figure 2.2: Wireless USB adapters are stand-alone devices that connect to the computer through a cable

Internal Expansion Cards

The most common internal wireless adapters are actually PC Cards mounted in PCMCIA sockets that fit a PCI or ISA expansion slot. The adapter fits a slot in one of the mounting plates on the back of the computer. This approach offers several advantages for the manufacturers: they can use the same PC Card adapter that they sell separately for use in laptops, combined with a socket that they obtain and relabel from some third party, and the metal housing of the PC Card provides an effective shield that keeps the radio signals away from the inside of the computer.

But it would be difficult to find a worse place to locate the antenna for a wireless adapter than inside a computer. If the adapter has a built-in antenna, you can't easily move it to a different position to improve the signal quality. The card sticks out from the back of the computer cabinet where you can't see the indicator lights. The backs of most desktop computers are usually rats' nests of other cables and connectors that can all affect the radio's radiation pattern. And the computer's metal backplane may act as either an obstruction or a source of multipath interference between the adapter and the nearest access point.

Of course, it's entirely possible that a PCI or ISA adapter will perform flawlessly, right out of the box; don't assume that it won't work until you have actually tried it in your own network.

If you do encounter problems, there are a couple of ways to work around them. If the computer has a USB port, then a wireless USB adapter is the obvious choice. Even if there's no obvious USB port on the outside of the computer, it's possible that the motherboard has a USB port; if it does, you can use an inexpensive cable and bracket to bring the port out to the backplane. For older motherboards that don't have USB ports, add-in USB ports on PCI or ISA expansion cards are a possible alternative.

If a USB adapter is not an option, go ahead and try an internal adapter. In spite of the shortcomings, it will probably work quite adequately in most places.

If signal quality is a problem, look for an adapter that has a connector for an external antenna, rather than an antenna built into the adapter itself. Adapters with external antenna connectors are available from Cisco, Orinoco, and Zoom, among others.

You may also want to consider a network adapter on a PC Card with a card reader that mounts in a spare external drive bay on the front of a desktop or tower computer, rather than the backplane. This makes the adapter much easier to reach than it would be at the back of the computer and moves it away from the tangle of other cables and plugs behind the computer.

Internal Adapters

Several major brands of laptop computers have begun to appear with internal 802.11b network interface adapters as an optional feature. These computers have an adapter module mounted directly onto the motherboard, with the antenna inside the "clamshell" section that also holds the display screen.

The obvious advantage of an internal adapter is that it doesn't force a user to carry (and possibly forget or lose) yet another accessory item along with the computer. The disadvantage, if there is one, is that it's not practical to move the same adapter to a different computer when it's time to repair or replace the original machine. If the backup unit doesn't have an internal adapter (which is likely, since it's probably older than the primary one), the user or the network manager will have to either provide a separate adapter on a PC Card or go without access to the network.

Internal wireless adapters will probably be extremely common in the next generation of portable computers. The cost is about the same as a separate PC Card for a much more convenient configuration. It doesn't make sense to replace your current laptop for a new one with internal wireless access, but when it's time to look for a new computer, it might be a feature worth adding.

If you do use an internal wireless adapter, make sure you have an easy way to disable the adapter when you aren't using it. Otherwise, the radio unit will drain your computer's battery more quickly than necessary, and it will produce radio signals that can interfere with other users of the same unlicensed 2.4 GHz frequencies.

Internal vs. External Antennas

Many access points and most wireless network adapters come with captive omnidirectional antennas. For most users, in most situations, those built-in antennas will send and receive a strong, clean data stream between an access point and a nearby computer. But if network adapters with built-in antennas don't provide a good enough signal, because of distance, obstructions, or interference from other radio signals, an external antenna may be the best way to solve the problem. As a rule of thumb, you can expect an external antenna to provide a signal at least 15 percent stronger than the antenna built into a PC Card adapter.

If you identify a dead spot in your coverage area, a network adapter with a connector for an external antenna instead of a built-in antenna may be the right choice for a network node that remains in that location, such as a desktop computer in a difficult location, but it's a lot more cumbersome to set up a separate antenna before you can log on to the network, so PC Cards with built-in antennas are generally the best choice for laptops and other portables.

Remember that there are two antennas in the link between a base station and a wireless network adapter—one at each end. A high-gain antenna at either end will have the same impact on the link, so it will be equally effective to replace the standard antenna on either the access point or the network interface. However, a directional antenna will focus most of the signal in one direction, so a directional access-point antenna can reduce the quality of links to other network nodes, as shown in Figure 2.3.

You can find more information about external antennas in the aptly named "External Antennas" section later in this chapter.

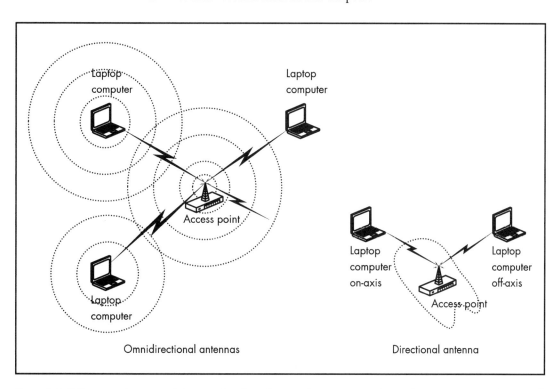

Figure 2.3: Different combinations of directional and nondirectional antennas can change the coverage area of a network

Interoperability

Wi-Fi certification is supposed to ensure that network adapters and access points from different manufacturers will work together seamlessly, but there are a few features and configuration options that can make it difficult or impossible to exchange data between certain combinations of hardware. For example, some devices come with 128-bit encryption keys, but others support only 64-bit keys. If an access point expects 128 bits, it won't work with the smaller key.

The easiest way to avoid this is to acquire all of your hardware from the same source and make sure you're not using incompatible models (such as the two types of Orinoco network cards with 64-bit and 128-bit WEP keys). Otherwise, test every new component type with the rest of your network as soon as you receive it, and make sure your vendor will accept a return if it isn't compatible.

Operating System Compatibility

Like every other peripheral device you use with your computer, a wireless network adapter requires specific driver software that contains the controls and interfaces that allow the adapter to exchange data with the computer's central processor. You can safely assume that the software disk supplied with the adapter includes a driver for Microsoft Windows, but that won't do any good if you're trying to link a computer that uses Linux or some flavor of Unix to your network. If you're a Macintosh user, Apple's AirPort adapters, or the more-or-less identical Orinoco adapters may be the best choice.

If you don't get the right driver software with your network adapter, you'll have to find it someplace else or choose a different adapter that does support your operating system. The first place to look is the manufacturer's own technical support Web site, which probably offers a variety of drivers for free download. If you can't find anything there, send a request for information to the manufacturer's tech support center; they might know of a third-party driver for your operating system or invite you to help test a new driver they haven't yet released.

Don't give up if the manufacturer can't help you. Many adapters contain similar internal circuits, so it may be possible to use a driver with one adapter that was originally created for a different brand. For example, the Xircom CWE1100 adapter uses the same drivers as similar adapters from Cisco. Take a look at Chapters 8 and 9 of this book for other sources of drivers for Linux and Unix from user groups and online archives.

Without a driver, your adapter is only useful as a paperweight. If you can't find the right driver for your operating system, look for a different adapter.

Ease of Use

Every wireless adapter uses a configuration utility program that controls the operating mode, the channel number, and all of the other configuration options that must match the settings for the other nodes on the same network. The manufacturer usually supplies the configuration program on a CD or diskette supplied with the adapter, but a more recent version may be available for free download from a Web site.

Each configuration program organizes the optional settings and status information displays differently. Some use a single window with all the options in one place, while others split things into several separate sections. Some display signal strength and quality as a numeric value, but others show the same data in graphic form. Figures 2.4 and 2.5 show two different approaches to presenting the same information.

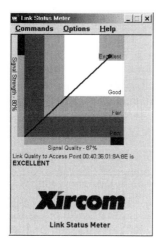

Figure 2.4: Xircom's Link Status Meter shows the signal strength and quality in a graphic display. Cisco uses a similar tool.

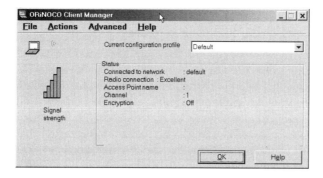

Figure 2.5: The Orinoco Client Manager shows the current network status as text

Under ideal conditions, a day-to-day user would never have to look at the configuration utility. But when that user wants to move to a different location or log on to a different network, the configuration settings and options will suddenly become very important. Unfortunately, it's about as complicated to configure a wireless network connection today as it was to set up a data link through a telephone modem years ago. In those days, it was necessary to worry about setting things like "stop bits" and "terminal emulation" every time you tried to place a call. Today, wireless network users have to deal with things like "preamble length" that are just as obscure and equally essential.

So the configuration utility and the status display should both be easy to understand and use. They all contain the same information and options, so the choice comes down to a subjective evaluation: Can you look at the configuration window and understand how to change the settings? Does the status display tell you at a glance whether or not you have a usable link to the network? As a famous cartoonist said about a long-ago election, "You pays your money and you takes your choice."

Security

The 802.11b specification includes a security scheme called WEP (Wired Equivalence Privacy) that uses either a 64-bit or 128-bit encryption key. The format of 64-bit encryption is a common standard, but there are some differences among the 128-bit encryption techniques provided by different manufacturers. Therefore, it may not always be possible for different brands of adapters and access points to exchange data when their enhanced security features are active.

If enhanced security is an important issue for your network, it may be necessary to standardize on a single brand of hardware or a group of brands that share the same kind of 128-bit encryption (such as Cisco and Xircom or Orinoco and Apple's AirPort).

Chapter 14 contains more detailed information about setting up and using the security features of a wireless network. Unfortunately, the WEP encryption standard is full of holes, so it's not adequate to truly protect your network against access by unauthorized users. The best choice, especially if your network has more than one brand of adapters and access points, could be to turn off WEP encryption and use one of the alternative security methods described in Chapter 14.

Documentation and Technical Support

Every company that makes and sells wireless Ethernet hardware offers some kind of technical support for its users. However, the quality and usefulness of that support varies wildly from one vendor to another. If you can't get the information you need from the manufacturer, you should find a different supplier.

At a minimum, an adequate level of technical support should include an accurate and clearly written user's manual, a support center that answers specific questions by telephone and email, a Web site with answers to frequently asked questions, and a download center that offers the latest versions of device drivers, configuration utilities, and status display software for free download.

Each adapter and access point should come with a detailed user's manual that contains instructions for installing, configuring, and using the equipment, written in clear, easy-to-understand language. It's always a good idea to look over the manual before you buy any piece of computer equipment; there's no excuse for a manual with confusing instructions or text that seems to have been badly translated from colloquial Swahili by somebody whose native language was an obscure dialect of Gaelic.

Even the greatest manual ever written won't include the answers to every possible question, so it should also be possible to telephone or send email to a technical support center. It's always nice when tech support has a toll-free telephone number, but it's not essential—you probably paid more for the product to support that "free" service. You should be able to reach a live human technician within a minute or two, or if you call at a busy time, you should be able to leave your telephone number for a callback within a couple of hours. There is never any excuse for endless time on "hold" (with or without sappy music), or incomprehensible menus that do not have the answers to your particular questions.

When you send a question by email, you should receive an acknowledgement within an hour or less, even if it's only an automated, "Thanks for your question. We will reply with a complete answer as soon as possible." You should expect an answer to your question no later than the next business day.

And of course, the people who answer your questions should provide information that actually solves your problem. Bad information is worse than no information at all.

Most computer hardware and software companies have technical support Web sites that contain answers to the most common questions they receive from users. If you have access to the Web when you need a quick answer, that's often the least painful way to find it. The Web site should also include a download center where you can find copies of the latest drivers and related software for every product that the company has ever sold, including discontinued models.

Reputation

It's almost always helpful to learn about other people's experience with a wireless adapter (or anything else you may be planning to buy) before you spend your own money. The manufacturer and the dealer who want to sell the product are happy to tell you about all the positive features, but you can't expect them to be completely objective.

Local users' groups, published product reviews, and Internet discussions can all be useful sources for information about wireless Ethernet equipment. It's not always safe to take every review and every horror story at face value, but when you see or hear a dozen or more reports about a driver that crashed Windows or a PC Card that overheated, you can often assume that there's some kind of pattern emerging.

The Practically Networked Web site (http://www.practicallynetworked.com) is one good place to look for reviews and users' evaluations of wireless Ethernet gear.

At least one major supplier of wireless network equipment has a reputation for bad tech support—long waits for a support technician by telephone, and longer waits for replies to email, combined with frequently unhelpful answers to questions. In a marketplace with as much competition as the wireless Ethernet business, you don't need to put up with a company that doesn't (or can't) provide decent support.

Adapters for Ad Hoc Networks

In an ad hoc network, every network adapter exchanges data with every other node through direct links, without an access point acting as a central node. Ad hoc networks are useful for small, isolated networks and direct peer-to-peer filesharing. For example, somebody who uses a laptop computer on the road and a desktop computer in the office can set up an ad hoc network to transfer files between the two. Or two laptop owners might use an ad hoc connection to share files.

Ad hoc wireless networks that connect two or more network nodes without the use of an access point are far less common than infrastructure networks, but they are part of the 802.11b specification, so just about every network interface adapter and wireless configuration program offers an ad hoc network option.

In general, any network adapter with a Wi-Fi logo will work well in an ad hoc network. It's essential that all of the nodes in the network are configured for ad hoc operation, and all of the other configuration options must be the same, but connecting directly to another computer should be no more difficult than connecting to an access point.

Dual-Purpose Adapters

Wi-Fi networking has become wildly popular, but it's not the only wireless technology out there. Several other systems, including Bluetooth (which provides very short-range connections for computer peripheral devices and accessories, such as headphones and keyboards) and 802.11a (which uses a different set of radio frequencies to provide higher-speed network links than 802.11b), are also available. Each offers solutions to a somewhat different set of problems, and each fills a different market niche.

Several manufacturers have announced new products that combine an 802.11b network interface adapter with an interface for some other wireless service. Some can detect and use both 802.11b (2.4 GHz) and 802.11a (5.4 GHz) networks, while others integrate 802.11b networking with Bluetooth. Still others might combine access to Wi-Fi LANs with cellular data or other wide area network (WAN) services. The benefits of a combined access point are obvious—one device is more convenient to carry and install than two, and it provides access to more networks and services. And because the same radio transmitter and receiver handles both services, the potential for interference is also reduced.

An ideal dual-service network adapter would automatically detect radio signals from all compatible networks within range and allow a user to set up an instant connection to any of them without the need to worry about the type of link the network is using. The cost of this combined adapter should be only slightly more than the price of an adapter that recognizes only one networking protocol. Such a perfect wireless networking device may actually appear some time in the next few years.

In the meantime, several interesting dual-mode products are on the shelves today. For example, GTRAN Wireless makes a PC Card adapter that works with both CDMA cellular data and Wi-Fi networks. It uses the cellular telephone network to send and receive data at relatively slow speed almost anywhere within most major metropolitan areas; when a user moves into a "hot spot" within range of a much faster 802.11 signal, the adapter can set up a new and much faster connection.

Other dual-mode products will use the Blue802 technology that was introduced by Intersil and Silicon Wave early in 2002. Blue802 allows Bluetooth and 802.11b connections to operate simultaneously through a single adapter, so a computer can use Bluetooth links to a mouse, keyboard, printer, or another computer at the same time that it is connected to the Internet or a LAN through a Wi-Fi network. This is a big deal, because both 802.11b and Bluetooth use the same 2.4 GHz radio frequencies, and each service can often create interference for the other. Blue802 coordinates the two types of radio transmissions to optimize the performance of both.

Numerous other combination devices are possible, even if they're not currently available. If the industry identifies a demand, you might see a network adapter with both an RJ-45 Ethernet connector and a wireless antenna, or a wireless adapter that shares the same package as a 56 Kbps modem.

The added cost of a dual-mode adapter might be justified if you know that you will be using both of the network services that the adapter supports. Blue802 is particularly attractive, because a combined adapter will provide better performance with less interference than two separate devices. But like most other electronic equipment, these adapters will come down in price over time, so there's not much reason to buy one unless you have an immediate need for it.

Access Points

Most wireless network interface adapters perform just one function: they exchange data between a computer and a network. Access points, in contrast, offer a wide variety of features and functions. They're available as simple access points and in combination with hubs, switches, and routers for wired connections to nearby computers and other devices. There's a whole category of wireless access points for home networks called *residential gateways.*

The physical design of an access point is less important than the design of an interface adapter, because access points don't have to fit into a computer's card slot or an expansion bay. Some are built into simple rectangular boxes, while others are in odd-shaped enclosures that may look more distinctive. The appearance of the package is less important that the features and functions inside, especially when the access point will be placed out of sight in a closet, or hidden behind a false ceiling. Regardless of the shape, most access points include mounting plates, brackets, or other hardware for attaching the device to a wall or shelf.

There are a handful of other general features that you may want to look for when you select an access point. If your site survey tells you that you will need high-gain antennas, or if you want to place an antenna outdoors or in some other isolated location, you should use an access point with an external antenna connector instead of a permanently mounted captive antenna. In a high-traffic network where you plan to use more than one radio channel at the same time, a single access point that contains two radio modules can replace two separate access points. And if the best location for your access point is not close to an AC power outlet, choose a model that offers an optional Power over Ethernet or Active Ethernet feature.

The best way to choose the type of access point for your network is to decide what kind of connections you're likely to need. Are you adding wireless access to an existing wired network? Or do you want to provide some new wired links along with the wireless service? Do you want to use the wireless network to share Internet access? The answers to all of these questions will help you choose the right access point for your network.

Pure Wireless LANs

When all the nodes in a LAN exchange data by radio, the access point acts as a hub that provides the central control point for the network, as shown in Figure 2.6. Strictly speaking, the "access point" in this kind of network does not provide access to anything except other wireless nodes. This kind of wireless arrangement is one of the basic functions of any access point, so if this is your design, you should select the simplest and least expensive model that can provide a usable signal to your coverage area.

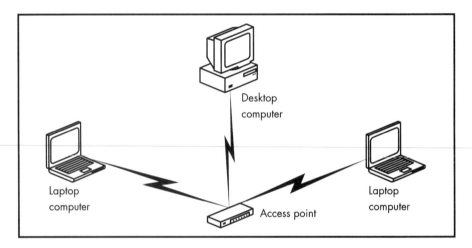

Figure 2.6: A simple wireless network without any external connections

This kind of simple wireless network is possible, but there's not much reason to use an access point in a purely wireless LAN. You can accomplish the same thing in an ad hoc wireless network that creates direct point-to-point links without the need to go through a central hub. About the only time a pure-wireless infrastructure network (with an access point) might make sense would be when you expect to start with wireless links and later expand the network to include a wired Ethernet connection to a file server, a shared Internet connection, or more computers and workstations, or when computers at the extreme ranges of the ad hoc network cannot communicate directly.

Wireless Access to a Wired LAN

Any access point can act as a base station, adding wireless links to an existing wired LAN, as shown in Figure 2.7. The access point presents the same appearance to the rest of the network as does a subsidiary hub or switch that connects wired nodes to the network.

In this kind of hybrid wired-and-wireless LAN, each device on the network can exchange data with every other network node, regardless of how it is con-

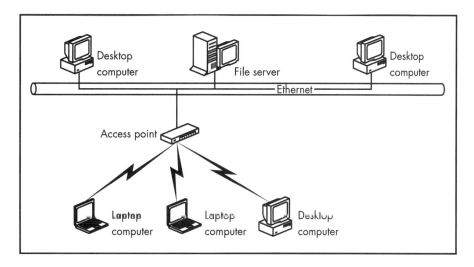

Figure 2.7: A wireless access point connected to a wired Ethernet network

nected. It doesn't matter whether a particular device is connected to the LAN through a wire or over a radio link; it's all one seamless network.

An access point that acts as a bridge between the wired and wireless sections of the network usually has a single 10 Mbps or 100 Mbps RJ-45 Ethernet port for connecting a cable to the wired LAN. There's often an additional serial port for a remote terminal that the network manager can use to enter configuration commands and receive status information.

Combining the Access Point with a Wired Hub

In a new LAN that includes both wired connections and wireless links, the best approach may be a single device that combines the functions of a wireless access point with a wired hub or switch, as shown in Figure 2.8. This kind of access point is sometimes described as a broadband router.

A broadband router typically has three kinds of network connections:

- Radio links to computers equipped with wireless Ethernet adapters

- One or more Ethernet ports for wired links to computers with network interface cards

- A broadband WAN port for connecting the router to the network backbone or for stacking the router with additional hubs or switches

Some routers also include a print server that can move documents directly to a network printer.

The major benefits of a combined access point and hub are convenience and economy in a home office or a small business where it's easy to run cables to some of the network computers. A combined unit may also be the quickest way to extend an existing network to both wired and wireless nodes in a remote location.

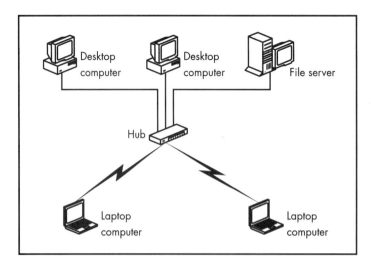

Figure 2.8: A wireless access point, combined with a broadband switch, controls both the wireless and wired segments of a hybrid network

Broadband Gateways

A *broadband gateway* is an access point that includes a port for a direct connection to a DSL or cable modem that supplies high-speed access to the Internet, as shown in Figure 2.9. Some gateway devices also include several RJ-45 Ethernet ports for wired connections to local computers.

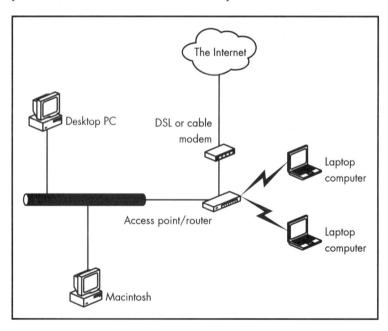

Figure 2.9: An access point combined with a broadband gateway supports a wireless network that shares a high-speed Internet connection

This approach is most practical in a home network or small business, where the wiring for the wideband Internet service runs all the way to the office, rather than stopping at a service entry or a telephone closet, because the access point must be placed in the best possible location to provide wireless network coverage.

Multiple Access Points

A single access point can be completely adequate to support a wireless LAN in an open, relatively small space, with a moderate volume of traffic. But when your network must cover a very large area (greater than about 100 feet in diameter), or a space with obstructions from walls, furniture, or other objects, or interference from other radios, you will probably have to add more access points.

Most home networks, and many networks in very small businesses, will need only one access point, so choosing an access point that supports *roaming* is only a problem for managers of large and complex networks.

The 802.11b specification includes a roaming function that automatically hands off a network link from one access point to another when the signal quality through the new access point is better than the original connection. After a network client associates with an access point, it automatically surveys all of the other radio channels to determine whether some other access point operating on a different channel will provide a stronger or cleaner signal than the one it is currently using. When the client finds a channel that can support a faster link than the current one, it drops the old association and immediately associates with the best available signal source.

Therefore, access points with overlapping coverage areas should be set to different channel numbers. For the least amount of interference from one access point to the next, the channel numbers of any pair of adjacent access points should be at least five channels apart.

In most cases, a network client will not associate with a different access point unless the client moves to a different location while the network link is active or the amount of traffic on the current channel increases. In other words, a hand-off may occur when a user carries a laptop or a PDA from one place to another, or when it becomes necessary for the network to balance the load among all of the available access points.

As Figure 2.10 shows, all of the access points must be connected together through a conventional wired LAN that may also include additional computers and servers that don't require a wireless connection.

In most cases, multiple access points should be placed to provide coverage that overlaps by about 30 percent from one access point to the next. However, when your wireless network must support a large number of simultaneous users, the best way to balance the load may be to install two or more access points in the same place, with each access point set to a different, non-interfering radio channel.

Roaming is covered by the 802.11b standard, so it should be possible to use different brands of access points in the same network. They're all supposed to work together. However, each access point includes a proprietary configuration utility, and each may have a somewhat different design, so a network with only one brand of access point will almost always be easier to configure and use than a mixed network. Building a wireless network is complicated enough; it's always a good idea to eliminate a possible source of confusion and finger-pointing.

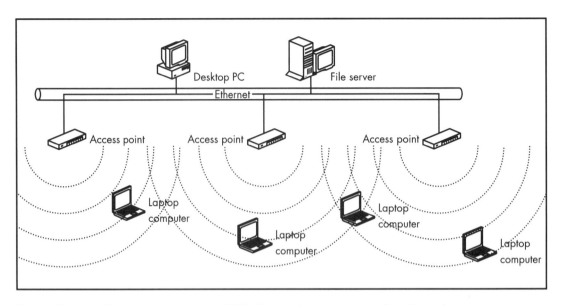

Figure 2.10: Multiple access points on a wired LAN allow wireless users to roam throughout a larger coverage area than any single access point can serve by itself

External Antennas

If you can establish a reliable high-speed data link to any location in your network's coverage area with the antennas built into your network adapters and the captive antennas attached to your access points, there is absolutely no reason to waste any time, money, or energy on external antennas. Once you have reached the maximum possible speed, better antennas won't move the data any faster.

But when reception conditions are less than perfect, and when you want to push a radio signal as far as you possibly can, a separate antenna can cut through interference, increase data transfer speed, expand the network's coverage area, and establish reliable communication links in places where they would be little more than a rumor with plain vanilla internal antennas.

At first glance, it would appear that the easiest way to improve the quality of a radio signal would be to crank up the power that comes out of the transmitter. Instead of the wimpy 30 milliwatts produced by most wireless adapters (that's 0.030 of a watt), why not boost it to 10 or 20 watts or more? Wouldn't that produce a much stronger signal?

Sure it would, but the FCC and the other agencies around the world that regulate radio services won't let you do it. More powerful radios would produce stronger signals that would create a lot more interference over wider areas, which would mean that fewer users could share the same piece of the radio spectrum.

By comparison, the television station that uses Channel 4 in New York City transmits with 100,000 watts of output power, but the nearest station that uses the same channel is in Boston, a couple of hundred miles away. The radios in a wireless LAN use less than a watt, so the signal is almost inaudible a few hundred feet away.

Since you can't increase the amount of power produced by the radio transmitters, the next best method for improving signal quality is to optimize the performance of the antennas.

Radio antennas come in two types: omnidirectional antennas that transmit and receive in all directions at equal strength, and directional antennas that focus their energy and their sensitivity in a specific direction. In a wireless LAN, an access point with an omnidirectional antenna is most useful when you want to cover a wide area. A network adapter with an omnidirectional antenna can communicate equally well with any nearby access point. If the coverage area you want to reach with your wireless LAN extends beyond the distance you can cover with internal omnidirectional antennas, you can expect to increase the coverage area by about 15 percent with an external antenna.

In other words, if the signal quality of your link begins to fade at a distance of 100 feet between a network node and the closest access point, you can extend the useful signal range to about 115 feet by using an external omnidirectional antenna on either the access point or the network adapter. If you use external antennas at both ends, you can expect to reach about 132 feet. Of course, that hundred-foot value is just an easy-to-calculate example. The actual signal range of a pair of internal antennas might be very different, depending on obstructions between the two devices and interference from other radio signals, but that 15 percent improvement rate for each antenna will remain about the same.

The shape of a directional antenna's coverage area and the amount of gain (signal strength from the transmitter and sensitivity to the receiver) depend on the exact design of each antenna. Some directional antennas can provide a moderate amount of gain over a broad pattern (like a floodlight), while others can focus three or four (or more) times as much gain over a much narrower area (like a spotlight).

Directional antennas can provide a huge improvement in signal quality over a tightly focused coverage area, and they can also reduce interference from "null" areas outside of that coverage pattern. This means they can have several uses in a wireless LAN:

- They can allow a user outside the "normal" coverage area to join the network.

- They can increase the effective coverage area served by an access point by limiting the coverage to one direction.

- They can reduce or eliminate the effect of off-axis interference from other radio signals.

- They can reduce the amount of interference that a wireless LAN creates for other radios.

- They can establish long-distance, stationary, point-to-point links between buildings.

Antenna Characteristics

External antennas come in many shapes and sizes. When you select an antenna, you should consider several items, including coverage pattern, gain, form factor, and weatherproofing.

Coverage Pattern

The specification sheet for every antenna includes a diagram that shows the shape of the antenna's coverage pattern. In general, the pattern will be either *omnidirectional* (an antenna that radiates or receives equally well in all directions), *directional* (with the strongest radiation or reception in one direction), or *figure-eight* (with strong coverage toward the front and back of the antenna, and weak coverage to and from the sides).

Catalog listings and spec sheets for directional antennas also usually include an aperture angle, beamwidth, or capture area, expressed in degrees. The aperture angle is the section of a circle that contains the antenna's maximum power coverage or sensitivity. For example, if an antenna has an aperture angle of 45 degrees, the maximum coverage or sensitivity extends outward from the front of the antenna at a 45-degree angle.

Directional antennas radiate in all directions, so most manufacturers will tell you the beamwidth in more than one plane. This may be important information when you're planning to place an access point's antenna on a wall, roof, or tower, and you want to exchange data with network nodes on the ground.

Gain

The *gain* of an antenna is the ratio of the transmitting power or receiving sensitivity when compared to a standard dipole antenna (a dipole is a straight, center-fed, half-wavelength antenna, such as the T-shaped twin-lead antenna supplied with many FM radios and tuners). The gain is usually expressed as dBi (decibels over isotropic). An antenna with a high dBi value has more gain than one with a lower value.

There's often a trade-off between an antenna's beamwidth and its gain. This occurs because an antenna with a tight aperture angle focuses the same amount of power (or sensitivity) into a smaller area.

Form Factor

A dipole antenna for a 2.4 GHz radio is only about an inch long, but the reflectors and other elements that add gain and directional characteristics may be much longer. Many antennas are supplied inside a protective cover that does not affect their performance, but which can keep the actual antenna clean and dry and make it easier to mount the antenna on a pole or a wall.

Omnidirectional antennas are almost always vertical whips or shafts, no more than two or three inches in diameter. Some high-gain omnis may be as much as two or three feet long. For indoor use, especially in rooms with dropped ceilings, special omnidirectional ceiling-mount antennas can be an excellent choice for a wireless network.

Directional antennas can take many shapes, including parabolic dishes and panels that include a reflector behind the active part of the antenna; antennas that resemble a shorter version of a rooftop TV antenna; and patch or panel antennas with several radiating elements, usually within a flat enclosure that resembles a smoke detector or mounted on a swivel that makes it possible to aim the antenna more precisely.

Weatherproofing

Outdoor antennas usually need some kind of protection from rain and snow and from ultraviolet radiation that can deteriorate the materials from which the antenna is constructed. Therefore, many manufacturers offer antennas with sealed elements inside weatherproof enclosures.

A weatherproof enclosure doesn't serve any purpose indoors, where the goal should be to make the antenna as unobtrusive as possible. Some antennas are advertised for "indoor/outdoor use," but the only thing they will do for an indoor installation is increase the cost.

How to Choose an Antenna

It's important to remember that there's no good reason to install an antenna with more gain than you can actually use. If you can establish a clean link with a low-gain antenna, your network won't perform any better, or move data any faster, just because the access point is sending and receiving stronger signals to and from the antenna. In fact, the signal quality might not be as good with a better antenna, because it will pick up more noise and interference from other networks and other 2.4 GHz devices.

The standard omnidirectional antenna should be your first choice, unless you have a good reason to use something else. If you do need a directional antenna, choose one that covers the area you want to reach as efficiently as possible. If you don't need to cover an enormous area, don't waste your money on a high-gain antenna; the least amount of gain necessary to reach all the nodes in your network will work as well or better than a bigger and more expensive antenna that pushes a signal out to places where nobody except unauthorized users will ever use it.

It's always a good idea to buy your antennas from the same supplier as the radios that you will use with them, in order to prevent unpleasant finger-pointing between two or more vendors when something doesn't work properly. However, if your network requires some kind of special antenna that you can't get from the people who make or sell your radios, don't be afraid to go to a specialist dealer.

Rolling Your Own

Some wireless network designers and experimenters have designed a whole class of homebrew antennas for 2.4 GHz operation, using such cheap and easily obtainable materials as an empty Pringles potato chips canister. We'll describe these antennas in more detail in Chapter 10.

Unless you already have a workshop full of tools and test equipment and you're really fond of salted snacks made out of potato flakes, these homemade antennas might not offer any particular advantages over a commercial antenna with well-defined performance characteristics. After you calculate the cost of materials and the value of the time needed to assemble and test a homebrew antenna (including the obligatory trip to your local big-box Home Center and Hardware Emporium, where you will spend at least 45 minutes searching for the right mounting brackets), the price of a store-bought antenna doesn't seem to be all that expensive. For example, you can buy a directional antenna with higher gain than the standard Pringles version from HyperGain (http://www.hyperlinktech.com/web/antennas) for about $50.

Where to Use a Directional Antenna

There are three ways to use directional antennas: on an access point, on a network adapter, or on both.

On an Access Point

A directional antenna on an access point will provide a stronger signal to all the network nodes within the access point's coverage area. Therefore, it will be possible to reach users who are farther away from the access point, and to improve the signal quality for users who are closer, at the expense of users who are not located within the antenna's coverage pattern.

In a network that requires several access points to provide complete coverage, an access point with a directional antenna at one end of the intended coverage area may be more efficient than an omnidirectional antenna. As Figure 2.11 shows, the directional antenna can concentrate all of the signal in places where it will be used, instead of flinging it out equally in all directions. In this example, the directional antenna's coverage angle is about 90 degrees, so it reaches the interior of the building, but it doesn't waste a lot of power on signals to other areas where nobody will want them.

Directional antennas can also be useful to extend coverage in one direction and to direct signals into dead spots and other places where the access points with omnidirectional antennas don't provide adequate signals.

On a Network Adapter

The second option is to place a high-gain directional antenna on a wireless network adapter and point the antenna at an access point with an omnidirectional antenna. This might be the best way to add a node to a network through an access point that is also serving other, closer network clients. To eliminate the cost and inconvenience of installing another access point or running an Ethernet cable to a single isolated user, try using a directional antenna on that user's network adapter.

On Both an Access Point and a Network Adapter

A network link that uses directional high-gain antennas at both ends can cover a *lot* of ground. A link from a rooftop to a hilltop location might reach several miles or more, if there's a clean line of sight without obstruction from trees or buildings. Aiming the two antennas at each other for maximum signal strength can be very critical for long-distance links; turning one antenna (or both) just a few degrees can make the difference between a strong signal and no signal at all. The coverage angles of dish and parabolic antennas can be extremely tight.

As you move the two ends of a radio link apart, two more complications arise. The curvature of the earth and an electromagnetic phenomenon called the Fresnel Zone can get in the way unless the antennas are high enough to avoid them.

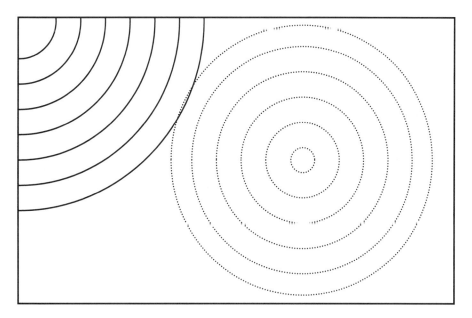

Figure 2.11: A combination of directional and omnidirectional antennas may be the best way to cover a large or odd-shaped area

At 2.4 GHz, the average height of the two antennas must be at least 13 feet above the ground or other obstructions for a one-mile link. At five miles, the minimum height increases to 35 feet, and at ten miles, the minimum height is 57 feet.

Antennas Are a Whole Other World

Long-range links are almost always required as solutions to specific problems, such as providing access to a place where no other network service is available or adding users in a remote building to a campus or corporate network. Adding a directional antenna that fills a dead spot in an indoor network, or a panel antenna that mounts on a roof or an outside wall to cover a parking lot, doesn't make your network much more complicated than using access points with omni-directional antennas. But when you start to think about antennas with complex patterns and very high gain, you're moving beyond what a book about wireless LANs can cover. You need expert help.

Before you can install a big, powerful antenna, you (or somebody working for you) must pay attention to things like wind loading (you don't want the antenna to fall down in a storm), local zoning ordinances (lots of people think antennas are ugly or dangerous), or both. So they have rules about where and how you can put them up. And you'll probably want to use an expensive piece of test equipment called a *spectrum analyzer* to aim the two antennas at each other.

If you don't have experience with this stuff, you'll need to either find help from somebody who does or spend a lot of time experimenting. If that's your idea of fun, have yourself a fine time. You can find more detailed information about long-range point-to-point links in Chapter 10.

It's Time to Buy

This chapter has described the different kinds of wireless network adapters, access points, and antennas that you will need to construct a new wireless LAN or add wireless access to your existing wired network. The next step is to make some choices and gather all of the hardware together. You're ready to install the wireless hardware.

In the next chapter, you will find step-by-step procedures for installing different kinds of adapters and access points, and for running the configuration utility programs that make all those pieces work together in a network.

3

INSTALLING AND CONFIGURING ACCESS POINTS

When you decide to start using a wireless network, you have at least two options: you can unpack all the boxes, hook up the radios to your computers, and try to make it all work, or you can do some advance planning and think about the best location for each component before you start playing with hardware. This chapter is for those conscientious and methodical people who plan first and install things later. It's also for the rest of us who tried to fire up our networks without any planning and now want to learn how to do the job properly.

An access point in a wireless network is the central transmitter and receiver that exchanges data with individual computers and other network clients. Every 802.11b network in infrastructure mode must include at least one access point. Additional access points can increase the size of the area served by the network and support a larger number of network clients, so the number and location of your network's access points defines its coverage and capacity.

The first thing to do when you start planning your wireless LAN — or for that matter, any LAN — is to spend some time thinking about exactly how you expect to use the network. Are all of the computers in your network in fixed locations, with easy access to cable runs? Are you thinking about wireless because it's the best way to add computers and users to your network or because it's the Flavor of the Month?

For example, I live in a one-story house with an unfinished basement. I could use wireless to extend my home network from the front room to the kitchen (and I did, when I was testing equipment for this book), but it's almost as easy, and a lot less expensive, to buy cheap Ethernet interface cards and string Cat 5 cable through the basement rafters instead. On the other hand, if I want to use my laptop computer on the front porch or in the backyard as well as the kitchen, or if I lived in a house with two floors or an apartment where I couldn't get to the basement or the attic, then it would make sense to install an access point in the front room and a wireless network card in the laptop machine, so I could carry the laptop from place to place.

You can apply the same kind of analysis to a business network. As long as all the computers in the office or plant are stationary, and you have an easy way to run cables, a wired network is usually the better choice. But if the salespeople all carry portables when they call on customers, or the engineers want to use their laptop machines in meetings or over lunch, or there's some other good reason to extend the network beyond the reach of the cables, it's probably time to add wireless access.

How Many Access Points?

A simple wireless network operates with just one access point and a handful of network nodes. However, when you're trying to cover a large space or a space with walls or other things that can obstruct the signal, you will probably have to add at least one additional access point.

The exact location of each access point in a complex network is no more or less obvious than the best place to put a single access point. If your network covers a big open space, you can place them at regular intervals, but finding the best way to cover an irregular space might be more difficult.

Placing access points is not an exact science. Perhaps the best method is to start with a single access point at one end of the building and confirm that it provides decent coverage within 50 or 100 feet, or up to the first major turn in the walls, by walking around with a computer running your site survey program. When the signal starts to fade, back up to a place where the signal is good and try to place the second access point about the same distance away in the opposite direction. If the second access point doesn't give you the necessary coverage for the rest of your space, you might have to add still more access points. Your goal should be a maximum of about 30 percent overlap in coverage between any pair of access points.

Locating three or more access points can become messy, because the positions might not be the same as they would be with one or two units. Remember, your goal in adding more access points is to fill in as much space as possible. With two access points in an open space, you would probably place both of them halfway between the side walls, each about a third of the way from the front and back. Add another unit, and you might want to put the third in the middle and move the other two closer to the front and back, or arrange them in some kind of triangle pattern.

When you need more than two access points in a complex space, you should start to think about using a combination of omnidirectional and directional antennas instead of the omnidirectional ones built into some access points. An antenna mounted high on a wall, beaming inward, might be the best way to fill in a dead spot or extend your network to that end of the building. Pay close attention to the antenna's coverage pattern, though, because it may be a tight cone rather than a broad arc (think of the difference between a floodlight and a spotlight).

Can you avoid climbing aimlessly around the ceiling, moving access points for more tests? The best advice I can offer is to work with a floor plan. Cut out some circles that cover the equivalent 150 feet or 200 feet in scale diameter, and others that match the pattern of directional antennas, and move them around the floor plan until you find a combination of locations that gives you maximum coverage. It's crude, but it ought to give you a starting point for your actual site survey.

The number of people using your network can also have an effect on the number of access points you need. As a practical limit, if more than half a dozen computers are trying to connect to the same access point at the same time, the data transfer speed from each wireless node will start to drop, but remember that most of your users won't be trying to move data at any given moment. "Half a dozen" at one time might translate to 20 or 30 users over the course of a day.

If the number of users on your network increases over time, you might discover that performance is deteriorating because your access points are operating at or near full capacity. When that happens, it's time to think about adding more access points to your network. You can place the new access points either midway between the existing access points or right next to the existing access points. Whenever possible, set the new access points to a different, non-interfering channel number, and reconfigure half of the network nodes to use that channel.

Operating in infrastructure mode, your network resembles a hub-and-spokes design, in which each node is communicating with the network through an access point. Therefore, it's not necessary for all the nodes on your wireless network to be using the same channel number. If you can distribute your nodes among two or three non-interfering channels, you will reduce the number of links on each channel, which will improve performance through the entire network.

Performing a Site Survey

General principles are fine, but you're installing a wireless network in a real location with real walls and real furniture (and most likely, real sources of real interference). Radio waves pass through some materials and bounce off others, so the general estimates of a radio's range and signal strength in an ideal environment are less important than the actual performance in the place you want to use it. What you need is a site survey that tells you how your own radios will operate in your own space.

The first step in doing a site survey is to identify the area that you want your network to cover. In most cases, that will be the entire area of your office, home, or campus, but there are other possibilities. For example, you might want to provide network access only in common areas, such as a conference room, a reception area, or a library, or you might want to share a single broadband network connection among a group of neighbors. Keep in mind that radio signals at 2.4 GHz can pass through many walls, ceilings, and floors, so they will probably reach adjacent spaces, even if you don't aim them at those spaces.

For a home or small office network, your site survey can be very simple. If the whole building is just 50 feet from front to back and 30 feet wide you can probably place the access point almost anywhere. Just connect the access point to your existing Internet connection, fire up a laptop or other portable computer as a network client, and carry the client device around while a network connection is active. If you can keep the connection alive everywhere in the house or office, you're ready to go.

The spaces covered by a single network don't have to be continuous (or contiguous), although that's the way most networks are constructed. For example, your business might occupy the third, fourth, and ninth floors of a building, but none of the floors in between. In this case, you can place access points in your own offices, connect them together with Ethernet cables, and ignore the other floors. If your LAN extends to more than one building, you can place access points in each building and link them together (if no link is already in place) with a leased line, a virtual private network (VPN) connection through the Internet, or a point-to-point radio link.

Make a Site Plan . . .

When you have a rough idea of the space you want your network to cover, it's time to create a more detailed floor plan. If your network will cover more than one floor of a building, and when the network will include space in more than one building, you will want a plan for each floor, a vertical diagram of each building, and another diagram that shows the network's entire coverage area.

Your floor plan should include the location of each wall and partition, along with every existing network connection and AC power outlet. If you know about potential sources of interference, such as a 2.4 GHz cordless phone, a Bluetooth network, or a microwave oven, mark their locations on the plan as well. Figure 3.1 shows a floor plan of a small office.

In general, you can get away with a single access point if you can find a spot with a clean line of sight to every location where somebody might want to place a computer or other network client. When that's not possible because of obstructions to the radio signals, you will need additional access points, but don't automatically assume that a clear radio path is the same as a line of sight. The only way to be sure is to fire up an access point and run your own test.

In this office, the best location for a line of sight to everywhere in the office would probably be at the corner of the L-shaped space. If that's not good enough, the next approach to try would be placing one access point at each end of the office. This office contains plenty of network drops and AC outlets, so connecting to the wired network should not be a problem. That's not always true. In many places, the logical place for an access point might be inside a false ceiling, but if

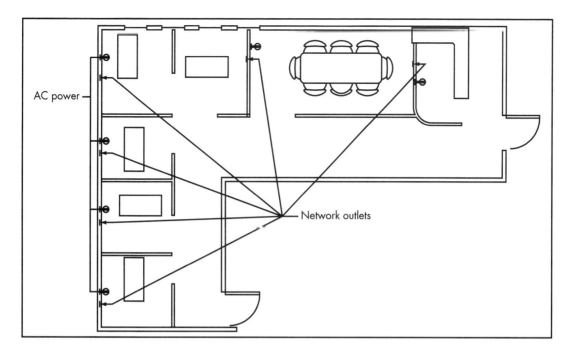

Figure 3.1: An office floor plan

you can't locate an AC outlet up there, you might have to find a different spot or use an access point that supports a Power over Ethernet (PoE) option.

It's less of a problem when the preferred access point location is close to an AC outlet but farther away from a network connection point. You can often solve the problem with a longer data cable, but don't drop a cable from a false ceiling into the middle of a room or over a partition that doesn't reach the ceiling; it looks messy, and somebody will almost certainly yank it out eventually. Your installation will look a lot better if you extend the data cable to a real wall and either drop the cable inside the wall or run it flush to a corner where two walls meet. Remember that high-speed data doesn't like to turn through sharp corners; be sure to allow for a broad curve when the cable run changes from horizontal to vertical.

When you want to use a single access point to serve two adjacent floors of a building, the best location would be as close to the shared ceiling and floor as possible. The location is less critical in most houses, because the radio signal will pass through wood and plaster more easily than concrete and steel.

If the anticipated coverage area of your indoor network extends more than about 150 feet from the access point, consider a network with more than one access point. Outdoors, you should be able to get a reliable signal from an access point at least 200 feet away, if a clean line of sight is available.

The antennas built into most access points and network interfaces are omni-directional, which means that they radiate equally in all directions. In other words, the useful signal range resembles a sphere or a doughnut, with the antenna at the center. Therefore, you will want to place your access point more or less in the middle of the space you want to cover. If you're using an access point with a connector for an external antenna, you can be more flexible. In some environments, a directional antenna at one end of the building might be more effective than an omni in the center.

The built-in antennas on many access points are whips mounted on swivels that allow you to change their positions relative to the box that contains the circuitry. It might not make much difference, but the usual practice is to place the antennas pointing down when the access point is placed near the ceiling and up when it's close to the floor. In general, you might get slightly better coverage when the antenna is vertical rather than horizontal.

Another potential cause of signal loss is multipath interference. Multipath loss occurs when the same signal reaches a receiving antenna both directly from the transmitter, and again a fraction of a second later after bouncing off a reflective surface. On a broadcast television signal, multipath appears on the screen as a "ghost" or "shadow" image. In a packet data network, the receiver treats multipath interference as noise, which can slow down the transmission speed.

Many access points and network adapters use two separate antennas in a *diversity* receiving arrangement to reduce or eliminate the impact of multipath interference. The receiver compares the strength of the signal from each antenna and automatically selects the better one. Even though the two antennas may be located just an inch or two apart, a diversity system can often provide a cleaner output than a single antenna. If the access point's built-in antenna is inside a package with an odd form such as a U-shaped bar, or if, as in some D-Link access points, it has two separate antennas, the device is probably using a diversity receiving system. The best way to find out if your hardware uses diversity is to read the specifications.

If your access point does have two captive antennas, you might want to experiment with different relative antenna positions. If your coverage is not adequate when the antennas are aligned north and south, try gradually turning the access point as you watch the signal strength display on a network client computer. If the antennas are on swivels, try moving them around rather than keeping them absolutely parallel.

Outdoors, the rule of thumb is "higher is better." If you possibly can, use an access point with a connector for an external antenna so you can place the box indoors and run a coaxial cable to the antenna. A weatherproof vertical antenna on a roof, or a flat-panel antenna mounted high on the side of a building, should provide decent line-of-sight coverage up to 300 feet away. When you place an antenna on a roof, try to mount it high enough to make it visible from the ground to prevent attenuation from the building itself, as shown in Figure 3.2. If you can't see the access point's antenna, the signal quality might suffer, but enough of the signal should pass through the structure to provide an acceptable signal. Don't be surprised if you get a stronger signal 20 feet away than you get right at the wall.

The amount of signal attenuation caused by a structure will be different for different building materials. At 2.4 GHz, radio waves can pass more easily through wood and glass than through concrete or structural steel. As a practical matter, if you're not trying to cover a large college campus or industrial park with your wire-

Figure 3.2: A rooftop antenna might not reach users close to the building

less network, you might produce an entirely usable outdoor signal from your indoor access points, especially if they're located near the exterior wall. As you run your site survey, try carrying a portable device away from the building while a connection is active; you might be surprised to discover how far the signal carries.

Remember that we're talking about digital signals. Once you achieve the minimum signal quality needed to provide a clean, high-speed data link, a stronger signal won't make any difference unless you have a problem with interference. Don't waste your time or money adding an outdoor access point if you can serve your outdoor picnic bench from an existing indoor access point. The signal might be stronger from an outdoor access point, but you won't transfer your data any faster.

Moving vehicles or other large metal objects (such as construction cranes) between the access point and a network client can get in the way of an otherwise clean signal and produce temporary dropouts. If you're trying to provide network coverage to a freight loading yard or some other space that has trucks or other large objects moving around, you will want to mount your antenna as high as possible or place a second access point at the other side of the area you want to reach with your network.

Testing, Testing . . .

After all the theoretical planning, you can't avoid real-world testing with actual hardware. A floor plan might give you a good idea of how your network *should* work, but the only way to find out how those radio waves actually move around the area you want to cover with your network is to set up a temporary installation and perform some real-world tests.

You have three options when you need to perform a site survey:

- Let somebody else do it for you—either a paid consultant or the vendor who expects to sell the network hardware to you.
- Use the site survey software supplied with some wireless hardware.
- Use the configuration program or the status program supplied with a network interface.

Allowing a consultant or sales tech to perform the survey for you has several advantages. First, you can let that person do the work, and you just have to read the report rather than having to run (or crawl) around the whole building with a test unit yourself. More importantly, the people who do this kind of site survey all the time have their own measurement devices that automatically store individual readings and produce detailed reports. Unfortunately, these measurement units are expensive, and they require some special training, so they're not practical for a one-time user.

If you can't find somebody else to do the job, you'll have to do it yourself. Several hardware vendors, including Cisco, Xircom, and Proxim, provide site survey software tools with their interface adapters and access points. Figure 3.3 shows the Xircom Site Survey program in action.

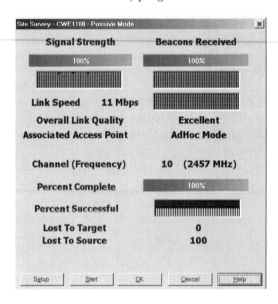

Figure 3.3: Site survey programs display the information you need to test a network

If your test hardware doesn't include one of these tools, you can pull enough information to perform a site survey out of the standard status and configuration programs that come with every wireless interface. It's a little easier with the survey tool, but the configuration programs will tell you what you need to know.

Most likely, the first access point you test will give you completely adequate network coverage, especially in a small network. But when you're setting up a more complex network, it can be very useful to convince your hardware supplier to let you test network interfaces and access points from more than one manufacturer. Because different manufacturers use different antenna designs and different configuration software, you might discover that one make of network adapters or access points works better than another in your network.

Here's what you should do to complete a site survey:

1. Choose a location for your access point. You might decide to change the location after the initial site survey is complete, but as a start, select a location with a line of sight to as much of your intended coverage area as possible.

2. If you already have a wired LAN in place, connect your sample access point to the LAN and plug in the power supply. If your site does not have an existing LAN, just connect the power supply. Turn on the access point.

3. Install a wireless network adapter in a laptop computer. If your access point is not connected to a wired LAN, install another network interface in a second computer. The second computer should be located close to the access point, so you can expect a clean signal path.

4. Use the configuration tools for your access point and your interface adapters to make sure that they are operating on the same channel numbers with the same SSID and the same preamble length. Set the adapter software and the configuration utility on the access point to infrastructure mode, and set the transmission rate to 11 Mbps or Automatic. For these tests, turn off Wired Equivalent Privacy (WEP) security.

5. Using your floor plan as a guide, prepare a site survey form like the one in Figure 3.4. Make an entry in the Location column for every room within your coverage area; make two or three entries for large spaces.

Location	Signal Strength	Signal Quality	Link Speed
Conference Room North End			
Conference Room South End			
Reception Area			
Mike's Office			
Sarah's Office			

Figure 3.4: A wireless network site survey form

6. Take the portable computer to the first location on your survey form.

7. Run the site survey program or the configuration or status program on your portable computer. The program should report a signal association between the network node and the access point, as well as the signal strength and quality. Some programs report only strength or quality, but not both. Figure 3.5 shows a configuration utility display that includes Link Quality and Signal Strength.

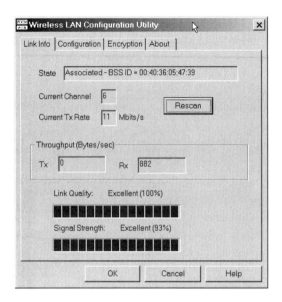

Figure 3.5: This display shows the signal strength and quality of a wireless link

8. Some configuration programs measure signal quality only when a file transfer is in progress. If the program doesn't show any signal, try opening the Windows Network Neighborhood window if you are using Windows. The wireless program should display the signal strength and quality as your computer polls the network. If your portable still can't associate with the access point, read the manuals that came with your hardware for more information about setting up your network hardware and configuring your computer to work with a wireless network connection.

9. Copy the signal strength, the signal quality, and the link speed for the current location to your survey form. If you're not using a site survey tool, your display might not include the link speed.

10. With the status or configuration program running, carry the portable computer to the next location on your list. If necessary, use the Refresh command in the Network window to obtain new readings. Note the strength, quality, and link speed on your survey form.

11. Repeat the process for each location on your list.

You might also want to wander around the building, noting changes in signal quality as you go. You can expect the signal strength to drop as you move farther away from the access point, but if the signal quality and ping-speed numbers remain good (a low ping speed is better), you shouldn't have any trouble using a wireless connection from this location.

Don't be surprised if you discover one or more unexpected dead spots where the signal strength or quality drops below a usable level. This might occur because of some kind of obstruction (like a metal filing cabinet) between the access point and the portable unit, or because some source of local interference (like a microwave oven, a Bluetooth device, or a cordless phone) is located nearby. Finding those dead spots is one of the reasons you're doing the site survey. In some cases, moving the test unit just a foot or two away from the original location might be enough to solve the problem. Be sure to note any dead spots on the survey form. If you find a lot of dead spots as you move around the building, or if any of the dead spots are in critical places, try moving the access point.

After you have tested the signal quality in every location on your list, mark the location of the access point on the floor plan and copy the test values for each room or other location. If you're working in a relatively small space, you will probably see consistent numbers for most locations. Don't be surprised to discover that the signal strength decreases as you move farther away from the access point. If signal quality and speed drop below a usable level, you might need to add one or more additional access points.

If the signal quality is not acceptable over most of the area you want to cover, try moving the access point to a different location, or if the access point has an external antenna, try moving the antenna. Once again, look for a place with a clean, unobstructed line of sight to as much of the area as possible. Repeat the survey with the access point in the new location.

Summary: Steps in a Site Survey

1. Identify the space you want your network to cover.
2. Prepare a floor plan and a vertical diagram.
3. Choose the ideal locations for access points and antennas.
4. Coordinate with other wireless networks.
5. Install the access points.
6. Test wireless links from many locations.
7. Try moving the access points or antennas.

Interference Problems

If nobody else is using a wireless network or any other 2.4 GHz device within about half a mile, you won't have to worry about interference on your network. That's becoming less likely every day. Other network services, along with cordless phones, microwave ovens, outdoor lighting systems, and radio-controlled toys, all use the same set of frequencies. Several nearby home or office networks might also be trying to use their own 802.11b networks. It's often a radio jungle out there.

The type of radio modulation used by wireless Ethernet networks is supposed to overcome interference from all those other services. That's the theory. The engineers who designed the various 2.4 GHz radio services are trying to cooperate, so we can all use our networks, phones, microwaves, and toys at the same time. In practice, however, the receivers in your access points and network adapters might listen to the channel that is supposed to contain a nice, clean Wi-Fi signal and perform the digital equivalent of throwing their hands into the air and shouting "Arrrgh!"

Or more accurately, it sends a message back to the source of the signal that says, "Huh? What did you say? I didn't understand that last packet." When that happens, the radio that transmitted the signal sends the same packet again and again until the receiver acknowledges that it has accepted a clean copy. The same thing happens with the next packet, and the one after that, and the one after that. This has the same effect as trying to conduct a voice conversation over a noisy phone line or a walkie-talkie, where . . . you . . . have . . . to . . . speak . . . very . . . slowly . . . and . . . listen . . . very . . . carefully. In other words, your nice, speedy network will feel like it's receiving data bits through a pipeline full of molasses.

If there's a lot of radio interference around you, you will probably discover it during your site survey. When you can't establish an 11 Mbps link within a clean line of sight to the access point, look for another signal source nearby. It might be something obvious like the microwave oven in the lunchroom or the cordless phone in the kitchen, but it could just as easily be something harder to find, like another network next door or a point-to-point radio link that's passing over your roof.

You can try a couple of things to reduce or eliminate interference: either remove the source of interference or move your own network to a different channel. Changing channels is often easier, but it's not always effective because your source of interference might be a frequency-hopping radio that jumps around the entire 2.4 GHz band, or a completely different source of interference might also be operating on the new frequency.

To try to eliminate interference, follow these steps, in this order:

1. Move to a different channel, at least five numbers away from the one where you encountered the problem. For example, if you can't use Channel 6, try dropping down to Channel 1 or jumping up to Channel 11.

2. Look for a cordless phone, a microwave oven, or some other device that radiates at 2.4 GHz. If possible, replace the offending device with one that operates at a different frequency, such as a 900 MHz cordless phone.

3. If you can change the output power of the radios in your access points and interface adapters, make sure they're set to the high (usually 100 mw) setting.

4. Ask your neighbors if they are using a wireless network. Because they're likely to experience the same kind of interference from your network that you're getting from theirs, they'll probably agree to cooperate on a channel assignment plan in which each network uses a different channel. Remember, if you can keep the networks at least five channel numbers apart, you will keep cross-channel interference to a minimum. If you're trying to coordinate more than three channels, spread the channel numbers across the band as widely as possible. Because the only set of three channels that don't interfere are Channels 1, 6, and 11, you might discover that they contain more interference from neighboring networks than one of the intermediate channels. You might have better luck with one or two of the intermediate channels instead.

5. Try replacing the omnidirectional antennas on your access point, your network adapters, or both, with directional antennas to increase the signal strength and the receivers' sensitivity. You might have to move the access

point to a different location or add more access points to cover the same area. If you can convince your neighbors to go to directional antennas, try to align the patterns for a minimum of overlapping coverage.

At this point, you can't do much more, except to either accept sluggish performance or replace your 2.4 GHz Wi-Fi network with an 802.11a wireless network that operates at 5.2 GHz.

You may encounter one more source of interference, but this one probably won't show up until your network has been in operation for a while. As the wireless network becomes more popular among your users, more and more of your own users may try to use the network at the same time, and the overall network performance will deteriorate. To solve this kind of problem, add more access points that operate on different channels.

Installing Access Points

As Chapter 2 explained, many access points are combined with other devices, such as network routers, broadband Internet routers, and traditional Ethernet hubs. At a bare minimum, every access point must include a radio transmitter and receiver, one or two captive antennas or connectors for external antennas, and an Ethernet port for connecting the access point to a wired network. The access point should also contain some kind of internal configuration software that displays the current settings and accepts commands to make changes.

Because each access point comes in a different package with different inputs, outputs, and controls, you will want to follow the specific installation and configuration instructions supplied with your own device. Unfortunately, the manufacturers' manuals don't always give you all the information you need. This section offers a general procedure for installing a generic access point, with occasional side comments about features and functions that don't exist in every product. It is intended to supplement the installation procedure provided in your own access point's manual.

Physical Installation

Here are the general steps for installing an access point:

1. If necessary, assemble the access point. The user's manual for your access point should contain specific instructions for the make and model you are using.

2. Based on the information in your site survey, place the access point in the location where you plan to operate it.

3. If the access point has a captive antenna on a swivel or other mechanism that allows you to move it around, adjust the antenna to a position as close to vertical as possible. If you are placing the antenna at or near the ceiling, place the antenna so that it points straight down, if possible. If the antenna is closer to the floor, point the antenna straight up. If you can't adjust the antenna's position, don't worry about it; the access point should work almost as well in its fixed position.

If the access point has a connector for an external antenna, install the antenna and run a cable from the antenna to the access point. Keep the cable between the access point and the antenna as short as possible without stretching it or turning any sharp corners.

4. Connect power to the access point. Most access points are supplied with "wall wart" DC power adapters, but some have AC power cords. Either way, connect the power cable to the access point first, and then plug the cable or power supply into an AC outlet.

    An access point does not draw a lot of power, so it's not necessary to use a dedicated AC power source, but if you use an uninterruptible power supply or a surge protector to protect your computers, you should also protect your access point.

    If you are using a PoE system to provide power to the access point, follow the PoE instructions supplied with your access point to connect the power.

5. Connect an Ethernet cable between the LAN connector on your access point and the nearest network hub, switch, or other network point of presence.

6. Consult the manual to find out how to connect a control cable to the access point. Some access points use a serial cable from a nearby computer, and others connect through the network. You will use this connection to set the access point's configuration.

    If the access point uses a serial connection, it might be easier to take a laptop computer to a temporary location near the access point where you can see the LED indicators light and go dark as you run the configuration routine, rather than running a longer cable to an existing computer.

7. Turn on the access point's power switch. You will probably see an LED indicator light. It could take a few minutes before the access point's internal processor is ready to operate. The access point's manual should explain the function of the LED indicators.

After the physical installation is complete, the next step is to configure the access point. If you are using the same brand of access point and wireless interface adapters, the default settings are probably the same, so you might be able to install an adapter into a nearby computer and test the network immediately.

Configuring the Access Point Through a Browser

Most access points have wired LAN ports, so they generally accept configuration commands through a dedicated local numeric IP address. You can use Microsoft Internet Explorer, Netscape Navigator, or any other graphic Web browser to view and change access point settings. Because the access point contains its own software, the configuration program will run on any operating system. You don't need different programs for Windows, Macintosh, Linux, Unix, or other operating systems.

Most people will find the graphic configuration utility easier to use than the command-line version, because it's not necessary to remember a bunch of cryptic commands every time you want to do anything.

The first time you turn on the access point, it will use the default settings that were set at the factory. Unless you change some of these settings, it might be possible for unauthorized users to gain access to your network and for network users (authorized or not) to make changes that should be made only by the network manager.

Once again, the specific configuration procedure is different for each type of access point, but the general principles are similar. Use this procedure as a supplement to the information in the access point's manual:

1. Confirm that the access point is connected to the LAN.

2. From a computer connected to the LAN, open the Web browser of your choice.

3. In the browser's Address field, type the default numeric IP address for the access point, as specified in the access point's manual, and then press ENTER.

4. The browser should find and open the access point's login window, like the one in Figure 3.6. Enter the information requested—usually a login name, a password, or both.

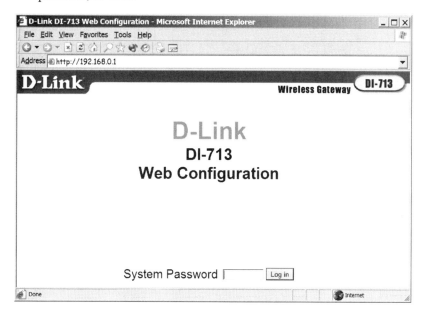

Figure 3.6: The access point's password window controls access to the configuration utility

5. You should see the top-level configuration page. Figure 3.7 shows a typical configuration page, this one for the ZoomAir AP11 access point.

If you get an "Unable to connect" message instead of a login window when you try to open the configuration utility, send a ping request to the access point. In Windows, open a DOS Prompt window and type

```
ping [IP address]
```

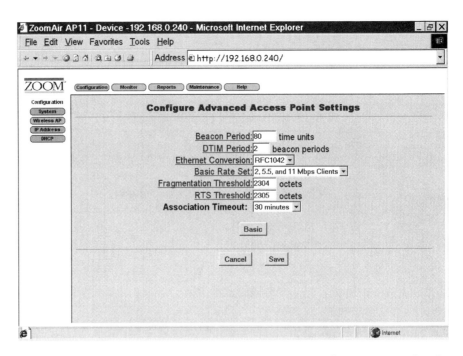

Figure 3.7: The configuration screen for a ZoomAir access point. Configuration screens for other access points display similar information, but they arrange the information differently.

using the access point's numeric IP address. If the network recognizes the address, you should see a response like the one in Figure 3.8. If the program reports "host unreachable," a conflict probably exists between the Dynamic Host Configuration Protocol (DHCP) server on your LAN and the default address for the access point. The next section explains how to deal with this problem.

DHCP and Other Disasters

DHCP (Dynamic Host Configuration Protocol) automatically assigns an IP address to each computer on a network. Because DHCP eliminates the need to manually assign a separate address to each computer, it can save a lot of time and trouble, but when the network hub or switch and the wireless access point both try to act as DHCP servers, or when a client device expects a specific address but the DHCP server assigns an address on the fly, trying to set up the network can become ugly.

Conflicting DHCP servers can cause problems when you add an access point to a LAN. Some stand-alone access points expect to receive requests for access to the Web-based configuration screens at a specific numeric IP address. When that access point is connected to a hub that is acting as a DHCP server, however, the server assigns a different IP address to the access point. So when a user tries to connect to the IP address listed in the access point manual, nothing happens (or the browser reports "unable to find this address," which is about the same thing).

Configuring an access point for DHCP would be a lot easier if every access point treated DHCP in the same way. But of course they don't. The only way that

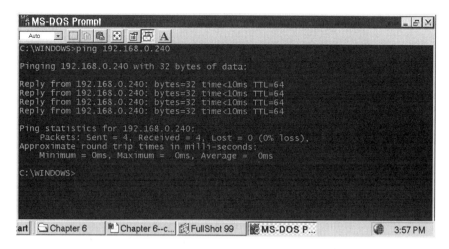

Figure 3.8: A successful ping request returns a series of timed echoes from the target device

could happen would be if all the engineers at all the companies that design and make access points were to come up with exactly the same solution to the problem. Fat chance.

There are several ways to deal with this. You can avoid it completely by using the console function of most access points and enter configuration commands through a serial port rather than the Web-based utility, but that means you must use an obscure command language that is likely to be harder to master than the graphic utility, and some access points don't accept commands through their serial ports.

The second possibility is to use the console function to change the numeric IP address of the Web-based utility from the default to the address assigned by the DHCP server. Most DHCP servers include a display of assigned addresses, like the one in Figure 3.9. After changing the access point's address, use your Web browser to reach the configuration utility.

If you don't want to mess with setting up a serial port connection to the access point, the next alternative is to turn off the DHCP server and use the access point's default IP address to display the configuration utility in your browser. This approach is okay as a temporary fix while you're setting up the network, but it disables the addresses of all the other client computers that receive them from the same DHCP server. Therefore, it will be necessary either to assign all the addresses manually or to make sure you turn the DHCP server back on after you finish configuring the network.

If all those methods seem too complicated, there's one more way to get to the configuration screens: run a *crossover* cable from the access point's LAN port to a computer with an Ethernet port. The crossover cable swaps pins on the cable connectors, so the devices at each end both send and receive data on the correct pins. With the cable in place, you can use your browser to open the utility at the default IP address. This approach is easy if you have the right kind of cable (a standard Ethernet cable won't work), but it does force you to disconnect the access point from the rest of the network.

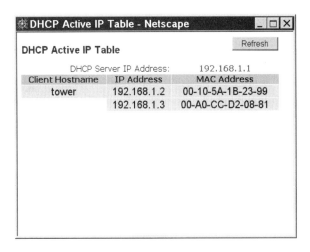

Figure 3.9: A DHCP server assigns numeric IP addresses to all of the nodes in the LAN. In this case, the access point's address is 192.168.1.3.

It's important to remember that a LAN can have only one DHCP server. If the LAN includes another DHCP server that assigns numeric addresses, it's best to disable the DHCP function in the access point and allow the main server to handle address assignments for the entire network, including both wired and wireless nodes.

This is one case where a generic description of the problem is less useful than the specific procedure provided with your particular access point. The hardware manual should contain setup instructions that cover both the access point's configuration utility and the Windows networking settings that apply to each client machine. Find the manual, and try to follow those instructions as closely as possible. When you do come up with a combination of access point configuration settings and Windows networking settings that actually works (and it's a safe bet that such a combination does exist), note those settings on paper and store them with the manual. You will need them later to add more computers and access points to the same network.

Configuring the Access Point Through a Serial Port

Most access points include a serial port that accepts a direct connection from a remote terminal (or more likely, from a computer running a terminal emulator program, such as the HyperTerminal program supplied with Windows). This provides an alternative to the common Web-based configuration utilities.

The serial port on an access point may be either a 9-pin DB-9 data connector or an RJ-45 connector that looks like a slightly fatter version of the RJ-11 connector commonly used on a single-line telephone. If your access point uses an RJ-45, the manufacturer probably provided a cable and an adapter. If the connector is a DB-9, it probably requires a straight-through cable from a computer's COM port. If the access point requires a null modem cable, that fact should be mentioned prominently in the manual.

At least one access point has a DB-9 connector that does not provide access to the configuration utility. The D-Link DI-713 Wireless Gateway has a serial port that connects to a modem and a dial-up phone line, as an optional backup to its WAN connection.

To send commands to the access point through the serial port, follow these steps:

1. Run a cable between the access point and one of the computer's COM ports.

2. Start a terminal emulator program, such as HyperTerminal (which is provided with Windows), and configure a connection through the COM port connected to the access point.

3. Open a connection to the access point.

4. If it is not already on, turn on the access point. You may see a start-up message on the terminal emulator, such as the one in Figure 3.10.

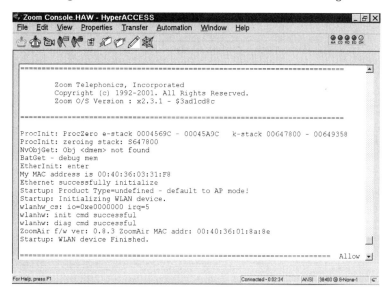

Figure 3.10: An access point's console program might display a start-up message when you turn on the unit

5. When the access point is ready to accept commands, it will display a prompt. To confirm that the terminal emulator is working, press ENTER. The access point should display another prompt on a new line.

At this point, the access point is ready to accept configuration commands. Each brand of access point uses a different command language, so you'll have to look in the manual to find the exact commands you must use to change your network settings.

Configuration Commands and Settings

Each configuration utility handles configuration commands and settings differently, but every access point that follows the 802.11b specifications should include the same basic set of options. As you set up your wireless network, you might want to change some of these options from the default values.

Many Web-based configuration utilities use tabs or menus to split the list of options into several screens. If the location of a particular command is not obvious from the layout of the top-level screen, either try opening lower-level screens until you find the one you want or look in the access point's manual for specific navigation instructions.

The command language for changing the configuration through the access point's serial point should also be described in the manual. In many cases, a help command will produce an on-screen list of other commands with their proper syntax.

In general, the configuration utility should include these options: IP address, subnet mask, wireless network ID, channel, security, and DHCP.

IP Address

The IP address field displays the numeric IP address currently used by the access point. This could be a default address assigned at the factory, an address automatically assigned by the LAN's DHCP server, or an address assigned manually by the network manager.

Subnet Mask

The subnet mask field identifies the subnetwork that includes the access point and the wireless clients that connect to the LAN through the access point. The address of the subnetwork is assigned by the network manager. If your LAN does not include a subnetwork, use the default value of 255.255.255.0.

Wireless Network ID (SSID)

The SSID (Service Set Identification) is the "name" of the wireless network that includes this access point. When a wireless client attempts to connect to a network, it searches for an access point with the same SSID as the one in its own configuration settings. If it finds a signal with a different SSID, it rejects the association and continues to scan for the correct SSID.

Therefore, the SSID serves two purposes: it acts as the first line of defense against unauthorized access to a wireless network, and in an environment where more than one wireless LAN is operating, it associates each client with the right network. However, the SSID by itself is not a particularly effective security tool, because some network adapters will accept an SSID of ANY, which will allow the client to associate with the first access point it finds, regardless of the access point's SSID.

Channel

The channel setting is the radio channel number that the access point will use to exchange data with the client devices in the wireless LAN. Each access point operates on a single channel, but most network adapters scan across all the channels to find the best available signal with the same SSID. If the clients in your network include the scanning function, you can assume that nearby client devices will find your access point, regardless of the channel setting. When one of your users tries to use a network adapter with a preset channel, however, the channel settings for the access point and the client must match.

In a noisy environment, some channels might perform better than others, because other networks and other 2.4 GHz devices could generate interference on some frequencies but not on others. If other wireless networks are also operating nearby, you might reduce interference and improve performance by using channel numbers that don't overlap. If that's not possible, use channels as far apart from one another as possible.

If your network includes more than one access point, you should set adjacent access points to different channels. To avoid overlap between signals, remember to use channels that are at least five channel numbers apart, such as Channels 1, 6, and 11.

Security

WEP (Wired Equivalent Privacy) is the security scheme that is supposed to keep people who do not have the proper electronic key code out of your network. As Chapter 14 of this book explains, WEP encryption is not particularly effective against a determined eavesdropper, but it's better than nothing. All 802.11b hardware comes with optional WEP encryption, so you ought to know how to use it.

Every access point can use a 64-bit WEP encryption key to restrict unauthorized access, and some offer the choice of either a 64-bit key or a more secure 128-bit key. Because the 64-bit key is actually a 40-bit key combined with a 24-bit initialization vector string, some configuration programs call it 40-bit encryption. Access points and network adapters that use 40-bit WEP encryption are completely compatible with those that use 64-bit WEP encryption.

Unfortunately, some manufacturers request a string of letters and numbers as a WEP key, and others expect you to provide a series of hexadecimal numbers, either as five groups of two or as a single ten-digit string. Still others will ask you for a passphrase and automatically generate the hex key for you.

It's generally easier to set up a wireless network with encryption disabled, but it's a very good idea to turn it on when you start moving real data through the network. The WEP keys must be identical in each of your access points' configuration utilities and all the client devices that you expect to use with each access point.

DHCP

As mentioned in the "DHCP and Other Disasters" section a few pages back, an access point can act as a DHCP server that automatically assigns numeric IP addresses to the wireless clients in the network.

Remember that only one DHCP server can be active at any time, so if the network already has an active DHCP server, disable the access point's DHCP function. If your network includes more than one access point, the DHCP server should be active in only one of them — and then only if no other server is already active.

When the access point's DHCP server is active, the configuration utility might display a list of currently active DHCP clients on the same screen that contains the enable/disable options, or the utility might offer to open another window or display another screen that contains the list of DHCP clients.

Other Settings

In addition to the settings listed previously, you might discover several other options in your access point's configuration utility. Some could control other non-wireless functions built into the same device, and others might be settings that allow a user to specify some arbitrary values that would otherwise be changed in the client device.

The access point's manual should give you the information you will need to set these options. When the purpose of a setting is not clear, or if it looks like it won't have any effect on your network, the safest approach is to accept the default value. In other words, when in doubt, leave it alone!

Multiple Access Points

Many wireless networks use more than one access point to extend the network's coverage beyond the signal range of a single base station. If the client device moves away from the currently active access point and closer to another one, or if the signal quality deteriorates because of interference from other radio signals, the original access point will hand off the link to the access point that is receiving the best signal from the client. This is similar to the technology that permits cellular telephones to roam without interrupting a conversation.

The 802.11b specification allows client devices to move a link to the network from one access point to another, but it does not explain how to hand off an association. In the absence of a standard, each access point manufacturer has come up with its own method, which may not be compatible with any other manufacturer's system. This will probably change at some point, but for the foreseeable future, it's essential to use just one type of access point in your network. You can expect a Wi-Fi–compliant network adapter to work with any brand of access point, but it's not safe to expect two different kinds of access points to work together.

To set up a wireless network with more than one access point, simply connect all the access points to the same wired Ethernet network, and configure all the access points to handle the same SSID and WEP keys. If you're not using a DHCP server that automatically assigns IP addresses, assign a different numeric IP address to each access point, but use the same subnet and gateway addresses for the whole network. If an access point is acting as a DHCP server, remember to disable the DHCP function in all the other access points in the network.

Each access point should operate on a different channel from the ones used by adjacent access points. If possible, use channel numbers that don't interfere with one another, such as Channels 1, 6, and 11. In a very large space, try to keep channel numbers widely separated by staggering the channel numbers over the entire area, like the arrangement in Figure 3.11.

Access Points Combined with Hubs and Gateway Routers

Several manufacturers offer products that combine the functions of a wireless access point with a network hub, switch, or router. Other combination products include network print servers or broadband (cable or DSL) Internet access along

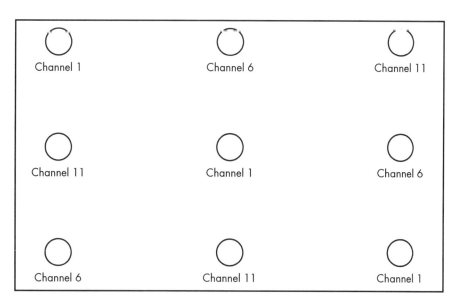

Figure 3.11: Keep overlapping access points separate from one another in a network with multiple base stations

with access points. A combination unit can be an excellent starting point for a new small network or for adding both wired and wireless clients to an existing network. Because a combined device doesn't require separate power supplies, enclosures, and interconnecting cables for each function, the cost is likely to be considerably less than the cost of separate components that perform the same jobs. The convenience of reducing the number of cables tying everything together can also be a huge attraction, especially for a small network that doesn't run everything back to a wiring closet.

To decide whether one of these combination units is the best way to meet your particular requirements, identify those requirements first, and then look at various manufacturers' product catalogs and Web sites to find a device that comes as close to your needs as possible. Among others, D-Link, Linksys, Intel, and Buffalo offer a wide variety of access points combined with other functions.

Installing the access point portion of a combination unit is not much different from installing a stand-alone access point. Each device uses a proprietary configuration utility that offers a place to set the access point's operating channel, the SSID, and other settings, along with other configuration options that apply to the device's added functions. Once again, the manual provided with each product is the only place to find the specific information needed to complete the configuration and setup routines.

In most Wi-Fi networks, the access points are just about invisible in daily operation. They sit on a shelf, or they're on the floor behind a desk where they move data between client computers and the wired network. Once you get the access point up and running, you can just about forget it until you need to change the configuration.

4

INSTALLING AND CONFIGURING NETWORK INTERFACES

In general, installing a wireless network adapter is easier than installing an access point, because most network adapters are Plug-and-Play devices. Regardless of the physical configuration, every network adapter requires both a device driver to act as a software interface between the adapter and the computer's operating system and a configuration utility that allows a user to set the adapter's operating parameters.

Installing PC Card Adapters

Network adapters on PC Cards plug into the PCMCIA socket on a portable computer or into the socket adapter that fits an expansion slot in a desktop computer (yes, that does mean that one kind of adapter plugs into another kind of adapter). To install the PC Card, just insert it gently but firmly into the socket. When it's properly seated, you should feel the pins inside the socket mate with the holes on the edge of the card.

Most wireless PC Card adapters contain internal antennas that extend an inch or more beyond the outer edge of the PCMCIA socket. However, a few adapters come with connectors for external antennas. If you are using an external antenna, place the antenna in the location where you want to operate it, and run the antenna cable from the antenna to the network adapter's antenna connector.

Installing USB Adapters

Most USB wireless adapters are compact devices with internal antennas. Because the adapter connects to the computer through a cable, it's easy to move the adapter around when the first position you try doesn't detect a strong signal from the access point.

To install a USB adapter, follow these steps:

1. Run a USB cable from the computer to the location where you plan to place the adapter. Note that the two ends of a USB cable have different types of connectors, so make sure the connector at the computer end of the cable mates with the computer's USB port.
2. Plug the cable into the computer's USB port.
3. Plug the other end of the cable into the network adapter.
4. Run the configuration program provided with your adapter, or use the Wireless Configuration Tool included with Windows XP.
5. Open the signal strength and signal quality display.
6. If the signal quality is not good or excellent, adjust the adapter's location for optimal performance.

Installing Internal Adapters

Adding an internal adapter to a desktop computer is a bit more complicated because it requires opening the case and inserting the adapter into an expansion slot. But it's no different from adding any other expansion card, which most network managers and serious home computer users have probably done more times than they care to think about.

You know the routine: Unplug the power cable. Open the case. Find a vacant expansion slot. Remove the metal backplane cover. Insert the adapter into the slot. Screw it down. Close the case. Plug the power cable back into the computer. Lather. Rinse. Repeat. Close cover before striking.

Most internal network adapters are actually PC Card adapters with PCMCIA sockets that fit into an expansion slot. Unless the adapter manual tells you otherwise, it's a good idea to remove the PC Card from the socket before you install the socket in your computer. It often takes a bit of twisting and pushing to seat the socket properly in the expansion slot, and the socket is more flexible without the card in place. After you reassemble the computer and confirm that Windows (or whatever operating system you may be using) recognizes the PCMCIA socket, insert the adapter into the socket and load the wireless adapter driver.

Many internal network adapters are not true PCMCIA to PCI bridges, but instead use a simpler and cheaper method called PLX. This means that while any PCMCIA card will fit into the PCI adapter, without special drivers they will not work.

Loading the Driver Software

Regardless of their physical format, just about all wireless adapters are Plug-and-Play devices, which means that Windows should automatically recognize the adapter as soon as you install it. However, the operating system needs to load a specific software driver for each type of adapter before it can use the adapter to send and receive data.

Drivers can come from several sources — they may be automatically provided by Windows, provided on diskette or a CD-ROM supplied with the adapter, or available at the company's technical support Web site. Often, the most up-to-date drivers are available from the company Web site. The same software disk or download that contains the driver for a wireless network adapter also includes the configuration utility program for that adapter. It should be possible to load the software and the driver before physically installing or connecting the adapter.

The first time you insert a PC Card into the PCMCIA socket or plug a USB adapter into the computer's USB port, Windows will identify the adapter and run its Add New Hardware Wizard, as shown in Figure 4.1. Assuming you have already loaded the latest version of the driver and the configuration utility, choose the automatic search option. Windows will find and install the driver.

Figure 4.1: Windows offers to load a driver the first time it detects new hardware

After it installs the driver, Windows will instruct you to restart the computer. Some configuration utilities run automatically whenever a wireless adapter is active; others require a user to start the program from the Start • Programs menu or from an icon on the Windows desktop. If the configuration program does not open in a program window, it will display a status icon in the system tray, next to the time display.

The driver for Apple AirPort loads on a Macintosh as part of the installation package. In Linux and Unix systems, you will have to install the driver manually. Chapters 7 and 8 describe Linux and Unix drivers in more detail.

Using the Configuration Utility Program

It should come as no surprise that every manufacturer of wireless access points uses a different configuration utility program. They all control the same settings and options, and they all display similar information, but most companies prefer to write their own software instead of licensing an existing program from somebody else. There are a few exception, but in most cases, you will see a different utility with each brand of adapter.

The major differences between configuration utilities have more to do with the layout of the options and status information than with the functionality of the program. Some manufacturers use one program to display the current status of the wireless link and a separate program to change configuration settings, and others use a single program with separate tabs or menu options for status and configuration information. For all practical purposes, though, every configuration utility does the same things.

Some configuration utilities run automatically when Windows starts, which is fine in computers that always use a wireless link. However, in portable computers that often run without an active network connection, loading the utility just increases the amount of time needed to boot the computer, and it wastes some small amount of system memory. To keep the configuration program from starting automatically in Windows 98, Windows ME, and Windows XP, use the Start • Programs • Startup menu or the msconfig program to identify and disable programs that start automatically.

The Microsoft Wireless Network Connection Utility

Windows XP includes a Wireless Network Connection utility that supports many of the most widely used wireless network adapters. When Windows supports a network adapter, it will automatically run the Wireless Network Connection utility unless you have disabled it in the Wireless Networks tab of the Wireless Network Connection Properties window, shown in Figure 4.2. If the Windows utility does not support the adapter, it will use the configuration utility supplied with the adapter.

If you are using an Orinoco adapter with Windows XP, the manufacturer recommends that you use the Microsoft utility instead of the Orinoco Client Manager. In practice, it doesn't appear to make much difference which one you use — they'll both display the information you need to select an access point, and both offer similar controls. You should try both programs and choose the one that seems easier to use. This may also be true with other brands of adapters, as Microsoft and the individual adapter manufacturers extend the Wireless Network Connection utility to support additional adapters.

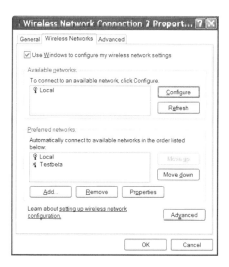

Figure 4.2: Use the Wireless Networks tab in the Properties window to enable or disable the Wireless Network Connection utility

Reading Status Information

Figures 4.3, 4.4, and 4.5 show status displays for two different brands of wireless adapters. Figure 4.6 shows the Windows Wireless Network Connection status display.

Each of these programs provides a somewhat different set of information. Most status displays contain most of these items:

- **Signal strength**   Signal strength is the amount of power in the radio signal that the adapter received during the most recent scan. Most programs show signal strength as a percentage, but some may offer the measured strength in dBm (decibels below 1 milliwatt). In practice, the signal strength value is most useful as a relative measurement to show how the signal changes in different locations, but it doesn't have much meaning between different manufacturers.

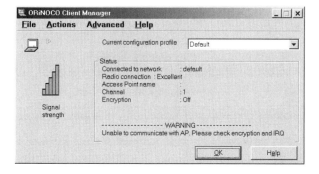

Figure 4.3: Lucent's Orinoco Client Manager arranges the same information as the Wireless Network Connection utility but in a different layout

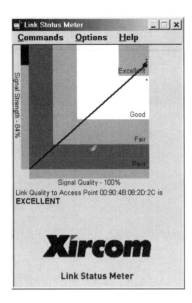

Figure 4.4: Xircom (and Cisco) show signal quality in one display and other status information in a separate window

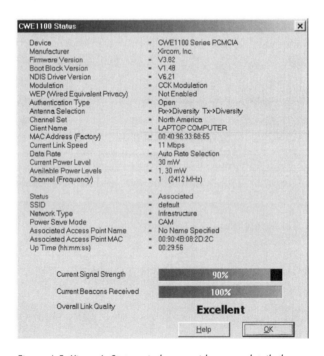

Figure 4.5: Xircom's Status window provides more details than some of its competitors

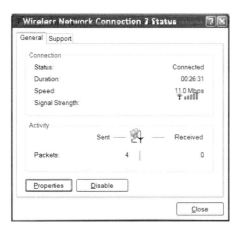

Figure 4.6: The Wireless Network Connection window in Windows XP shows the same information in another format

- **Signal quality**   Signal quality is the quality of the data packets the adapter received during the most recent scan. A 100 percent reading indicates that all of the received packets are good.

- **Overall quality**   Overall quality is a calculated value based on the signal strength and signal quality. It is usually expressed as Excellent, Good, Fair, or Poor.

- **Link speed or data rate**   The link speed is the nominal data transfer speed that the adapter and the associated access point are currently using.

- **Association**   This field confirms that the adapter has established an association with a wireless LAN.

- **MAC**   This field identifies the network adapter's unique MAC address.

- **SSID**   The SSID is the name of the LAN with which this device is currently associated. All nodes and access points in a wireless LAN must use the same SSID.

- **Network type**   If the network uses one or more access points, the network type is *infrastructure*. If it's a peer-to-peer network, the type is *ad hoc*.

- **Channel**   This field shows the radio channel that the adapter is currently using.

- **Encryption**   This field shows whether the adapter is currently using WEP encryption, and if the adapter can handle both 64-bit and 128-bit encryption, which type of encryption is in use.

- **Activity**   The activity display shows the number of outbound and inbound packets that the adapter has sent and received.

Wireless Configuration Tools

The configuration tool is the place to set or change the local settings that your adapter uses to communicate with the network. Some utilities show the status information in one window and provide a place to change those settings in a separate window.

The network type, SSID, and WEP encryption key settings must all be the same for every node in a network. The numeric IP address for each adapter in a network must be unique, but the subnet address should be the same for all adapters.

If your adapter does not automatically scan for the active channel, or if more than one access point are within range, you must use the configuration tool to set the channel number to the channel used by the nearest access point.

The easiest way to configure a whole network full of adapters is to start by configuring the access point and then note the wireless configuration settings that you must match in the individual adapters. If you expect your users to configure their own adapters, you will want to prepare a standard information sheet or card that lists these settings:

- The network's SSID
- Network type (infrastructure or ad hoc)
- DHCP on or off
- If DHCP is off, the IP address and subnet assigned to this adapter
- Type of WEP encryption (none, 40/64-bit, or 128-bit)
- WEP encryption key (or the telephone number of the help desk that can provide it)
- Channel number
- Preamble length
- URL, login, and password for access to the network (if necessary)

No matter how clear you make the written instructions, some people will have trouble connecting to the network without help. So, your instruction sheet should also include the name or telephone number of the people who can help set up an adapter and talk a confused user through the configuration process.

If most of your users have the same kind of adapter, you might want to include screen captures of that adapter's configuration window and the Windows Network Settings window, with step-by-step instructions for opening those windows.

Moving from One Network to Another

If you use your portable computer on more than one wireless network, you may want to prepare your own cheat sheet for configuring your network adapter to work with each network that you regularly use: home, office, coffee shop, airport, and so forth. Some configuration utilities offer two or more preset configuration profiles, but if yours does not, you will have to set all the options each time you move to a different network.

The Wireless Network Connection utility in Windows XP includes an automatic wireless configuration feature that detects every wireless network within range and automatically configures your wireless adapter. If your adapter is compatible with the Windows utility, this can save a lot of time and trouble. However, if Windows doesn't detect a network that ought to be there, it won't hurt to use a sniffer tool, such as Network Stumbler, to perform your own search.

To use the automatic wireless configuration feature in Windows XP, follow these steps:

1. Open the Wireless Network Properties window by clicking the network icon in the System Tray next to the clock, or open Start • Settings • Network Connections, right-click the icon for the wireless network connection, and select Properties from the pop-up menu.

2. Select the Wireless Networks tab.

3. Enable or disable automatic configuration by selecting the Use Windows to Configure My Wireless Network Settings option.

4. Click the Advanced button to open a window where you can set the type of networks that Windows will automatically detect. Figure 4.7 shows the Advanced window.

Figure 4.7: The Advanced Wireless Network Connection Properties window lets you specify the networks that Windows will automatically detect

5. Choose the type of network that you want your computer to detect. To instruct Windows to detect and connect to any nearby network, even if it's not in the Preferred Networks list, turn on the Automatically Connect to Non-preferred Networks option.

On Beyond Windows

Every adapter manufacturer provides software for the most popular versions of Microsoft Windows, but that's not the only operating system you can use with a wireless network adapter—if you can find the right drivers. Drivers for less-common operating systems may be available from the adapter manufacturer's technical support Web sites or from user groups devoted to the operating system in question.

For Macintosh users, your best bet is to use Apple's AirPort adapters and the software provided with them, which are fully compatible with other 802.11b networks. However, some other adapters will also work with a Mac if you have the right drivers. Apple's AirPort adapters are private-label versions of Orinoco products, so you can often use Apple software with Orinoco adapters. Chapter 6 explains how to use AirPort software with a Macintosh.

If you have some other make of PC Card or USB wireless adapter, don't give up hope. Cisco and other manufacturers also offer Mac OS drivers and configuration software. Check the adapter maker's Web site for the latest versions.

Drivers for some adapters are also available for Linux, FreeBSD, NetBSD, and other varieties of Unix, either directly from the manufacturer (for example, both Orinoco and Cisco offer Linux drivers through their Web sites) or through user groups. Some recent releases of several flavors of Unix and Linux include drivers for several widely used 802.11b chip sets. Chapters 7 and 8 contain more detailed information about using Linux and Unix on a wireless Ethernet network.

Signal Strength and Signal Quality

Most wireless utilities show signal strength and quality in bar graphs or as a percentage value, but they don't tell you what a signal at 100 percent strength is 100 percent *of*. It's important to understand that signal strength and signal quality are not the same thing; a wireless adapter does not have to receive a signal at "full strength" to move data at the maximum possible speed. As long as the receiver can capture a clean signal, the network's performance should be acceptable. But even a strong signal can suffer if the receiver also picks up interference from other wireless networks or from other devices that use the same radio frequencies, such as wireless telephones and microwave ovens.

Even if the data transfer speed is slower than the maximum possible rate, it might not make any difference. For example, if you're using a Wi-Fi network to connect your computer to the Internet through a DSL line (at about .5 Mbps or less), it won't make any difference if your local network speed drops from 11 Mbps down to 2 Mbps; that's still a lot more bandwidth than you need.

The spread-spectrum radio signal used in a Wi-Fi network is not the same as an FM radio signal, but the interference and signal quality problems are similar. If you live in or near a big city, you can probably receive a dozen or more FM radio stations on your kitchen radio. Some of these stations might have transmitters close to your house, and others may transmit from the other side of town or even farther away. But as long as your radio can capture a station at a minimum useful level, the radio reproduces the music reasonably well; the signal from the little teakettle college radio station a mile away sounds just as good as the big commercial station with a much more powerful transmitter up in the hills (this is a technical discussion—the quality of the programming is a whole other question). On the other hand, if you're out on the fringes of the station's coverage area, or if there's another nearby station using the same frequency, the sound of the station you want to hear will be noisy and hard to understand. In the same way, the overall quality of a wireless network link is affected by both signal strength and the presence or absence of unwanted noise.

The technical definition of *noise* in an information channel is "any unwanted energy or information." The only thing you want your network adapter to receive is the digital signal that came from your own network's access point, so everything else that shows up at the receiver is noise. This can include interference from other wireless data networks and other radios using the same frequencies and interference from natural sources such as lightning. Up to a point, the digital technology and spread-spectrum radio system used in an 802.11b network can do a pretty good job of ignoring interference, but when the noise is just as strong as the signal you want, the network will apply its error-correction features until it can confirm that an intelligible signal has made it from the transmitter to the receiver.

A stream of noise or another pair of radios trying to use the same channel at the same time can reduce a link's data transfer speed, but so can a weak signal. As the distance between the transmitter and the receiver increases, the amount of energy that the receiver detects will decrease, until the signal is simply too weak for the receiver to decode the data. If there are physical obstructions that absorb some of the radiated energy between the transmitter and the receiver, the useful signal range will be even shorter. It's possible to use a high-gain antenna to increase the signal strength, and you can raise the antenna to the top of a tower or a tall building to increase the useful distance that it will travel, but at some point, the signal strength will be too weak to be useful.

When signal problems do occur, you can use the signal strength and quality measurements to help identify the source of the problem: if the signal is strong but the quality is low, the problem is probably caused by some kind of interference, but if both the signal quality and signal strength are low, it's likely that you're too far away from the nearest access point or there is some kind of obstruction. Any time the network fails to transmit a data packet successfully, the device at the receiving end instructs the transmitting device to send the same packet again. This may happen when there is noise or interference on the link (radio or wired), when other users are trying to use the same channel at the same time, or when a radio signal is too weak for the receiver to decode the data contained in the packet. One or two repeated packets in a data stream won't make any real difference, but when it becomes necessary to send almost every packet several times before the receiver accepts it, the actual data transfer speed will be half of the nominal speed or less. A pair of 802.11b radios might try to compensate for a poor signal by dropping the transmission speed (this is the same kind of approach as speaking slowly and distinctly over a noisy telephone line), but the effect is often the same: it takes longer to receive the data.

Slow data transfer is not always caused by the radio portion of the network; it can also happen when there's heavy traffic on a server or some kind of noise on the wired portion of the network, so several problems can all produce the same symptoms. When data speed appears to slow down, the cause could be in the radio link or the server, or someplace else in the network. To isolate the source of the problem, run the configuration utility or the status report program on the client computer. If the signal strength is low, try moving to a different location, away from obstructions between your computer and the access point; if the signal strength is adequate but signal quality is poor, the network adapter is probably receiving noise along with the network data; and if both signal strength and signal quality are adequate but the data speed is slow, the cause is probably in the server or someplace else in the network.

5

WI-FI FOR WINDOWS

In a world of ideal networks, it would be possible to plug a wireless network adapter into a computer, fire it up, and connect to the network right away. No fuss, no bother (and no need for a book like this one). When Windows identifies a network adapter during startup, it should automatically place a Network icon on the desktop and configure a set of standard network resources.

Unfortunately, nothing is ever that simple. Before you can start to move data across a wireless network, you will probably have to tell Windows exactly how and where to find the network and how to connect through the wireless LAN to the Internet. This chapter contains an explanation of the general principles involved in making Windows work with a wireless LAN and the specific procedures you will need to configure the networking tools and features in different versions of Windows. This is tedious, nitpicky stuff, but if you don't get it right, your network won't work properly.

In Windows XP, all of this configuration nonsense is supposed to happen automatically, if (and it's a big *if*) your network adapter contains firmware compatible with Microsoft's automatic configuration tool. Many of the most popular brands of adapters don't, so there's an excellent chance that you'll need to configure your wireless network connection by hand. Even if Windows does recognize your adapter, it can be useful to understand what's happening below the visible surface.

If you have experience setting up Windows networks, you shouldn't have much trouble with wireless. As far as Windows is concerned, a wireless adapter is just one more type of network interface that exchanges data with applications and the operating system. Up until Windows XP, the "wireless" stuff happens in a separate utility; in XP, there's a tab for wireless-specific settings in the network properties dialog box. Configuring Windows for wireless is a matter of making this particular computer aware that it's connected to a network and then setting the addresses of the network servers and services.

Unfortunately, Windows spreads the configuration options all over the virtual map, so a set of pointers to each of those options can be extremely helpful. You will find those pointers later in this chapter.

Windows Network Configuration in General

Different versions of Windows use somewhat different configuration tools, but they all accomplish the same thing: the computer's IP address, subnet mask, and gateway address settings must all match the values that the rest of the network requires. It's entirely possible to set these values without understanding what they mean, but it's always helpful to know something about how the network actually works.

IP Addresses

The numeric IP (Internet Protocol) address of a network client is the formal identity that the other computers in the same network use to reach that device. Every computer on a network must have a different address.

The agencies that administer the Internet have established a complex numbering system with a unique address for every device connected to the Net. Numeric IP addresses always appear as four groups of numbers within the range 0 to 255, so the total universe of IP addresses runs from 0.0.0.0 to 255.255.255.255. These numbers are sometimes called "octets" because they use eight binary digits (binary 11111111 equals decimal 255).

A numeric IP address can identify a single computer, or it can be a gateway to a LAN (or a larger network) with two or more computers connected to it through a router. When the LAN connects to the Internet through a gateway, each local computer must also have a unique numeric IP address. Depending on how your network is designed, every computer on the LAN may have a real IP that is reachable from the Internet, or it may have an IP in one of ranges designated for private use and a gateway that connects the LAN to the Internet and translates between private and public addresses.

To prevent conflicts between local IP addresses and Internet addresses, several ranges of numbers have been reserved for use by local networks:

- 10.0.0.0 to 10.255.255.255
- 172.16.0.0 to 172.31.255.255
- 192.168.0.0 to 192.168.255.255

Assigning Addresses

In some networks, a DHCP (Dynamic Host Configuration Protocol) server assigns a different IP address to every client device on the network. The server assigns an address to each client device whenever the client joins the network, so the same client might have a different local address from one session to another; that's why it's called *dynamic host configuration*.

The DHCP server is usually in the router that controls all the devices in the network. In a pure wireless network, that's probably in an access point; in a mixed network that has both wireless and wired links, the DHCP server is likely to be in the Internet gateway. Figure 5.1 shows the server in a typical network.

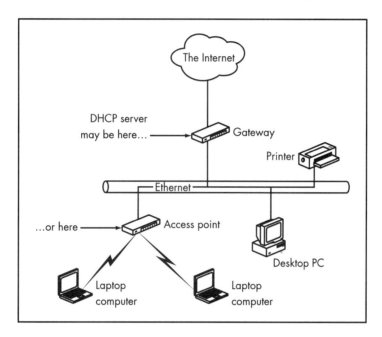

Figure 5.1: A DHCP server provides local IP addresses to all the devices in a LAN

When a DHCP server is active, all of the users on the LAN should instruct Windows (and other network operating systems) to obtain an IP address automatically. If a network does not use a DHCP server, the network manager must assign a permanent address to each client. If you assign addresses manually, keep a copy of the list of addresses in a text file, with a backup copy on paper.

The manual for your access point should specify the default range of addresses for client devices. If you use DHCP, the server will assign them automatically. If you don't use DHCP, you must use a different address within the specified range for each device on your network. If you are connecting a wireless network to your wired LAN, you may need to configure the range that the access point hands out as a range of addresses in the same range as your LAN.

The Subnet Mask

The *subnet mask* is a string of four numbers that specifies which part of a larger network contains a computer or other network node. Each of the four numbers is usually either 255 or 0. The numbers specify which parts of the IP address identify the network or the local subnetwork (the *subnet*), and which parts identify individual computers or other nodes on the network. For example, if the subnet mask is 255.255.255.0, then all the numeric IP addresses in the network must be XXX.XXX.XXX.ZZZ, where XXX.XXX.XXX is the same for all addresses, and ZZZ is different in each address.

The subnet mask must be identical for all of the access points and all the wireless clients served by those access points. In small and medium-size networks, the subnet mask is almost always 255.255.255.0.

Gateways

The *gateway* is the wireless access point, router, or other device that acts as the interface between the computers on a LAN and other devices or networks that are not part of the local network. Any time a computer that is not part of the local network tries to communicate with a device on the network, it must move data through the gateway.

The gateway address (sometimes called the *default gateway*) is the numeric IP address of the gateway server. Depending on how your wireless network is set up, this will often be the address that has been assigned to the access point, but if your wireless equipment is configured to function as a simple bridge, it may be the same IP address as the gateway for your wired network.

If an access point doubles as a hub or router, the gateway address that the access point uses for wired and wireless clients is not the same as the gateway address that it uses to communicate with a LAN or Internet server. When you configure a network client, remember to use the access point's LAN IP address as the default gateway, not the address of the WAN gateway.

DNS Servers

A DNS (Domain Name System) server is a computer that converts domain names, such as nostarch.com or hard-cider.com, to the numeric IP addresses of the computers or other devices that use those addresses. Some DHCP servers provide a DNS server address automatically, but others require each user to add the DNS server to each client's TCP/IP configuration by hand. If you are not using DHCP, you must specify at least one DNS server address.

Most networks and Internet service providers use two or more DNS servers in order to provide an automatic backup when the primary server is offline. Your network manager or your Internet service provider should give you the addresses of your network's DNS servers.

Some access points and network gateways also request a DNS server address. The list of servers in the access point or gateway should be identical to the list of servers on each client.

File and Printer Sharing

When File Sharing is active, other network users can read and write files to and from your computer. Printer Sharing allows other users to send files and documents to a printer connected to the shared printer. In Microsoft Networking, a folder that contains files that are available to other users is called a *share*.

The access level of a shared file or folder specifies whether other users can read a file but not change it, or that they have permission to add, remove, or change the contents of a file.

Network Interface Adapter Options

If you can't find a setting or option in the configuration utility, look in the Properties window for your wireless adapter. The driver for each type of network interface adapter includes a set of options that controls the specific features of that adapter, such as the name that the client will use on the network, the data transfer speed, the operating mode, and the power-saving mode. Figure 5.2 shows a typical list of adapter properties.

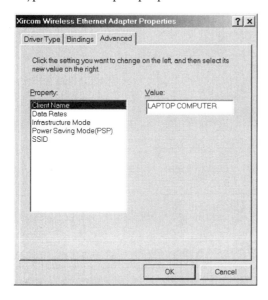

Figure 5.2: The adapter properties control many configuration options

To open the Properties window, go to the Windows Control Panel, double-click the System icon, and choose the Device Manager. Then open the list of Network Adapters and double-click the entry for your wireless adapter. The list of options is under the Advanced tab.

Many of the same adapter options also appear in the configuration utility supplied with the adapter and in the Wireless Configuration Utility in Windows XP. When you change an option in one place, that change should also appear in the other location the next time you open it.

Name Your Computer

The network uses a numeric IP address to find and identify your computer, but the human users of the network will want a name that is easier to recognize and remember than one of those strings of numbers and dots. Most users won't know or care that 192.168.0.34 is the computer in your office, and 192.168.0.37 is the laptop in the kitchen. So you (or the network manager) must assign a name to each computer in the network. This name will appear in all of the directories and lists of computers that can be reached through your network, as shown in Figure 5.3. Each computer must have a unique name, with a maximum length of 15 characters and spaces.

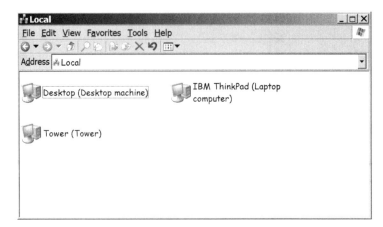

Figure 5.3: The name and description of each computer on the network appears in a network window

The Computer Description field is not required, but it can provide more detailed information about a network client to other users than the 15-character Computer Name limit allows.

Windows also provides a space to assign each computer on the network to a *workgroup*. In a small LAN, you will probably want to assign all of the computers to a single workgroup. Therefore, the Workgroup Name setting should be identical on every computer in the network.

In some wireless networks, the name of the workgroup must be the same as the SSID used by the access point, especially when the network configuration utility doesn't display a list of nearby networks. If you're having trouble connecting, try changing the workgroup name to the SSID of the network you want to join.

Configuring Windows 98 and Windows ME

Windows 98, Windows 98 SE, and Windows Me all have similar network configuration tools.

IP Address and Subnet Mask

Follow these steps to set the IP address and the subnet mask:

1. From the Control Panel, double-click the Network icon.

2. In the Configuration tab, scroll down to the TCP/IP entry for your network adapter and click the Properties button.

3. If it's not already visible, click the IP Address tab. The Properties window shown in Figure 5.4 will be displayed.

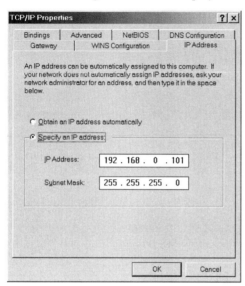

Figure 5.4: The IP Address tab controls network connection options

4. If the DHCP server in your access point or some other network device is active, select the Obtain an IP Address Automatically option. If you are not using a DHCP server, choose the Specify an IP Address option, and type the IP address assigned to this computer in the IP Address field.

5. The Subnet Mask field is in the same TCP/IP Properties tab that controls the IP address. If you are not using a DHCP server on your network, type the same subnet mask as the one used by the access point.

Gateway

Follow these steps to set the gateway address:

1. In the TCP/IP Properties window that you used to set the IP address, click the Gateway tab to display the dialog box shown in Figure 5.5.

2. Type the wireless access point's LAN IP address in the New gateway field and click the Add button.

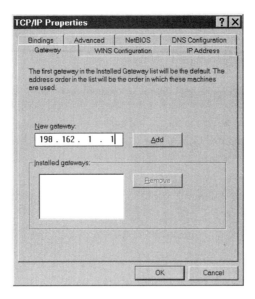

Figure 5.5: Use the Gateway tab to set the gateway address

DNS Servers

Follow these steps to set the DNS options:

1. In the TCP/IP Properties window, click the DNS Configuration tab to display the dialog box shown in Figure 5.6.

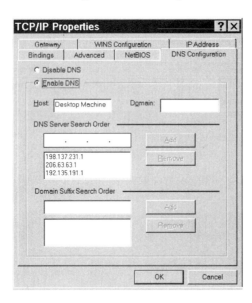

Figure 5.6: Use the DNS Configuration tab to set the name server options

2. If a DHCP server assigns DNS addresses to network clients, select the Disable DNS option. If the network uses a static DNS server, select the Enable DNS option.

3. If it is not already visible, type the name assigned to this computer in the Host field.

4. If the LAN, the access point, or the DHCP server uses a domain name, type the domain name in the Domain field.

5. Type the address of each DNS server that your network uses in the DNS Server Search Order field, and click the Add button. Your network manager or Internet service provider can supply the correct DNS addresses for your network.

6. Click the OK button in the TCP/IP Properties window and again in the Network window to save the new configuration settings. Windows will store the changes and ask you to reboot your computer. When the reboot is complete, the new settings will be active.

File and Printer Sharing

To make the contents of a folder or an entire drive available to other network users, right-click the folder or drive's icon and choose the Sharing option from the drop-down menu. The Properties dialog box shown in Figure 5.7 will open.

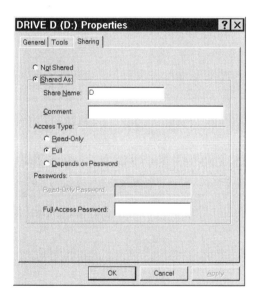

Figure 5.7: Use the Sharing tab to change the sharing characteristics of a folder or drive

To restrict access to this folder or drive to users on this computer, select the Not Shared option. To make it available to users on other computers, choose the Shared As option and select the type of access you want to offer for this resource.

When you have allowed shared access to a drive or folder, the icon for that item changes. When sharing is permitted, the icon includes a hand "serving" the item to the network.

Network Interface Adapter Options

To change the network interface adapter options, follow these steps:

1. From the Control Panel, double-click the Network icon. The Network window will appear.
2. Click the Configuration tab to display the list of installed network components.
3. Near the top of the component list, select the first entry for your network adapter and click the Properties button. The Adapter Properties window will open.
4. Click the Advanced tab. A list of properties like the one in Figure 5.8 will be displayed.

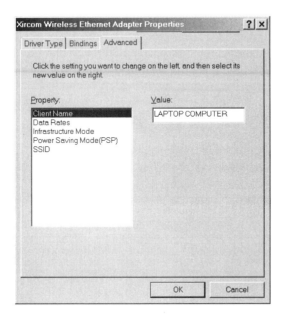

Figure 5.8: Use the Advanced tab in the Adapter Properties window to configure your network adapter

5. Highlight each of the items in the list of properties to see the current setting in the Value field. Some values are text fields, and others are drop-down menus. To change the current value in a text field, select the current text and type the new value. To change a value in a menu, open the drop-down menu and select the new value you want to use.
6. Click the OK button to save your changes and close the window. Click the OK button in the Network window to return to the desktop.

Some wireless network adapters, including some Orinoco products, do not accept any option settings. If you don't see an Advanced tab in the Adapter Properties window, use the configuration utility program supplied with the adapter to change adapter settings.

Network Identity

Before you can connect to a network, you must assign a name to your computer. In Windows 98 and Windows ME, the option settings are located in the Identification tab of the Network window. Follow these steps to change these settings:

1. From the Control Panel, double-click the Network icon. The Network window will open.

2. Click the Identification tab to see the page shown in Figure 5.9.

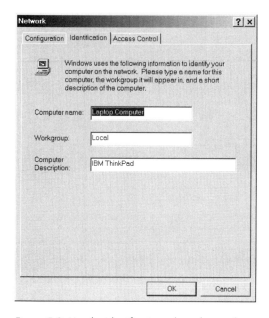

Figure 5.9: Use the Identification tab to change the computer's name and the network's SSID

3. Type the name that identifies this computer on the network in the Computer Name field.

4. Type the network's SSID in the Workgroup field.

5. If you want to provide a more detailed description of this computer to other network users, type the text in the Computer Description field.

6. Click the OK button to save your changes and close the Network window.

Configuring Windows 2000

Windows 2000 contains all of the same configuration options as earlier versions of Windows, but some of them are located in different places.

IP Address and Subnet Mask

Follow these steps to set the IP address and the subnet mask:

1. From the Control Panel, double-click the Network and Dial-Up Connections icon. A window with icons for each network connection profile will open.

2. The network connection profile for your wireless Ethernet connection is the Local Area Connection. Right-click the icon and select Properties from the pop-up menu. A properties window like the one in Figure 5.10 will appear. Confirm that the name of your wireless network interface adapter is visible in the Connect Using field.

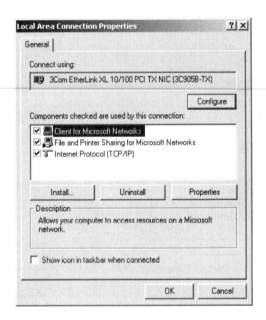

Figure 5.10: Choose the Internet Protocol (TCP/IP) item to set network options

3. In the list of installed items, select the Internet Protocol (TCP/IP) item and click the Properties button. A TCP/IP Properties window like the one in Figure 5.11 will appear.

4. If the DHCP server in your access point or some other network device is active, select the Obtain an IP Address Automatically option. If you are not using a DHCP server, choose the Use the Following IP Address option, and type the IP address assigned to this computer in the IP Address field.

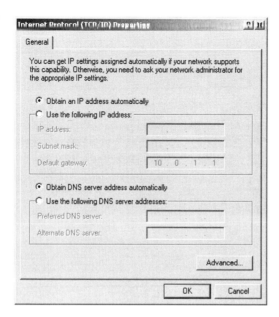

Figure 5.11: The TCP/IP Properties window controls network connection options

5. The Subnet Mask field is in the same TCP/IP Properties tab that also controls the IP address. If you are not using a DHCP server on your network, type the same subnet mask as the one used by the access point.

6. Type the wireless access point's LAN IP address in the Default Gateway field.

7. If a DHCP server assigns DNS addresses to network clients, select the Obtain DNS Server Address Automatically option. If the network uses a static DNS server, select the Use the Following DNS Server Addresses option, and enter the DNS addresses supplied by your network manager or Internet service provider.

File and Printer Sharing

To make the contents of a folder or an entire drive available to other network users, right-click the folder or drive's icon and choose the Sharing option from the pop-up menu to view the dialog box shown in Figure 5.12.

To permit access to this folder or drive to other users on the same computer, select the Share This Folder option. To permit other users on the network to edit or delete files, select the Allow Network Users to Change My Files option.

When you permit sharing, the icon for the shared item changes. A shared folder or drive has an icon with a hand "serving" the item to the network.

Network Interface Adapter Options

To change the network interface adapter options, follow these steps:

1. From the Control Panel, double-click the Network and Dial-Up Connections icon. The Network Connections window will open.

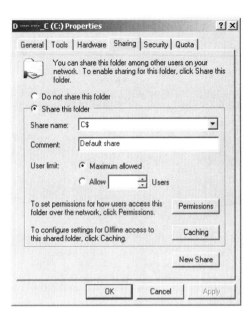

Figure 5.12: Use the Sharing dialog box to change the sharing characteristics of a folder or drive

2. Right-click the icon for the wireless interface adapter's network connection profile. Choose Properties from the pop-up menu.

3. In the General tab, click the Configure button. The Adapter Properties window will open.

4. Click the Advanced tab. A list of properties will be displayed.

5. Highlight each of the items in the list of properties to see the current setting in the Value field. Some values are text fields, and others are drop-down menus. To change the current value in a text field, select the current text and type the new value. To change a value in a menu, open the drop-down menu and select the new value you want to use.

6. Click the OK button to save your changes and close the window. Click the OK button in the Network window to return to the desktop.

Some wireless network adapters, including some Orinoco products, do not accept any option settings. If you don't see an Advanced tab in the Adapter Properties window, use the configuration utility program supplied with the adapter to change adapter settings.

Network Identity

The identification option settings in Windows 2000 are located in the Network Identification tab of the System Properties window. Follow these steps to change these settings:

1. From the Control Panel, double-click the System icon. The System Properties window will open.

2. Click the Network Identification tab. The dialog box shown in Figure 5.13 will open.

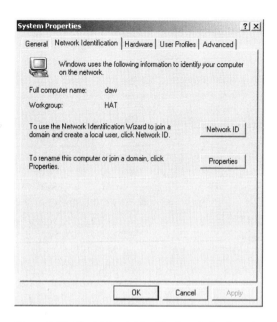

Figure 5.13: The Network Identification dialog box shows the current identity for this computer

3. Click the Properties button to open the Identification Changes window shown in Figure 5.14.

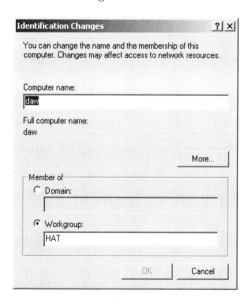

Figure 5.14: Use the Identification Changes window to set the computer's name and the network's SSID

4. Type the name that identifies this computer on the network in the Computer Name field.

5. Type the network's SSID in the Workgroup field.

6. Click the OK button to save your changes and close the window.

Configuring Windows XP

Microsoft has introduced specific support for 802.11b wireless networking in Windows XP that is supposed to integrate wireless configuration with other Windows configuration settings. In theory, this should make it easier to set up and use wireless networks, but it's still not a simple Plug-and-Play process.

The goal is automatic wireless configuration; Windows should automatically detect your wireless network adapter and search for accessible wireless network signals. When it detects a nearby network, Windows should allow a user to join the network with just a few mouse clicks. If you replace your adapters with a different brand (provided it's supported by Windows XP), you won't have to learn a new set of commands and controls.

That's the goal, but the current reality doesn't always meet it, for several reasons. First, the automatic configuration feature requires compatible firmware in the network adapter, and that firmware is not yet available for many adapters. Second, there are still a few obscure configuration settings buried in the Device Manager rather than the wireless configuration tool. It may be necessary to use the configuration tool supplied with your network adapter and the less obvious network configuration settings and options, until the Windows XP support improves and more adapters support it.

Do You Have the Latest Firmware?

Because it has taken a while for many network adapter manufacturers to develop firmware compatible with Windows XP, it's even more important than usual to make sure that you're using the most recent software and firmware with your adapter. Just about every manufacturer of network adapters offers the latest upgrades on their Web sites as free downloads.

Using the Windows Wireless Tools

If your wireless adapter supports the Microsoft configuration tool, it's worth a try. Some vendors have integrated the Windows Wireless Properties controls with their own programs, and others have turned the whole process over to the Windows utility. For example, Figure 5.15 shows the Orinoco Client Manager. When you select the Add/Edit Configuration Profile option from the Actions menu, the Windows Wireless Networks Properties window opens.

Other adapters allow you to choose between their own programs and the Windows tools. Both programs probably do the same things, so the correct choice is to use the one you like best. Try both, and use the one that seems easier to understand and use.

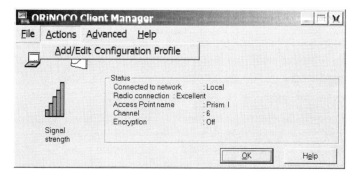

Figure 5.15: The Add/Edit Configuration Profile option in Orinoco's Client Manager opens the Windows Wireless Networks Properties configuration tool

Wireless Network Connection Status

To open the status window, double-click the network icon in the system tray next to the time display.

The Wireless Network Connection Status window shows the current state of your wireless link, including the connection status, the amount of time the current link has been active, the data transfer speed, the signal quality, and the number of bytes the adapter has sent and received since the adapter connected itself to the network. Figure 5.16 shows the status window.

To turn off the radio link, click the Disable button at the bottom of the status window. To change the most common network settings, click the Properties button.

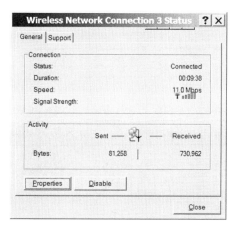

Figure 5.16: The Wireless Network Connection Status window in Windows XP

Network Configuration Settings

To set wireless network configuration options, select Start • Settings • Network Connections and double-click the icon for your wireless connection. The Wireless

Network Connection Properties window is similar to the properties windows for wired network connections, with an additional tab for wireless options, as shown in Figure 5.17.

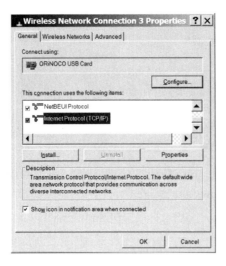

Figure 5.17: Choose the TCP/IP item to set network options

To configure your wireless connection, follow these steps:

1. In the list of installed items, select the Internet Protocol (TCP/IP) item and click the Properties button. A TCP/IP Properties window like the one in Figure 5.18 will appear. Click the General tab if it is not already selected.

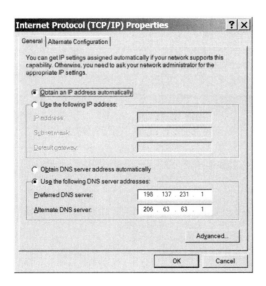

Figure 5.18: The TCP/IP Properties window controls network connection options

2. If the DHCP server in your access point or some other network device is active, select the Obtain an IP Address Automatically option. If you are not using a DHCP server, choose the Use the Following IP Address option, and type the IP address assigned to this computer in the IP Address field.

3. The Subnet Mask field is in the same TCP/IP Properties window that controls the IP address. If you are not using a DHCP server on your network, type the same subnet mask as the one used by the access point.

4. If you are not using a DHCP server, type the wireless access point's LAN IP address in the Default Gateway field.

5. If a DHCP server assigns DNS addresses to network clients, select the Obtain DNS Server Address Automatically option. If the network uses a static DNS server, select the Use the Following DNS Server Addresses option, and enter the DNS addresses supplied by your network manager or Internet service provider.

6. Click the OK button to save your settings and close this window.

File and Printer Sharing

To make the contents of a folder or an entire drive available to other network users, right-click the folder or drive's icon and choose the Sharing and Security option from the drop-down menu. The Properties window shown in Figure 5.19 will open.

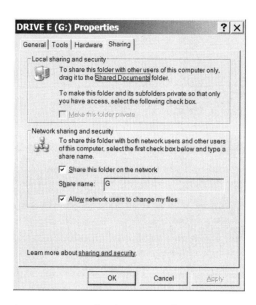

Figure 5.19: Use the Sharing tab of the Properties window to change the sharing characteristics of a folder or drive

To permit network access to this folder or drive, select the Share This Folder on the Network option. To permit other users on the network to edit or delete files, select the Allow Network Users to Change My Files option.

When you permit sharing, the icon for the shared item changes. A shared folder or drive has an icon with a hand "serving" the item to the network.

Network Interface Adapter Options

To change the network interface adapter options, follow these steps:

1. From the Wireless Network Connection Properties window, click the Configure button. The Adapter Properties window will open.

2. Click the Advanced tab. A list of properties like the one in Figure 5.20 will be displayed.

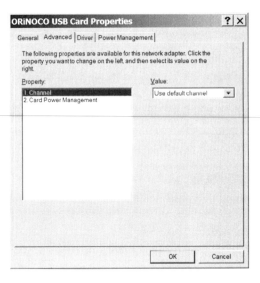

Figure 5.20: Use the Advanced tab in the adapter's Properties window to configure your network adapter

3. Highlight each of the items in the list of properties to see the current setting in the Value field. Some values are text fields, and others are drop-down menus. To change the current value in a text field, select the current text and enter the new value. To change a value in a menu, open the drop-down menu and select the new value you want to use.

4. Click the OK button to save your changes and close the window. Click the OK button in the Network window to return to the desktop.

Some wireless network adapters do not accept any option settings. If you don't see an Advanced tab in the adapter's Properties window, use the configuration utility program supplied with the adapter to change adapter settings.

Network Identity

To set or change the name assigned to your computer in Windows XP, open the Computer Name tab of the System Properties window. Follow these steps to change the settings:

1. From the Control Panel, double-click the System icon. The System Properties window will open.

2. Click the Computer Name tab. The dialog box shown in Figure 5.21 will appear.

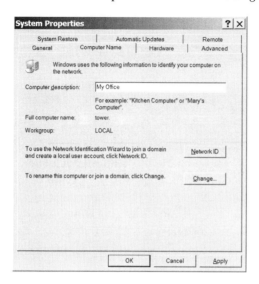

Figure 5.21: Use the Computer Name tab to change the computer's name and the network's SSID

3. Type the name that identifies this computer on the network in the Computer Description field.

4. Click the Change button. The Computer Name Changes window, shown in Figure 5.22, will open.

5. Type the network's SSID in the Workgroup field.

6. Click the OK button to save your changes and close the window.

Configuring the Wireless Network in Windows XP

The wireless configuration tools in Windows XP are intended to be a common interface that can control many brands of network adapters. Some adapter makers use the Windows utility exclusively, and others treat it as part of their own more extensive network configuration packages.

To open the Wireless Network Connection Properties window, follow these steps:

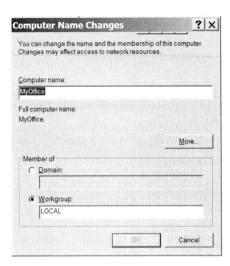

Figure 5.22: Use the Computer Name Changes window to set the computer's name and SSID

1. Double-click the Network icon in the Windows system tray, next to the clock at the lower-right corner of your screen. The Wireless Connection Status window will open.

2. Click the Properties button at the bottom of the window. A Properties window similar to the one in Figure 5.23 will open.

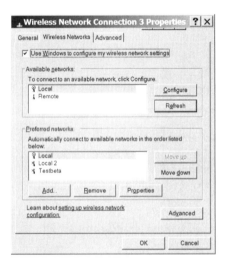

Figure 5.23: The Wireless Network Connection Properties window

Selecting a Network

If your computer is within range of more than one network, you must choose the one you want to use. The Wireless Properties utility includes a list of preferred networks, but it doesn't limit you to the networks on that list.

The list of available networks in the Properties window shows the SSIDs of all the networks that will accept a link from your wireless adapter. If the adapter detects just one network, Windows will automatically connect to that network. When a network adapter detects more than one network, it compares the SSID of each network to the names in the Preferred Networks list and automatically connects you to the network with the highest priority. You can change the order in which Windows searches for networks with the Move Up and Move Down buttons in the Properties window.

Microsoft has carefully hidden the dialog box that specifies whether or not Windows will limit itself to the networks on the list of preferred networks. If your adapter detects a network that's not on your preferred list, it will set up a connection, *if* the non-preferred option in the Advanced window is active. Click the Advanced button in the Properties window to open that window.

Of course, it's possible that the computer will make the wrong choice — if it detects two or more networks, it might not automatically connect to the network you want. When that happens, select the SSID of the correct network in the Available Networks list and click the Configure button. This will open another window with more information about that network, and it will set up a connection with that network.

Turning Encryption On or Off

The Local Properties window, which you can open from the main Properties window with either the Configure button or the Properties button, includes a set of WEP encryption options. If you're using a network with WEP encryption active, turn on the Data Encryption option.

Summary: Making the Connection

Whether you're using Windows XP or some earlier version of the operating system, it ought to be possible to set up a link to a wireless network. If the automatic connection function doesn't work, don't assume that you've done something wrong — more likely, you're a victim of somebody's bad design. Here are some things to check:

- Is the SSID used by your computer exactly the same as the SSID of the network you want to join?
- Is WEP encryption turned on or off? If it's on, are you using the correct encryption key? Is encryption set to 64-bit or 128-bit?
- Does the access point use MAC address filtering? Is your wireless adapter on the list of qualified users?
- Does the workgroup name match the SSID?
- Does your access point use a DHCP server? If not, are the IP address, subnet mask, and default gateway settings correct?
- Is the preamble length setting correct?

6

WI-FI FOR MACINTOSH

Apple's AirPort family of wireless networking products is the logical choice for Macintosh users who want to connect their computers through a wireless network and those who want to connect their Macs to an existing wireless network. Because Apple controls both ends of the network link — the access point and the network client — an AirPort network is a lot easier to set up than a generic 802.11b network. The AirPort Base Station (Apple's name for its access point) automatically loads its Internet configuration settings from an existing Macintosh connection and transfers those settings to all the other computers on the same network.

Apple is a member of the Wi-Fi Alliance, and both the AirPort Base Station and the AirPort Card carry Wi-Fi certification. So a Macintosh with an AirPort Card can join any 802.11b network almost as easily as it can join an AirPort network. A mixed-platform wireless network that includes Macs, Windows-based PCs, and Unix or Linux machines can use one or more AirPort Base Stations as access points.

The radios used in AirPort Cards and AirPort Base Stations are private-label versions of Orinoco PCMCIA wireless network adapters. The AirPort Base Station is made by KarlNet, which sells a similar product called the Wireless KarlRouter.

Apple uses different names for some of the features and functions in its wireless networks, but the general rules for designing, configuring, and using an AirPort network are the same as the rules for setting up generic wireless nets. The only difference between an AirPort network and any other Wi-Fi network is some of the terminology and the software that moves configuration data from a network client to the AirPort Base Station.

This chapter explains how to set up and use a wireless AirPort network on Macintosh computers, how to add a Macintosh with an AirPort Card to an existing 802.11b network that does not use an AirPort Base Station, and how to add a computer running Windows to an AirPort network.

AirPort Components

The AirPort product family includes two components: a wireless network adapter called the AirPort Card and an access point called the AirPort Base Station. The AirPort Card is a PCMCIA card, which is supplied with a mounting bracket that fits into Macintosh models that don't already support PC Cards. The AirPort Base Station is a stand-alone access point that manages the wireless network. The latest version includes an internal PCMCIA socket that contains an AirPort Card (or an identical WaveLAN or Orinoco wireless adapter card), two 10/100Base-T Ethernet ports, and a built-in 56 Kbps telephone line modem. Figure 6.1 shows an AirPort Base Station.

Figure 6.1: Apple's AirPort Base Station are wireless network devices that have been optimized for use with Macintosh computers

The AirPort Base Station has three indicator lights on the case that display its current operating status:

Light	Color	Status
1	Flashing green	Communication in progress
2	Steady green	Power on
3	Flashing green	Ethernet or modem port in use

Along with the AirPort hardware, Apple provides several software tools:

- The AirPort Setup Assistant is an automated configuration tool that automates the process of setting up most network installations.

- The AirPort Admin Utility provides direct access to configuration options for setting and changing more complex networks.

- The AirPort Control Strip is a simple tool for monitoring and controlling network activity from the desktop.

- The AirPort Application offers more detailed control and monitoring of network performance.

- The AirPort Software Base Station program is an alternative to using the separate base station; it converts a network client into a software-controlled access point.

Setting Up an AirPort Network

Most AirPort users can use the AirPort Setup Assistant to create and configure their networks without the need to worry about complex configuration options. However, when local conditions require direct control of advanced settings, and when the network manager wants to monitor the network's operation, the AirPort Admin Utility offers more complete control of all network settings.

Using the Setup Assistant to create a network is fast and easy: just configure a client, click a couple of buttons, and let the software make all the decisions for you. The Setup Assistant automatically loads all the settings and fires up the network for you.

Installing the Hardware

Some recent Macintosh models come with built-in AirPort adapters and AirPort software bundled with the operating system. If you are using an older Macintosh that does not already have an AirPort Card, you must install the AirPort Card before you try to run the AirPort Setup Assistant.

To install an AirPort Base Station, follow these steps:

1. Place the AirPort Base Station in the location where you plan to operate it. Like any other wireless network access point, a single AirPort Base Station should be close to the center of the area you want to reach with your network. If you are installing more than one base station in order to cover a large area, spread them evenly through the entire space.

2. Run a cable between the base station's Ethernet port and an existing wired Ethernet hub or a broadband Internet router, such as a DSL modem or a cable modem. If you do not have access to a wired LAN or a broadband Internet service, or if you want to use a telephone line as a backup to your broadband connection, run a modular telephone cable from the base station's modem port to a wall outlet for the telephone line.

3. Plug the power cable into the base station's power outlet and an AC outlet.

The AirPort Base Station's antennas are built into the enclosure, so it's not possible to move them without moving the entire unit. After running the AirPort Setup Assistant, if you discover that the signal level is not adequate for reliable data exchange with all of the network clients, it might be necessary to move the base station to a different location for better signal coverage.

Running the AirPort Setup Assistant

The structure of the AirPort Setup Assistant has changed between OS 9 and OS/X, but the commands are similar, even if they're in different locations.
Follow these steps to use the AirPort Setup Assistant in OS 9:

1. Set up a direct connection from the local computer to the Internet. The AirPort Setup Assistant will transfer the configuration settings from this computer to the base station.

2. If it is not already in place, install an AirPort Card in this computer.

3. Confirm that the AirPort Base Station is connected to a telephone line, a broadband connection, or both, and that power is connected to the base station. The number 2 (middle) green light on the base station should light.

4. Open the top-level menu of directories.

5. Open the AirPort Setup Assistant, which is located under (Mac OS 9) Applications/Apple Extras/AirPort or (in Mac OS X) Applications/Utilities. The Introduction screen of the AirPort Setup Assistant will appear.

6. Choose one of the three options in the Introduction screen, as shown in Figure 6.2.

7. Set up the local computer to join an existing wireless network.

8. Set up an AirPort Base Station.

9. Set up a Software Base Station.

The Introduction screen offers the Set Up Your Computer to Join an Existing Wireless Network option first, but in practice, at least one base station (or other access point) must be running within the AirPort Card's signal range before you can successfully set up the local computer. When you're creating a new network, you must set up at least one base station first, so we'll explain the Set Up an Air-Port Base Station option first.

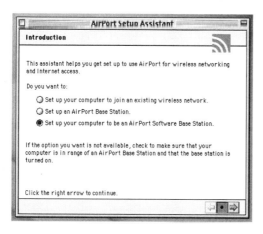

Figure 6.2: The AirPort Setup Assistant offers options to set up the local AirPort Card, the AirPort Base Station, or a Software Base Station

Set Up an AirPort Base Station

The Internet Choice option specifies which way to configure the base station. If the computer where the Setup Assistant is running already has an Internet connection, the program can use those settings to configure the base station. If there is no Internet connection present, the Setup Assistant will open the Internet Setup Assistant, which will request all of the TCP/IP configuration settings necessary to connect the wireless network to the Internet.

Set Up Your Computer to Join an Existing Wireless Network

The Set Up Your Computer to Join an Existing Wireless Network option automatically detects radio signals from active networks and configures the local machine to connect to one or more of those networks. When the setup is complete, the computer displays a Conclusion screen that reports that the AirPort Setup Assistant is done, and it displays a list of the networks that it has detected. To join a network, select the name of the network from the list and click the Connect Now button.

When the AirPort Card associates itself with a network, the computer automatically runs the AirPort application program.

Set Up Your Computer to Be an AirPort Software Base Station

A Software Base Station performs all the functions of an AirPort Base Station from one of the computers in the network. This approach can provide the benefits of a wireless network without the added cost of a separate base station, but it places an additional drain on the resources (including processing power and memory) of the computer running the base station software, and it means that the entire network will not work when the base station computer is turned off. A separate AirPort Base Station also allows the network manager to be more flexible with the location of the base station.

If you decide to use a Software Base Station, choose a computer in as central a location as possible to run the base station software, because every other wireless client on the network will exchange radio signals with the base station.

To install a Software Base Station, choose the Set Up Your Computer to Be an AirPort Base Station option. The Setup Assistant will offer the choice of either automatically importing the network configuration data from your computer's Internet settings, or opening the Internet Setup Assistant.

The AirPort Application

The AirPort application is Apple's version of the Windows-based configuration and status software supplied with other makers' wireless network adapters. Figure 6.3 shows the AirPort application.

Figure 6.3: The AirPort application shows the current status of the local computer's wireless network connection

The AirPort application has three sections: Status, AirPort, and AirPort Network.

Status

The Status display shows the name of the network currently associated with this computer, the connection status, and the quality of the signal the AirPort Card is currently receiving.

AirPort

The AirPort section shows whether the AirPort Card is currently on or off and provides a button to turn the card on or off. The AirPort ID is the MAC address of the local AirPort Card.

When a network is configured as a closed network, it does not appear on the list of detected networks. In order to connect to a closed network, a user must enter the network's name in the AirPort Application or the Control Strip. This is a security feature that prevents unauthorized users from joining a network.

AirPort Network

The Choose Network menu under AirPort Network is a list of all the wireless networks that this network client has detected, except for closed networks.

The Computer-to-Computer Network option configures the local client as a member of an ad hoc network.

The Base Station ID is the MAC address of the AirPort Base Station or other access point that controls the network currently connected to this client.

The AirPort Control Strip Module

The AirPort Control Strip module, shown in Figure 6.4 has five circles that show the quality of the current signal; when more circles are filled, the signal quality is better. The AirPort module is also a control button that opens a menu from which a user can perform several common functions:

- Turn the wireless network connection on or off
- Select a network connection when more than one wireless signal is within range
- Set up a connection through the base station's modem
- Monitor and control modem activity
- Display the AirPort ID (MAC address) of the local computer and the base station

Figure 6.4: The AirPort Control Strip module provides access to basic AirPort network controls from the desktop

The AirPort Admin Utility

It's often entirely possible to set up an AirPort network from the Setup Assistant, using nothing but default configuration settings, but the AirPort Admin Utility provides a method to establish or change those settings when the Setup Assistant doesn't give you enough options.

The AirPort Admin Utility window in OS 9 has four tabs, each of which contains controls for a different part of the AirPort programs. In OS/X, there are six tabs, but the commands and functions are similar.

The AirPort Tab

The Admin Utility's AirPort tab contains controls for the AirPort Base Station and for the network as a whole. These controls are accessible from any Macintosh computer currently connected to the network. Figure 6.5 shows the AirPort tab.

The information in the Identity section of the window specifies the name of the AirPort network, which is the same as the SSID in any other 802.11b network. To connect a computer with a non-AirPort wireless network adapter to an AirPort network, use the network name as the SSID.

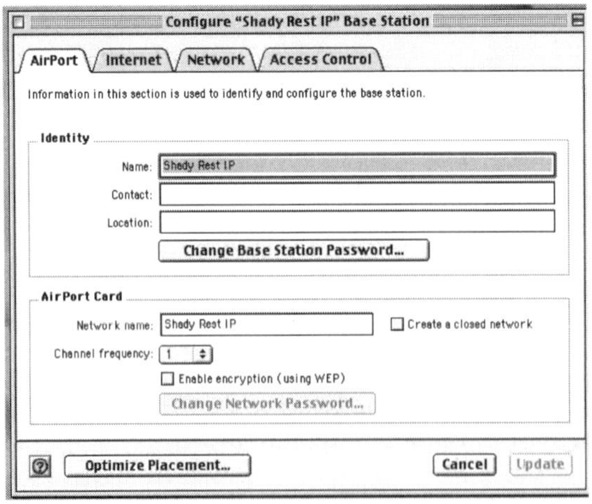

Figure 6.5: The AirPort tab contains network controls

The Contact and Location fields are optional settings that display additional information about the network. Typically, the Contact field can contain the name, telephone number, and email address of the person who maintains the network, and the Location field shows the physical location of the base station.

The AirPort Card section repeats the network name and provides a place to change the Channel Frequency, which is Apple's name for the radio channel number. The default setting for an AirPort network is Channel 1, but that's no better than any other channel. In an environment with more than one AirPort Network in operation, each network should use a different channel. All of the usual rules about preventing interference from other 802.11 networks and other 2.4 GHz radio services apply to AirPort networks, so it's often a good idea to change to a channel number that isn't used as widely as the default. When the base station changes channels, all of the AirPort clients connected to the network will automatically shift to the new channel. In a mixed-platform network, most 802.11b network adapters scan for active network signals, so you can expect the network clients to automatically shift to the new channel. If any of the adapters in the network don't change automatically, it will be necessary to change the channel numbers manually.

The Create a Closed Network option allows a network manager to create a wireless network whose name does not appear in the lists of accessible networks in the AirPort Setup Assistant, the AirPort application, and the AirPort Control Strip module. In order to connect to a closed network, a user must type the name of that network rather than selecting it from a list.

The Optimize Placement button opens the Placement window shown in Figure 6.6.

The Placement Window
The Placement window provides a graphic display of signal strength and signal quality for each network client currently connected to the base station. This dis-

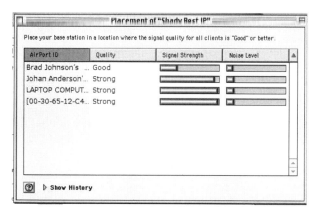

Figure 6.6: The Placement window shows the quality of the signals from each network client

play can help a network manager choose the best location for a base station or a client computer.

The AirPort ID column shows the name of each computer currently connected to the wireless network. If no name has been assigned to a computer, the AirPort ID column shows the computer's MAC address.

The Quality column lists the quality of the radio link detected by the base station. Quality is a combination of signal strength and noise level, so a strong but noisy signal might have lower quality than a weaker signal in a quieter location. If the signal quality of a link is "Good" or better, the link should be able to exchange data at full speed.

The Signal Strength column shows the measured strength of the radio signal from each network client to the base station.

The Noise Level column shows the amount of interference from other networks and other radio services that the base station is receiving on each link. When the noise level approaches the signal level, the performance of the network will deteriorate.

The Show History option opens another graphic display that shows the quality of network signals over time.

The Internet Tab

The Internet tab, shown in Figure 6.7, specifies the information that the base station uses to connect the local wireless LAN to the Internet. The AirPort Setup Assistant loads these settings automatically.

Some settings can change over time (when, for example, an Internet service provider re-configures its network servers), so the AirPort Admin Utility provides access to the network configuration settings:

• The Connect Using option allows the network manager to specify a connection through the base station's Ethernet port or the built-in modem. When Connect Using Modem is active, the base station places a telephone call to connect the wireless network to the Internet. When Connect Using

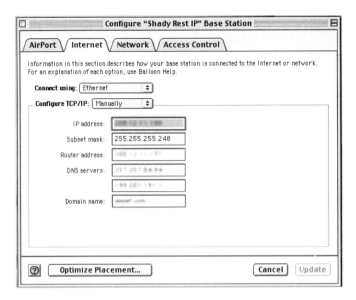

Figure 6.7: The Internet tab contains TCP/IP connection options and selects the type of Internet connection

Ethernet is active, the base station uses the LAN connection to connect the network clients to the Internet.

- Two Configure TCP/IP options are available: DHCP, which instructs the base station to assign an IP address and subnet mask to each network client; and a Manual option, which requires the user to enter those settings into each computer by hand.

- The IP Address field shows the numeric IP address of this network client's Internet connection.

- The Subnet Mask field shows the subnet mask settings that the base station uses to connect multiple clients through a single Internet connection.

- The Router Address is the address of the network's Internet gateway server.

- The DNS Servers fields contain the addresses of the Domain Name System servers that convert internet domain names to numeric addresses.

- The Domain Name is the name of the Internet domain that connects this client to the Internet.

The Network Tab

The Network tab, shown in Figure 6.8, controls the bridge between the wireless AirPort network and a wired LAN.

When the Distribute IP Addresses option is checked, the computers on the wireless network can either share one numeric IP address (which the network translates internally to separate local addresses) or use a separate numeric address for each computer.

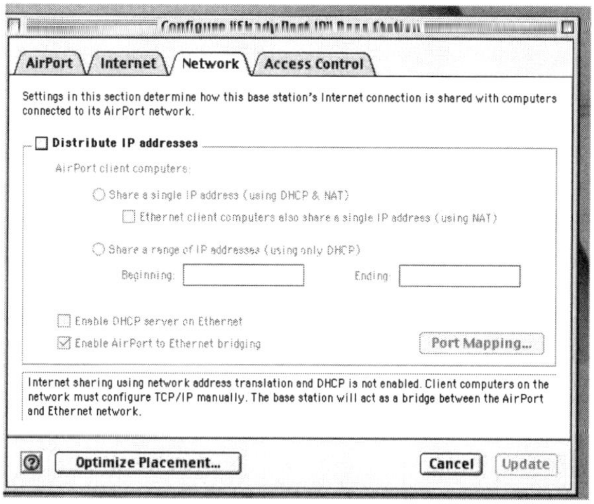

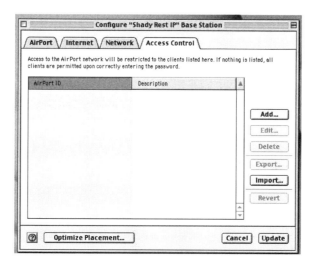

Figure 6.8: The Network tab controls the bridge between the wireless AirPort network and a wired Ethernet LAN

The Access Control Tab

The Access Control tab, shown in Figure 6.9, provides a way to limit the use of a network to specific computers, rather than allowing the base station to accept a connection from any client within usable signal range. The list of accepted computers shows the AirPort IDs of those computers. To add a non-AirPort device to a restricted-access network, use the MAC address of the wireless network adapter.

Figure 6.9: The Access Control tab is a security tool that restricts access to the network

Using an AirPort Network

Once the AirPort network is up and running, a Macintosh treats the computers connected to the network through wireless links just like any other network resource. File transfers, Internet access, remote printers, and other services show up on directories the same way they would appear if they were connected through Ethernet cables.

For most users, the only indication that a wireless connection is active will be the indicators in the AirPort Control Strip module at the bottom of their screens that light and go dark as the quality of the wireless signal changes due to interference and network activity. Unless a networked computer is on the edge of the base station's coverage area or it is receiving a lot of interference, the connections to the local network and the Internet should be just about as fast and clean as they would be through a 10Base-T network.

Connecting Macintosh Clients to Other Networks

Apple hopes that most Macintosh users will use their AirPort Cards to connect their computers through an AirPort Base Station to other Macs. But that's not the only possible way to use a wireless network with a Macintosh. Because the Setup Assistant automates the process, it's easier to connect Macs to an AirPort network than it is to build a mixed-platform wireless network that can use access points, network adapters, and configuration software from different sources, but AirPort Cards do meet the Wi-Fi specification for interoperability, so they can also communicate with 802.11b access points (and in ad hoc networks) made by many other manufacturers. Therefore, it is not a problem to use a Macintosh computer in a new or existing wireless network that also includes network clients that run Windows or other operating systems.

For example, PowerBook owners who carry their computers to offices and public spaces served by wireless networks can connect to those networks just as easily as the owners of Windows-based laptop computers. And a wireless network in an office or household can provide service to both Macs and PCs without any changes to the network configuration.

Most Macintosh owners will probably want to use an AirPort Card rather than some other brand of network adapter, because the AirPort software is so closely integrated with the Mac OS networking functions, but it's also possible to install a different brand of PC Card or USB-based wireless network adapter, if you can find driver and control software for the Mac OS version used by your computer. Among others, Macintosh drivers are available for network adapters sold by Orinoco, Proxim, and Buffalo. The Orinoco adapters are a very similar design to the AirPort Card (which is not surprising, considering that they are made in the same factory), and some users have reported that they have been able to use the Orinoco control software with their AirPort Cards.

Connecting an AirPort Card to a Non-AirPort Access Point

When a Macintosh with an AirPort card is within range of a signal from a non-AirPort access point, the AirPort Card should detect the network signal and display the access point's SSID in the AirPort application's Choose Network menus and the AirPort Control Strip menu. When a user selects that network from the menu, the AirPort Card should associate itself with that access point, just as it would associate with an AirPort Base Station. The Control Strip module and the AirPort application will show the quality of the signal from the access point in their graphic displays the same way they show a connection to an Apple Base Station.

In most large business networks and public wireless services, the network manager has probably prepared a "how to connect to our network" document for employees and visitors who want to use their portable computers and other devices on the wireless LAN. This document might be a printed information sheet or brochure or an online Web page. Either way, it will include some specific settings that users must change in their configuration utility programs. The configuration program for an AirPort adapter is the AirPort Admin Utility, but Apple has chosen to use different names for some of the settings, including "Network Name" for the SSID and "AirPort ID" for the network adapter's MAC address. Fortunately, the AirPort utilities will detect the network name and ID automatically, so it's not necessary to change them by hand.

If the wireless network uses a DHCP server in the access point or someplace else in the network to assign IP addresses to network clients, open the Internet tab of the AirPort Admin Utility and set the Configure TCP/IP option to accept DHCP addresses.

If the network does not use DHCP, the network manager will provide a list of configuration settings assigned to this client. To configure an AirPort client to connect to the network, set the Configure TCP/IP option to Manually and enter these addresses in the Internet tab of the AirPort Admin Utility. Copy the IP address, subnet mask, DNS servers, and domain name provided by the network manager directly to the fields in the Admin Utility. The setting that AirPort calls a "Router Address" is known to the rest of the world as the network gateway. Use the gateway address supplied by the network manager in the AirPort Admin Utility's Router Address field.

Connecting Other Wi-Fi Clients to an AirPort Network

Just because a wireless LAN uses an AirPort Base Station as its access point, that network is not limited to AirPort clients. Every client computer on an AirPort network does not have to be a Macintosh. There is absolutely no difference between an AirPort network and any other 802.11b network, so a computer that uses some other brand of network adapter and a different operating system will have no trouble detecting an AirPort network.

An AirPort Base Station appears to the network adapters in computers that use other operating systems as a standard 802.11b access point. The adapter will use the AirPort network to exchange data with other computers and as a gateway to the Internet. From the adapter's point of view, connecting to an AirPort Base Station is just like connecting to any other brand of access point.

Detecting the radio signal is one thing, but configuring a network client to use the network is a bit more difficult, because Apple uses different names for some of the standard network configuration settings. If you don't know how to translate between AirPort and 802.11b terminology, you may have trouble getting the network to work properly. Don't panic. We're here to help. It's not as bad as it seems, once you have the translation keys that are all revealed in the next few pages.

Network Properties

In Windows, the Network Properties window contains the settings and options that a computer must use to connect to a TCP/IP network. On a Macintosh, the same information is in the AirPort Admin Utility.

If the AirPort Admin Utility is set to use DHCP to configure TCP/IP, the configuration utility on the client must also be set to accept DHCP (in Windows, select the Obtain an IP Address Automatically and the Obtain DNS Server options).

If the AirPort Admin Utility is set to configure TCP/IP manually, the owner of a Windows, Unix, or Linux client must enter these TCP/IP Properties settings:

IP address   Use the IP address provided by the LAN manager or ISP.

Subnet mask   Copy the address from the AirPort Admin Utility's Internet tab. If you don't know the address, try 255.255.255.0.

DNS servers   Copy the DNS server addresses from the Admin Utility's Internet tab.

Host   Copy the network name from the Admin Utility's AirPort tab.

Domain   Copy the domain name (if any) from the Admin Utility's Internet tab.

Gateway   Copy the router address from the Admin Utility's Internet tab.

Wireless Network Configuration

As you know, every wireless network adapter comes with a different configuration utility program. There's a standard wireless configuration utility in Windows XP, but if you're using an older version of Windows (or some other operating system), you will have to use the program supplied with the adapter hardware.

Some configuration utilities automatically scan for nearby wireless networks and display a menu that lists the SSID of each one, while other programs require users to specify the SSIDs of the networks they want to use. When a network adapter detects an AirPort network, it will display the Network Name value as its SSID. If the configuration utility requests an SSID, use the Network Name that appears in the AirPort tab of the Admin Utility.

If the adapter doesn't select an operating channel automatically, set the channel number to the Channel Frequency set in the AirPort tab.

If the network uses an AirPort Base Station, it is an infrastructure network. To set up an ad hoc network between a Macintosh and a Windows (or other) client, set the AirPort Network option in the Settings screen of the AirPort Setup Assistant to use a Computer-to-Computer network.

Once the network configuration is set and the client associates with the base station, the signal quality display on the network client should show the quality of the link, and the AirPort Placement window should show the name of the network client and the quality of the radio link, along with all the other computers on the wireless network. At this point, all of the computers on the network—regardless of operating system—should appear on the other computers' lists of available network connections.

Configuring an AirPort Base Station from a Non-AirPort Client

The manager of a mixed network that includes both Macintosh and non-Mac operating systems has two options for setting up the base station: either use a Macintosh to configure the base station or use one of the AirPort configuration programs that Apple and other software developers have created for Windows and Unix.

At least three software developers offer alternatives to Apple's own AirPort Base Station configuration software. Most of these programs are written for Windows or other operating systems, but at least one is also available for the Macintosh.

These programs perform all of the same functions as the Apple software, but they organize the configuration options differently. These programs use standard 802.11b and TCP/IP terminology, so they might be a little less confusing for experienced wireless network managers.

AirPort Admin Utility for Windows

Apple's own Admin Utility for Windows is available for free download from http://docs.info.apple.com/article.html?artnum=120093. The program won't work with the original (Graphite) AirPort Base Station, but it's a useful tool for the newer (Snow) version.

As the name suggests, the AirPort Admin Utility for Windows performs the same functions as the AirPort Admin Utility for the Macintosh.

AirPort Base Station Configurator

Jon Sevy's AirPort Base Station Configurator is a Java application that will run on any host computer that has a Java Runtime Environment, including most versions of Windows, Unix, and Mac OS. The program (including a complete manual) is available for download from http://edge.mcs.drexel.edu/GICL/people/sevy airport. Figure 6.10 shows a typical screen from the program.

Several other AirPort utilities are available from the same source, including a program that monitors modem activity on the base station, a utility that measures signal strength and quality on wireless links, and a Wireless Host Monitor that displays a list of client computers currently connected to the base station.

FreeBase

FreeBase is an AirPort Base Station configuration program for Windows that is available online from http://freebase.sourceforge.net. The FreeBase Web site also includes a "guided tour" of the AirPort Base Station that explains how to replace the internal adapter card and provides some extensive details about the base station's internal communications protocols and configuration block.

Figure 6.11 shows a FreeBase screen. Like the AirPort Base Station Configurator, FreeBase organizes everything into a single tabbed window.

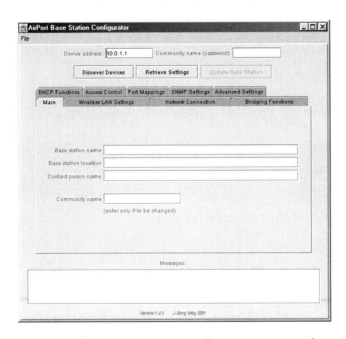

Figure 6.10: The AirPort Base Station Configurator organizes configuration options in a logical presentation that some users may prefer to the Apple AirPort software

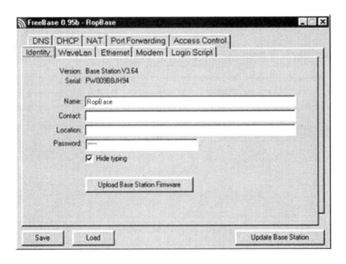

Figure 6.11: FreeBase is another AirPort Base Station configuration program for Windows

KarlNet Configurator

As we mentioned earlier in this chapter, the AirPort Base Station is a version of an access point designed by KarlNet. KarlNet does not promise that its own KarlNet Configurator software will work with the AirPort Base Station (probably because it doesn't want to compete with a major customer), but there's every reason to expect that it will indeed work. The Windows version of KarlNet Configurator is available online at http://www.karlnet.com/download. However, the KarlNet program is considerably more limited than the other two configuration programs for Windows, so there's not much reason to choose it instead of either FreeBase or AirPort Base Station Configurator.

Is AirPort the Answer?

Because Apple could control both ends of their AirPort design — the access point and the network clients — it has come up with a system that automates the configuration hassles that confront most other wireless networks, without losing compatibility with other Wi-Fi networks. We can hope that the wireless tools in Windows XP will move in the same direction, but for the moment, it's still faster and easier to connect a batch of Macs to an AirPort network than to connect them to a network that uses some other brand of access point. And once you know the secret handshake (in the form of AirPort's oddball names for some standard features and functions), your non-AirPort network adapters will also be perfectly happy on an AirPort network.

An AirPort network is indeed the obvious choice of wireless network in a business or household where most of the computers are Macintoshes. For the rest of us, the AirPort Base Station (with third-party software, if necessary) is a completely adequate access point that's comparable to several others. Regardless of your position in those tedious religious disputes among people who use different operating systems, it appears that Apple has gotten this one right.

7

WI-FI FOR LINUX

Every wireless network adapter (except the Apple AirPort Card) comes with drivers and configuration tools for Microsoft Windows, but that doesn't mean that Windows is the only operating system that will work with that adapter. A TCP/IP network doesn't care what kind of operating system the computers connected to the network are using. It's just receiving bits and bytes from a computer port and moving them around. It's possible to use a wireless network with any kind of computer, as long as you can find the right driver for your network adapter. That's as true for Linux and various versions of Unix as it is for Windows and Macintosh systems. This chapter contains information about connecting your Linux-based computer to a Wi-Fi network and describes some utilities and other tools that can make things easier. In Chapter 8, you can find similar information about using Unix computers on a Wi-Fi network.

Finding the right driver is not always as easy as it sounds. This chapter will explain how to find the right Linux drivers for several adapters and how to install and use them to connect to a wireless network. If you're not already using Unix or Linux, access to a wireless network is probably not a good reason to start. This chapter is written for users who already have enough Linux experience to set up and use a wired network connection. If you need more help using your Linux clients, you should ask for help from your neighborhood guru or find a more general how-to book on Linux.

Drivers, Backseat and Otherwise

Before we go any deeper into the wonders of connecting Linux devices to wireless networks, let's take some time to review exactly what a driver does and why drivers are important. Later in this chapter, you can find advice about finding the right drivers for different kinds of wireless network adapters and how to use them to connect Linux computers to a wireless network.

A device driver is the software interface between a computer's operating system and the inputs and outputs of a peripheral device connected to the computer. The driver contains the instructions that translate incoming commands and data from the device into a form that the operating system can understand, and it translates outbound instructions from the operating system into specific device controls. It handles memory management and timing, and it specifies the input/output (I/O) port and the interrupts that the device will use to communicate with the operating system. Figure 7.1 shows the relationship between a computer and a very generic device driver.

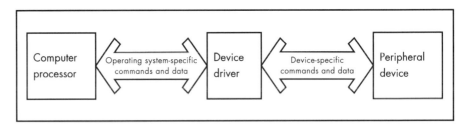

Figure 7.1: A device driver is the data and control interface between a computer and a peripheral device

Every peripheral device, including a wireless network adapter, requires a driver that converts standard instructions from the computer into controls that handle the specific features and functions of that device. Without the driver, the device won't operate. A device without the right driver is useful only as a paperweight or a doorstop.

For example, the driver for a keyboard tells the computer which I/O port carries data to and from the keyboard, it converts keystrokes into input data, and it turns the CAPS LOCK, NUM LOCK, and SCROLL LOCK lights on or off. A printer driver includes the specific controls that make the difference between an impact printer and a laser printer. A driver for an input or output device will specify whether the device uses a serial or parallel port, a USB port, a PCMCIA socket, or one of the internal expansion slots on the computer's motherboard. The driver for a wireless network adapter specifies things like the channel number that the radio will use to send and receive data, the amount of power the radio will transmit, and the data transmission speed that the adapter will use to transfer data.

The drivers for wireless Ethernet adapters handle the physical layers of TCP/IP communication—just the information the adapters need to set up and use radio links to a network while other layers handle data formatting and content. This ensures that the adapter can handle many data formats and the data can pass through many different adapter types.

Drivers also make it possible for the same piece of hardware to work with different operating systems. A driver converts the input and output signals produced by the operating system to and from commands in the device's "native language." Drivers written for different operating systems that control the same device start with instructions in different forms, and they convert those instructions into the same set of device controls. Therefore, if your computer runs Linux, it requires device drivers written specifically for that operating system.

It might be useful to think of a driver as the instruction manual for a device. Manuals written in English, Danish, and Malay all contain the same set of instructions, but they are provided in languages that different users will understand. Computer device drivers are similar, except the languages are operating systems instead of human speech.

The device driver is separate software from the configuration utility, but many software designers combine the two in a single installation. The configuration utility provides a set of commands that send instructions and displays that receive data in both directions through the driver to the network adapter.

Where to Find Drivers

So you need a driver for your computer's operating system before you can use your wireless network adapter. If you're lucky, or if you have done some careful shopping, the right driver is on the CD-ROM supplied with the adapter or bundled with the operating system.

A large proportion of the wireless adapters out there are private-label products that were actually made by somebody whose name does not appear anywhere on the package or the device itself. It's often necessary to do some detective work to identify the right driver for a particular adapter. Orinoco and Cisco are particularly active in the private-label adapter business. The adapter manufacturers might not want to tell you whose hardware is lurking inside their boxes, but the people who develop third-party Linux drivers have often figured out which brands work with which drivers.

The first place to look for a Linux driver for your wireless adapter is on the CD that came with the adapter. A few manufacturers do include them along with their Windows drivers, but don't count on it. If there is a driver in the package, though, you don't have to waste your time searching for one from another source, but you might find a newer version online.

If you have a choice, it's better to buy an adapter that comes with the driver you need for your operating system. Adapter manufacturers who have produced Linux drivers have generally done a good job of making them available to potential users, but at this point in the development of the wireless network marketplace, adapter drivers for anything except Windows are not common. Drivers supplied by manufacturers have also presumably been tested by those manufacturers, and they won't subject you to finger-pointing between the hardware and software developers when you ask for help. Few things in the world are more irritating than some tech support drone in a call center refusing to answer any questions because "we don't support that software."

As Wi-Fi networks become more popular, there will be more incentive for adapter manufacturers to include drivers that appeal to a relatively small portion of the market. When the total number of wireless users is in the tens of millions, the 5 percent or less who want to use wireless with Linux will become a significant number of potential buyers.

If a driver did not come with the adapter, check the manufacturer's Web site for drivers that may be available for free download. Many manufacturers print Web site addresses on their adapter labels and in their manuals, but if you can't find an address, try http://www.[*brand name*].com, or look in one of the online device-driver directories, such as http://www.windrivers.com, http://www.driverzone.com, or http://www.driversplanet.com. The directory sites tend to concentrate on drivers for Windows, but once you follow a link to a manufacturer's driver page, you can generally find its drivers for other operating systems, if they exist at all.

If you already have an adapter made by a company that doesn't support Linux, you'll have to move from the relatively sane and stable world of commercial software to the wide open universe of users' groups, email lists, and Web sites. Communities of users are out there, made up of people who are eager to improve the performance of their favorite operating systems and others who spend vast amounts of their own time (and their employers' resources) sharing information and answering questions. Within those communities, dozens of software developers have created device drivers and configuration tools for wireless adapters.

Linux Drivers

More than 80 different brands of wireless network adapters carry Wi-Fi certification labels, but almost all of them use one of just four or five internal chip sets. Therefore, only a few Linux drivers are necessary to control just about every possible adapter.

A few companies, including Cisco, Intel, Orinoco, Addtron, and Samsung offer their own Linux drivers for their wireless network adapters. If you can't find a Linux driver from your adapter maker, you can probably use one of the drivers supplied in Linux distribution packages or download a separate driver from a third-party developer. Table 7.1 contains a partial list of Linux drivers.

Table 7.1: Wireless Adapter Drivers for Linux

Adapter	Driver Source
Adapters that use the Intersil Prism II chip set (including Actiontec, Addtron, Bromax, Compaq, D-Link, GemTek, Linksys, Nokia, Samsung, SMC, Z-Com, ZoomAir, and others)	Download the latest version of the wlan-ng drivers from http://www.linux-wlan.com/pub/linux-wlan-ng or try the HostAP drivers at http://www.epitest.fi/Prism2
Orinoco	Linux drivers are included on the CDs provided with the adapters and at http://www.orinocowireless.com. For information about alternative drivers, see http://www.hpl.hp.com/personal/Jean_Tourrilhes/Linux/Orinoco.html.
Apple	AirPort adapters are private label versions of Orinoco products. Try downloading drivers from http://www.orinocowireless.com or see http://www.hpl.hp.com/personal/Jean_Tourrilhes/Linux/Orinoco.html.
BreezeCom DS11	http://www.xs4all.nl/~bvermeul/swallow
Cisco 340 and 350	http://www.cisco.com/public/sw-center/sw-wireless.shtml A somewhat different version of this driver is included in the Linux PCMCIA package and Linux kernel as airo.o (for PCI and ISA versions) and airo_cs.o (for PCMCIA)
Dell TrueMobile 1100	See Cisco 340
D-Link DWL-500	ftp://ftp.dlink.com/Wireless/DWL-500/Driver/DWL500_linux_driver_034.tar.gz
Ericsson 11Mb DSSS WLAN	http://www.ericsson.com/wlan/su_downloads11.asp
Intel PRO/Wireless 2011	http://appsr.cps.intel.com/scripts-df/Product_Filter.asp?ProductID=450
Lucent	See Orinoco (above)
Nokia C110/C111	http://www.nokia.com/phones/productsupport/wlan/c110_c111/
Samsung MagicLan	http://www.magiclan.com/product/magiclan/download/mlist.jsp
Symbol Spectrum24 High Rate	http://sourceforge.net/projects/spectrum24
3Com AirConnect	http://sourceforge.net/projects/spectrum24
3Com WLAN XJack	http://www.xs4all.nl/~bvermeul/swallow
D-Link DWL-650+ and 22 Mbps from other vendors	Nearly all of these cards use a new TI chip set which, at the time of writing, has no support in Linux. For future drive developments, see http://www.hpl.hp.com/personal/Jean_Tourrilhes/Linux.

If you can't find your adapter on this list, take a look at the "Wireless LAN Resources for Linux" Web site at http://www.hpl.hp.com/personal/Jean_Tourrilhes/Linux. This site serves as a central clearinghouse for information about making wireless LANs work with Linux. Not all of the information on the site applies to 802.11b networks, but there's plenty of useful material there.

The Linux community is famous for offering help to new users. Somebody who knows which driver will work with your Whoopie-Matic Lightning Bolt Wireless Adapter has probably posted pointers to exactly the information you need in a Linux newsgroup. The comp.os.linux.networking newsgroup is the place to ask questions about finding drivers for wireless network adapters. Before posting your own questions, it's always a good idea to scan the newsgroup's archives for previous answers that will solve your problem — user groups are usually more helpful if they know you've at least tried to find the answer yourself. Look in the comp.os. linux section of http://groups.google.com for a searchable archive of old questions and answers.

Intersil's Prism chip sets are used in a large number of wireless network adapters that carry many brand names. Intersil's Web site has a current list of Prism users at http://www.intersil.com/design/prism/prismuser/index.asp. If your adapter contains a Prism chip set, you can use the linux-wlan driver, which is available for download at http://www.linux-wlan.com/download.html.

If your adapter isn't on the Prism list, and none of those other sources can tell you where to find a Linux driver, the next step is to identify the chip set inside the adapter and find a driver for that chip set. You can almost always find this information by entering the FCC ID code from the adapter's label into the Federal Communications Commission's FCC ID Search Page at http://www.fcc.gov/oet/fccid. This database provides links to a database with copies of the paperwork that the manufacturer filed with its application for type approval, usually including a technical description and one or more circuit diagrams. A few minutes' reading of those documents should tell you who made the adapter's chip set, which should be enough to let you find the applicable driver.

Other Linux Wireless Programs

Some of the Linux drivers for specific wireless adapters come with configuration utilities that control channel assignment, SSID selection, and so forth. Separate wireless application packages are also available that can simplify the processes of setting up and using a wireless connection to a wireless network.

Several of these packages are based on the Wireless Extensions for Linux API that are included in most recent Linux releases and on the Wireless Tools programs that use the wireless extensions. The combined documentation for both Wireless Extensions and Wireless Tools is online at http://www.hpl.hp.com/personal/Jean_Tourrilhes/Linux/Linux.Wireless.Extensions.html.

As other wireless software for Linux appears, the Wireless Tools for Linux Web page (http://www.hpl.hp.com/personal/Jean_Tourrilhes/Linux/Tools.html) will probably be one of the best places to learn about it.

If a driver supports wireless extensions, the user can change the network configuration without the need to restart the driver. The wireless extensions are disabled by default, so a user must enable the CONFIG_NET_RADIO option in the kernel configuration.

Wireless Tools

Wireless Tools is a set of programs that manipulates the wireless extensions. It is available for download from http://www.hpl.hp.com/personal/Jean_Tourrilhes/Linux/Tools.html. The Wireless Tools are command-line programs, but they also provide a foundation for other programs that add a graphical user interface (GUI) to their controls and statistics.

Wireless Tools contains a /proc entry and three programs: iwconfig, iwspy, and iwpriv. The Wireless Tools programs are more of a framework for software developers than easy to use resources for end users. They do the actual work for other programs (described shortly), so it's useful to know that they exist and what they do. In actual operation, programs like KOrinoco and gWireless are a lot easier to use for everyone except the most hard-core command-line geeks.

/proc/net/wireless

The /proc entry is a listing in the /proc pseudo file system that shows some statistical information about the wireless interface. The /proc entries act as files, so the command cat /proc/net/wireless will display wireless statistics:

```
>cat /proc/net/wireless

Inter-|sta| Quality       |Discarded packets
face  |tus|link level noise| nwid crypt  misc
  eth2:  f0   15.  24.   4     181    0     0
```

It looks cryptic, but it can be understood:

- The status listing shows the current state of the network device.
- The Quality values show the signal quality of the link, the signal level at the receiver, and the amount of noise at the receiver when no signal is present.
- The Discarded packets values show the number of packets discarded due to an invalid network ID (nwid), or because the adapter was not able to decrypt the contents of the packets.

iwconfig

The iwconfig program controls the wireless adapter's configuration options. In an 802.11b network, it includes these parameters:

- channel   The channel number that the adapter will use.
- nwid   The network identification. In an 802.11b network, the nwid is the same as the SSID.
- name   The name of the type of wireless network or protocol in use on this network. This may be the type of adapter or a generic name such as "802.11b".
- enc   The encryption key currently in use.

The command iwconfig, with no argument, produces a list of current iwconfig and /proc/net/wireless values.

iwspy

The iwspy program sets and displays the local computer's IP address and the MAC address.

iwpriv

The iwpriv program provides additional support for device-specific extensions.

KOrinoco

KOrinoco is a program that uses the information and configuration settings from Wireless Tools in a set of graphic displays and dialog boxes for the KDE graphical desktop environment, and it mimics the Orinoco Client Manager for Windows. Even though the program looks like the one supplied with Orinoco network adapters, it should also work with other brands, provided the drivers support the Linux wireless extensions. Information about the program and instructions for download are online at http://korinoco.sourceforge.net.

The main KOrinoco status window shows essential information about the current connection, including the signal strength, the channel number, and the SSID of the current network connection. The KOrinoco Configuration Editor provides all the options necessary to associate with a wireless access point or join an ad hoc network.

gWireless

gWireless is another set of wireless programs that uses information from Wireless Tools. It includes a Gnome panel applet that changes color from red to orange to green as the quality of the current network connection improves, and a graphic interface for the options and information controlled by iwconfig. The graphic interface is still in development, but the project looks very promising. The home page for information about gWireless is http://gwifiapplet.sourceforge.net.

NetCfg

NetCfg is a network configuration tool for the Gnome environment. It allows a user to create and mange connection profiles and change network settings in real time. The NetCfg home page is at http://netcfg.sourceforge.net.

Wavemon

Wavemon uses ncurses to monitor and configure wireless adapter settings. It includes an Overview screen with all the important information from Wireless Tools in graphic form, a "level alarm" that triggers when signal strength drops below a preset level, and a full-screen history display that shows changes in signal level, noise level, and signal quality over time. There's also a configuration tool that uses menus for easy setup.

For more information about wavemon and links to the most recent version of the program look at http://www.jm-music.de/projects.html.

Status Display Programs

Several programs import the information from the /proc/net/wireless listings into graphic displays. The major difference among these programs appears to be the display format.

Wvlanmon

Wvlanmon is another Gnome panel applet that displays link quality as a color bar. You can find wvlanmon at http://tobi.tildesoftware.net/index/projects/wvlanmon/.

E-Wireless

E-Wireless is an Enlightenment epplet that monitors and displays signal quality information from the /proc/net/wireless listings. The program is online at http://www.bitshift.org/wireless.shtml .

Wmwave

Wmwave is a dockapp that shows link quality, signal level, and noise level in a small on-screen window. It's available at http://www.schuermann.org/~dockapps/.

GKrellMwireless

The GKrellM monitor stack is a graphic display of system information that can use themes to match the appearance of many window managers. The GKrellM wireless plug-in adds information about wireless network connections to the monitor stack. For general information about GKrellM, go to the main Web site at http://web.wt.net/~billw/gkrellm/gkrellm.html. For details about the wireless plug-in, go to http://gkrellm.luon.net/gkrellmwireless.phtml.

WireStat

WireStat displays wireless network connections in Xload format. Download the program from http://www.bogor.net/idkf/idkf/software/linux-hack/wlan/.

Remote Monitoring

The /proc/net/wireless entry looks like a file, so it's possible to retrieve status information about remote network clients through the network. Steven Hanley's Signal Level Server and Clients programs present this information in a graphic display. For details and downloads, go to http://wibble.net/~sjh/wireless.

Configuring an Access Point

Except for the Apple AirPort Base Station, most configuration utilities for wireless access points use a Web-based interface, an internal command-line interface from a remote terminal, or both, so it should not make any difference what operating system you use on the host computer that connects to the access point. The access point's commands, controls, and status displays will be the same on any system.

The Apple AirPort Base Station access point presents a different set of problems. The internal software supplied with the AirPort Base Station assumes that you're configuring it from a Macintosh, using the AirPort Setup Assistant and the AirPort Admin Utility.

To set up an AirPort Base Station from a Linux host, you need a Linux configuration program. At this time, only one program, the AirPort Base Station Configurator, appears to fit this description. Separate program versions for the two versions of the AirPort Base Station ("Snow" and the older "Graphite") are available from http://edge.mcs.drexel.edu/GICL/people/sevy/airport.

Because it was written as a Java application, the AirPort Configurator program will run on any computer with the Java Runtime Environment (JRE) in place. This includes Windows, Solaris, and Linux platforms. You can obtain a copy of JRE from http://java.sun.com/products/jdk/1.2/jre.

8

WI-FI FOR UNIX

The number of wireless options for people who use various flavors of Unix is limited, but they do exist. The universe of wireless adapter drivers and network software for Unix systems is not as large as the one for Linux, but there's enough support out there to connect computers running many major versions of Unix to a wireless network. It's even more important with Unix than with Linux to find out if a driver is available *before* you buy an adapter, because drivers for some adapter types simply don't exist for every version of Unix. Orinoco, Cisco, and the most widely used internal chips are often supported, but you might not have as much luck with a more obscure brand of adapter.

Unix Drivers

If you already have a wireless adapter that you want to use in a computer running Unix, you can try the standard drivers, or you can search for information in the archives of the newsgroups and mailing lists that cater to your Unix version. The FreeBSD search page at http://www.freebsd.org/search/search.html is a particularly good resource for learning which driver works with which adapter, even if you're using a different Unix type. But don't be surprised to discover that the best solution is to buy a different brand of adapter.

If you don't already have an adapter, the best choices for a Unix client appear to be the ones supported by the wi and an drivers. It might be possible to get other adapters to work, but it will probably require a lot more time and trouble. The man pages for each Unix version provide the exact syntax and detailed information about using the wi and an drivers.

FreeBSD, OpenBSD, and NetBSD all include similar drivers and related utilities for many widely used wireless adapters. The wi driver supports Orinoco adapters and adapters that use the Intersil Prism chip sets, including products from 3Com, Samsung, SMC, Addtron, Linksys, and Microsoft, among others. The an driver (for Aeronet, a company that has since been absorbed by Cisco) in OpenBSD works with Cisco 340 and 350 adapters.

If you can identify the chip set inside your adapter, you can usually figure out which driver to use. In most cases, the name of the chip set used in the adapter will show up someplace in the paperwork that was submitted to the FCC. If you don't know what kind of chip set is inside your adapter, use the FCC's online ID number search tool at http://www.fcc.gov/oet/fccid to find detailed technical descriptions of most adapter designs.

Configuration Tools

Each BSD Unix version also includes configuration programs that control the settings and options of the adapters that use the an and wi drivers. Some of the commands have slightly different names, but the functions are essentially the same. Table 8.1 lists the configuration commands for different versions of BSD Unix.

Table 8.1: Unix Configuration Programs

Unix Type	wi Configuration	an Configuration
FreeBSD	Wi wiconfig	Driver not used
NetBSD	wiconfig	ifconfig and ifmedia
OpenBSD	wicontrol	ancontrol

As Wi-Fi networks become more common, more versions of Unix will probably support wireless Ethernet services. As always, the official and unofficial mailing lists, newsgroups, and Web sites dedicated to each version will have the news of new drivers and network support as soon as they become available and people start discussing them.

wiconfig and wicontrol

The configuration programs for the wi driver can set all the network and adapter options. The syntax for the wiconfig and wicontrol commands are identical in all three Unix versions that contain them.

The syntax for wiconfig in an 802.11b network is:

```
wiconfig [interface] [-o] [-e 0|1] [-k key [-v 1|2|3|4]]
    [-t tx rate] [-n network name] [-s station name] [-p port type]
    [-m MAC address] [-d max datalength] [-r RTS threshold]
    [-f frequency] [-A 0|1] [-M 0|1] [-P 0|1] [-T 1|2|3|4]
```

The syntax for wicontrol is exactly the same.

The interface argument identifies the logical interface name of the network adapter. The names are typically wi0, wi1, and so forth. Assuming you have just one wireless adapter in the computer, it will show up as wi0.

To view the network adapter's current settings, type the command (either wiconfig or wicontrol) and the interface name, with no other flags. The WEP encryption key will appear only if you have root access to the system.

The other options are listed in Table 8.2.

Table 8.2: wiconfig and wicontrol Options

Option	Description
-o	Displays the statistics counters for this interface.
-e	Enables or disables WEP encryption. Enter -e 0 to turn off encryption, or -e 1 to turn it on. The default is for encryption to be disabled.
-k key [-v 1/2/3/4]	Sets the WEP encryption keys. If the command omits the -v setting, the command will set the first key.
-T 1/2/3/4	Identifies the WEP key that the adapter will use to encrypt outbound packets.
-t tx rate	Sets the transmission rate. The tx rate values are 1 1 Mbps 2 2 Mbps 3 Automatic rate select (default value) 4 4 Mbps 5 6 Mbps 11 11 Mbps
-n network name	Sets the name (the SSID) of the network that this client will join. The default setting is an empty string, which will instruct the client to associate with the first access point it finds. The -p option must be set to BSS mode for this option to work.
-s station name	Sets the name that will identify this client on the network.
-p port type	Identifies the operating mode that this network client will use. Use -p 1 for infrastructure mode or -p 2 for ad hoc operation.
-m MAC address	Changes the MAC address of the network adapter. There is rarely a good reason to change the factory-assigned MAC address.
-d max_data_length	Changes the maximum frame size, in bytes. The default is 2304.

Table 8.2: wiconfig and wicontrol Options (continued)

Option	Description
-r RTS threshold	Sets the RTS/CTS threshold, in bytes. The default is 2347.
-f frequency	Sets the adapter's operating channel number. In infrastructure mode, most network adapters automatically scan through all available channels to search for an access point, so this option should be omitted unless you want to select a specific channel in an environment where more than one signal is present.
-M	Enables or disables the option that reduces interference from microwave ovens. Use 0 to disable this option or 1 to enable it.
-P 0/1	Enables or disables power management.

This all looks a lot more complicated than it really is. In practice, if the kernel recognizes the card, and if the adapter settings match the settings for the access point and other adapters in the same network, you ought to connect without any trouble. If the kernel doesn't find the card, rebuild the kernel.

When you set up a new connection, it's easier to enter each option as a separate command than to try to run a whole string at once. Here are the commands that you will use most often:

wiconfig -p 1	Sets the network client to operate in infrastructure mode with one or more access points.
wiconfig -s Sally's Laptop	Identifies the network node as "Sally's Laptop."
wiconfig -e 1	Turns on WEP encryption.
wiconfig -k [WEP key]	Sets the WEP encryption key.

Along with the wireless settings, it's also necessary to set the standard network configuration options that apply to any TCP/IP connection. The ifconfig command handles these settings in most Unix versions.

Once you have configured your wireless network adapter and your network connection, they operate just like any other network connection. You can run network utilities like ping, Web browsers, email clients, and other applications, and connect to network resources just as you would run them and connect to them over a wired connection.

And, of course, you can connect through your wireless link from a Unix platform to any other computer on the same network, regardless of the operating system that the remote computer is using. If the computers are all connected to the same network, they will have no trouble exchanging radio signals and data.

Utilities for Unix

A few of the Linux configuration tools and status-display programs described in the previous chapter have been ported to one or more versions of Unix, but there aren't anything like the number of choices that exist under Linux or Windows. Original utilities are even more rare, but at least a couple are out there in Unix land.

Xwipower

Xwipower is a utility that shows wireless signal strength in an on-screen icon and includes a bar graph that tracks signal strength over time. As Figure 8.1 shows, the signal-strength icon shows a set of bar graphs that correspond to the strength of the received signal. The icon displays a message in Japanese when the adapter fails to detect a signal (roughly translated, it means "outside of signal area").

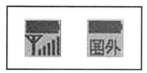

Figure 8.1: Xwipower shows the strength of a wireless signal as an on-screen icon

The same icon also shows the current battery level. When the tiny battery in the icon is solid, the battery is fully charged, or the computer is using external power. The battery icon appears as an outline when battery level drops below 10 percent.

Xwipower works in FreeBSD and NetBSD. It's available for download at http://iplab.aist-nara.ac.jp/member/masafu-o/xwipower.

WEP

WEP is a tool for setting WEP encryption in FreeBSD. It's available from the same source as Xwipower.

Bsd-airtools

Bsd-airtools is a package of BSD tools for detecting and analyzing 802.11b networks, and for controlling Prism-based wireless adapters. The home page for the bsd-airtools package is at http://www.dachb0den.com/projects/bsd-airtools.html.

Bsd-airtools includes these programs:

dstumbler A utility that detects and displays information about wireless access points within range of the wireless adapter's receiver

dweputils A set of utilities for auditing and securing WEP-encrypted networks, and recovering (a polite word for "cracking") WEP encryption keys

prism2ctl An interface to the Prism2 chip set's debug modes, including monitor mode

prism2dump A protocol analysis tool for 802.11 network traffic

9

WI-FI FOR PDAs AND OTHER HANDHELD DEVICES

Wi-Fi networks are not limited to full-size computers running full-size operating systems. Today, Palms, Handspring Visors, Pocket PCs, and other handheld personal digital assistants (PDAs) can all use Wi-Fi links to synchronize data with other computers, send and receive mail, and download data from the Internet. Tomorrow, a new category of hybrid devices will automatically switch between relatively slow cellular networks with wide coverage areas and much faster Wi-Fi networks that only extend a few hundred yards from their access points.

Some PDAs are built to operate with other radio services, such as the GSM (Global System for Mobile communications) cellular telephone network, but as a general rule, if your PDA can connect to a traditional wired LAN, there's probably a way to make it work over a Wi-Fi link. If no adapters are currently available, there's an excellent chance that somebody will introduce one soon.

Wi-Fi–enabled PDAs can be particularly useful in locations away from your own home or office, when you want to exchange email messages or consult an online information source from a public hot spot at an airport, a coffee shop, or even on the street.

Using a Handheld in a Wi-Fi Network

In a Wi-Fi network, the same network structure that supports laptops and desktop computers also works with handheld devices. One or more access points operate as hubs for the wireless network and double as bridges to the wired portion of the LAN and to the Internet. A single network can include both handheld units and larger computers, so it's entirely practical to use a wireless link to synchronize a PDA with another computer.

In order to use a PDA in a wireless network, the PDA must have a network adapter, driver software for the adapter, and tools for configuring the link. The world of handheld devices has no universal set of hardware interface standards, so every type of PDA requires an adapter that is specifically designed for it.

Handhelds come in many shapes and sizes, with several competing operating systems. Therefore, there isn't any single standard type of network adapter package (such as a PC Card) that fits all of them. The CompactFlash format is the most common design, especially among Pocket PCs, but many PDAs require adapters or modules that are specifically designed to fit their own proprietary interfaces. So, for example, if you're using a wireless module with your Palm m500, you can't use that same module in an iPAQ or a Handspring Visor.

Connecting a PDA to a wireless network takes the same basic steps as setting up a link to a laptop or desktop computer: install the adapter and change the network settings to match the requirements of your wireless LAN. As far as the access point is concerned, the PDA is just one more network node. The data format inside each packet might be different, but the network doesn't care; it's working with the frames that the network adapter adds to the beginning and end of each packet.

Windows CE

Windows CE, and more recently Windows CE .NET, are Microsoft's operating systems for pocket and handheld computers and embedded devices. The most widely used computers that use Windows CE include the Compaq iPAQ, Casio's Cassiopeia, Hewlett-Packard's Jornada, and the URThere's @migo-600C. Handheld PCs are larger than Pocket PCs but smaller than traditional laptop computers. The Handheld PC operating system is used in computers with a variety of form factors, including tablets and fold-over "clamshell" screens with keyboards. The latest Windows CE .NET release includes built-in support for 802.11 networks.

There's no single standard for input and output ports or sockets in Windows CE devices, so wireless adapters are not universally interchangeable. Each make (and sometimes each model) requires a particular type of adapter. Some use the same PC Cards that work with laptop computers (with different driver software), while others require a smaller CompactFlash adapter. Table 9.1 lists some popular Windows CE PDAs and the adapters they use for wireless network access.

Table 9.1: Popular Windows CE PDAs and Their Wireless Network Adapters

Maker	Model	Adapter Type
Audiovox	Maestro	CompactFlash
Casio	Cassiopeia BE300	CompactFlash
Compaq	iPAQ	CompactFlash *or* PC Card
Hewlett-Packard	Jornada	CompactFlash *or* PC Card
URThere	@migo-600c	PC Card
NEC	MobilePro	CompactFlash, PC Card, or both
Toshiba	Pocket PC e740	Built-in

Just about all Windows CE devices also have USB ports, so it ought to be possible to use a USB wireless adapter to connect to a Wi-Fi network, but it's not really practical to hang a USB cable and an outboard adapter that's bigger than the PDA itself onto a device designed to fit in the palm of your hand. In practice, nobody offers wireless USB drivers for Windows CE, so it's not a real option. On the other hand, a USB link between your PDA and a larger computer can be very useful when you want to load drivers and other software into the PDA.

You can think of a CompactFlash adapter as a smaller version of a PCMCIA (PC Card) adapter. The CompactFlash form factor is about the size of a matchbook — less than a quarter the size of a PCMCIA card — but wireless adapters are usually a little bigger than that, because the built-in antennas extend beyond the edge of the socket. Among others, CompactFlash Wi-Fi adapters are available from Intel, Kyocera, D-Link, Pretec, Socket, and Symbol. Figure 9.1 shows a Symbol adapter.

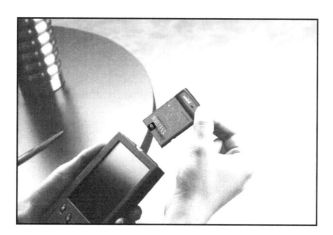

Figure 9.1: The Symbol Wireless Networker is a CompactFlash adapter

Several larger Pocket PCs, including some of the offerings from NEC, Hewlett-Packard, and Compaq, have PCMCIA sockets rather than CompactFlash slots, so they can use the same PC Card wireless adapters that are used with laptop PCs, if you can find a Windows CE driver. Fortunately, almost all the major manufacturers (and many of the minor ones) offer drivers for Windows CE. For an up-to-date list of adapters with links to driver downloads, go to Chris De Herrera's Windows CE Web site at http://www.cewindows.net/peripherals/pccardwirelesslan.htm.

If you already have a PC Card adapter that you want to use with your Windows CE device, check the adapter maker's Web site for the latest drivers. If the manufacturer doesn't offer a Windows CE driver, look on the back of the adapter for an FCC ID number, and run that number through the database at http://www.fcc.gov/oet/fccid to learn if it's a private-label version of an adapter for which a driver is available.

Installing and Configuring a Wireless Adapter

The software that accompanies each driver always includes a wireless network configuration utility. The specific procedure for downloading and installing the new driver and configuration software is different for different adapters, but they all include the same general steps:

1. Insert the adapter into the PDA.
2. Connect the PDA to a Windows desktop or laptop computer.
3. Use the Microsoft Active Sync utility to transfer the software from the larger computer to the PDA. In some cases, you must download the software from the manufacturer first; in others, it's all one process.
4. Enter the configuration settings for your PDA's connection to the wireless LAN and the Internet. If the LAN uses a DHCP server, set the PDA to automatically accept an IP address; if it doesn't use DHCP, enter the address assigned to the PDA and the address of the gateway server by hand.
5. Specify the wireless network's SSID, or instruct the PDA to detect and display all nearby SSIDs.
6. If your network uses WEP encryption, set the encryption key.
7. Disconnect the cable between the PDA and the computer.
8. Try to establish a network link to confirm that the network is operating properly. If your configuration utility includes a ping command, that's a good choice.

When installation and configuration are complete, choose Start • Programs • Connections and select the new network connection. Your PDA should connect to the network. You can now run all the same network applications and utilities that you could run through a modem or a wired network.

Palm OS

Owners of Palm handhelds and other PDAs that use the Palm OS platform don't have as many wireless options. Because each type of Palm handheld requires a different package for the network interface, the Palm OS category is not as attractive a market for wireless adapters, compared with the Windows CE arena, where a single CompactFlash or PCMCIA product can work with many different devices.

Intel's Xircom division offers 802.11b adapters for the Palm m500 and m125 series and for Handspring Visors, and Symbol's Palm-based SPT series of handhelds has wireless interfaces embedded within the devices. Symbol also has a license to make Palm OS bar-code scanners that use Wi-Fi networks to relay data back to a host computer. However, if you have some other model of Palm, or maybe a Sony Clié, you could be out of luck.

Palm m500 and m125

An 802.11b wireless link to the Internet offers a faster alternative to the Palm.Net service that connects through the cellular telephone system. Intel's Xircom Wireless LAN Module for Palm Handhelds replaces the standard Palm cradle that connects the handheld unit to a PC. When the Palm is mated with the wireless module, a user can use a Wi-Fi link to connect the PDA to a host computer for a HotSync data exchange and for access to the Internet. Figure 9.2 shows the Xircom module with a Palm m500.

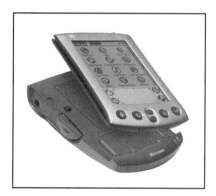

Figure 9.2: The Xircom Wireless LAN Module is a snap-on cradle for a Palm m500 or m125

Wi-Fi network connections through a Xircom adapter or a Symbol PDA require the same kind of configuration settings as every other wireless network client. The client settings (such as DHCP, WEP encryption, and IP addresses) on the Palm must match the configuration of the network access point.

Handspring Visor

Handspring Visors are yet another type of Palm OS device in a completely different package from Palm's own handhelds. Therefore, they can't use the same wireless adapters. Xircom's SpringPort Wireless Ethernet Module plugs into the top edge of the Visor case; the module has its own battery, so it doesn't increase the power drain on the Visor's internal battery.

To use a SpringPort, plug the module into the top of the Visor. The Visor will automatically recognize the SpringPort and display a configuration screen with five options: Client Settings, Network Settings, HotSync Settings, Status, and Tips.

The Client Settings screen includes the configuration options that identify the Visor to the network and set up a link. Use this screen to assign a client name, specify the SSID of the network, and enable or disable WEP encryption and power management.

The Network Settings screen provides instructions for adding the current SpringPort options to the Visor's network configuration.

The Status screen displays the state of the current link. It shows signal strength and the condition of the two batteries (in the Visor and the SpringPort). The Advanced Status option opens a menu with IP Information and Software Information options. The IP Information option opens a screen with the Spring-Port's current IP address, the subnet mask, the addresses of the DNS servers, the current DHCP status, and the SpringPort's MAC address.

Other Handhelds

If anybody is currently making 802.11b network adapters for Blackberries, Psions, or other varieties of PDAs, they're keeping them a secret. This might change as the demands for wireless LANs increases and new handheld models appear, but many current models won't ever have access to Wi-Fi networks, and of course, many handhelds, such as the Blackberry and some Palms, have been designed around built-in radios that use some other wireless service, so adding a 2.4 GHz radio to the same package would be extremely awkward. Other handhelds have such a small market share that it's simply not practical for any manufacturer to devote design time and money to creating a Wi-Fi interface, because the potential sales would never be enough to recoup the cost of research and development.

Therefore, it may not be possible to add your particular PDA to your Wi-Fi network. If you run your life out of one of those devices, your only options are to replace the PDA with a different model or use some other method to gain access to the rest of the world. Sometimes, it's best to recognize that You Can't Get There From Here, and just get on with your life.

Bigger Isn't Always Better

The standard Palm OS screen is just 160 x 160 pixels. Windows CE screens can be larger (up to 640 x 480), but the physical size of the display is a lot smaller than a laptop with similar numbers. Therefore, an image that looks fine on a conventional monitor could be useless on a handheld device. As more devices with tiny screens connect to the Internet, many Web sites and services will be introduced to fit those screens—it's not realistic to expect to see the same amount of information in a couple of square inches that you can display on a full-size computer monitor, so Web services for PDAs generally use screens designed to meet the specific needs of their target audiences. In practice, this means that successful Web services for users of handheld devices restrict themselves to a small amount of data on each screen, rather than large pages that force the user to scroll down or across. A large number of nested pages is a common approach.

Because the displays are smaller, and because most PDAs were designed to work with relatively slow network connections, you should not expect to use your Palm or iPAQ online the same way you use your laptop or desktop computer. The network functions are pretty much identical, but the content is likely to be quite different.

Coming Attractions

The next generation of Wi-Fi interfaces will be even smaller than the ones used in CompactFlash adapters today. SyChip, a Bell Labs spin-off company, has introduced a reference design for a tiny interface module that will add internal 802.11b capabilities to cellular telephones and other appliances and devices, and several companies are developing new "smart phone" products that will combine the functions of a cellular phone, a PDA, and a Wi-Fi client in a single pocket- or purse-size package. These devices will allow users to establish a high-speed Internet connection when they're within range of an 802.11b hot spot and drop back to a slower cellular connection when that's the only available wireless network access. Others might combine Wi-Fi services with Bluetooth, for wireless links to nearby peripheral devices.

Remember that a Wi-Fi network doesn't care what kind of data is moving through it, or what kind of client device is sending and receiving it. As long as the frames, packets, and radio modulation methods meet the 802.11b specifications, the network will pass the data along, so the same technology that connects your laptop computer to the Internet today will appear in embedded modules that perform completely new services. For example, home appliances, office machines, and cars will transmit diagnostic information to central monitoring centers that will identify problems and dispatch a repair technician before the problems become visible to the people using those machines. And pollable water and electric meters will allow a remote data collector to gather billing information without the need to send a human meter reader to every account location. Some of these applications will probably use Bluetooth rather than Wi-Fi, but we'll probably see some kind of embedded Wi-Fi devices within the next few years.

In spite of the efforts of the 3G wireless interests, Wi-Fi and its successors appear to be headed for very wide use on all kinds of devices.

10

EXTENDING THE NETWORK
BEYOND YOUR OWN WALLS

The original idea behind the 802.11b specification was to provide wireless connections to LANs in limited areas such as businesses, homes, and public institutions. Wi-Fi was supposed to be a simple extension of traditional Ethernet to laptops and other computers that could not be conveniently connected to a cable. Other radio services would provide wireless access to the Internet from public spaces.

That was the plan, but Wi-Fi gear is inexpensive, it doesn't require a license, and it's relatively easy to set up and use, so an entire culture of "guerilla networkers" has emerged to develop alternative uses for the technology that extend the reach of 802.11b networks beyond their own offices, classrooms, and homes. Hobbyists and community organizers are installing antennas on rooftops and hillsides where they can provide entire neighborhoods with public or private wireless access to the Internet and create point-to-point data links over distances of several miles. Many colleges and universities have added outdoor wireless access points to their campus-wide networks, and a few cities have started to build public Wi-Fi networks that will eventually cover their entire downtown areas.

This is still a grassroots movement mostly made up of enthusiastic techno-geeks and network hackers, but it has the potential to offer some serious competition to the multi–billion dollar 3G (third-generation cellular) wireless networks that were supposed to be the next wave of mobile connectivity. If these noncommercial networks that have been thrown together with duct tape and antennas in coffee cans ever come close to providing widespread reliable and cheap wireless network access at 6 Mbps, the 3G cellular folks will have a lot of trouble convincing people to buy their expensive 384 Kbps services. Therefore, the commercial cellular and wireless network operators are watching the community network movement very carefully.

It's relatively easy to install and use a Wi-Fi network to move data between buildings or to provide network access to your backyard, parking lot, or other open space. Outdoor antennas are widely available, or if you prefer, you can build your own.

This chapter contains information about the legal and practical issues related to operating and using a wireless network outside your own property, and it provides technical information about outdoor access points and antennas. In the next chapter, you can learn how to use Wi-Fi equipment to construct and use point-to-point network links.

Legal Issues

Wi-Fi networks do not require licenses, but the FCC and other regulatory agencies have established some rules about the radio transmissions that make those networks possible. Most of these rules exist to minimize the likelihood of interference among wireless networks, cordless phones, and other services that share the same radio frequencies, so nobody has an unfair advantage over other nearby users.

When you're trying to create an 802.11b network with the largest possible footprint, rather than just reaching all the computers in your own building, the strength of the radio signals from your access points and network adapters becomes a lot more important. There's a direct relationship between the strength of your signal and the distance it can travel, so it's essential to understand just exactly what the regulations allow.

The specific rules that apply to 802.11b wireless devices in the United States appear in Part 15, Section 15.247 of the FCC's regulations. Here's what they say:

(b) The maximum peak output power of the intentional radiator shall not exceed the following:
> *(1) For[…]all direct sequence systems: 1 watt.*
> *(3) Except as shown in paragraphs (b)(3)(i), (ii) and (iii) of this section, if transmitting antennas of directional gain greater than 6 dBi are used the peak output power from the intentional radiator shall be reduced below the stated values in paragraphs (b)(1) or (b)(2) of this section as appropriate, by the amount in dB that the directional gain exceeds 6 dBi.*
> > *(i) Systems operating in the 2400 – 2483.5 MHz band that are used exclusively for fixed, point-to-point operations may employ transmitting antennas with directional gain greater than 6 dBi provided the maximum peak output power of the intentional radiator is reduced by 1 dB for every 3 dB that the directional gain of the antenna exceeds 6 dBi.*

What does that all mean? First, the rules allow the radio transmitters in access points and network adapters to have a maximum power of 1 watt. And second, the maximum amount of antenna gain is 6 dBi, unless you reduce the transmitter power as you increase the gain. Highly directional point-to-point systems are permitted to use more antenna gain than point-to-multipoint systems. The maximum power *to the antenna* can't be more than one watt, but you can use a directional antenna to increase the effective radiated power to 4 watts.

To stay strictly within FCC regulations, each antenna must be certified with the specific access point you wish to use it with. These certifications should be available from the company selling the antennas.

When you calculate the output power of a radio, you must also consider the signal loss in the cable between the radio and the antenna. For example, the output of an access point might be 20 dBm (equal to less than half a watt), but a particular cable to the antenna might lose 6 dB at 2.4 GHz. Therefore, the antenna would receive only 14 dBm from the radio. That's a lot less than a watt, so there's room for some gain in the antenna.

The radios built into most Wi-Fi access points and adapters transmit at only about 0.030 watt, so they're well within the legal limits, unless you connect one to a huge antenna with a tremendous amount of gain. An RF (radio frequency) amplifier between the radio and the antenna could boost power beyond the 1 watt limit, but of course, that would violate the FCC's regulations.

Two different types of Wi-Fi signal could benefit from more transmitter power: point-to-point signals, where the added power could increase the distance between the two sites; and point-to-multipoint, where increased power at the access point could expand the footprint within which client devices could successfully join the network. A point-to-point link typically uses high-gain directional antennas at both ends; in a point-to-multipoint system, the access point usually uses an omnidirectional or sectional antenna that covers a broad area, but the client adapters might use directional antennas.

If anything, the FCC's power restrictions on radio transmitters in the 2.4 GHz band are too conservative. It would be nice to be able to push, say, 5 watts into a high-gain antenna to create a clean and reliable data link over a distance of five or ten miles or more, or use a single access point to cover a larger area. However, the telephone companies and other service providers who sell data services have enough influence with the regulators to keep the low-power rules in place, so the 1 watt limit is probably here to stay, except in rural areas.

As a responsible, law-abiding citizen, you should always take those federal regulations very seriously. And as a responsible, law-abiding author, I would never encourage you to do anything else. However, it's extremely unlikely that a hypothetical individual or small business who used a hypothetical high-gain antenna to boost the signal strength of a hypothetical wireless LAN would ever attract any attention from the FCC or other law enforcement types, unless that hypothetical signal created significant interference to somebody else's network or other radio service, or if it attracted attention from a local telephone company or a major Internet service provider. And even if there were a complaint, it could be difficult to identify the source of an illegal signal (unless the oversize antenna was right out in the open on the roof or the side of a building). Operating your

Wi-Fi network within the FCC's power restrictions is the right thing to do, but that's too bad, because it would not be difficult to boost the strength of your signal.

As a general rule, the FCC doesn't care to spend its time and resources dealing with interference complaints on unlicensed frequencies like the 2.4 GHz ISM band used by Wi-Fi networks. But the law is the law, so as a matter of principle, nobody with the good sense to buy and read this book would ever consider blatantly boosting the power from their access points and network adapters or using very-high-gain antennas. Of course not.

If you're reading this outside North America, remember that the FCC's rules apply only to the United States. The regulators in other countries have set their own limits, which are sometimes even lower than the American numbers, and their enforcement policies might be a lot more severe. It's important to consult technical and legal experts in your own country before you try to install a high-gain antenna or an RF amplifier in your network.

While the power output of most wireless networks—even with high-gain antennas—should be well within safe levels, it's generally not a good idea to operate a high-gain or amplified antenna next to you. Many access points contain warnings about operating the equipment near your body or especially your eyes, and when using amplifiers and high gain antenna equipment, this should definitely be kept in mind.

Outdoor Antennas and Access Points

Several factors contribute to the signal strength (and therefore the maximum distance) of a radio link between an access point and a network client in a Wi-Fi network:

- Antenna gain
- Transmitted power
- Antenna height
- Cable attenuation

Keep in mind that a Wi-Fi link moves data in both directions: from the access point to the network adapter and from the adapter to the access point. So the antennas and radios in the link must be able to both transmit and receive radio signals. Fortunately, the gain and directional characteristics of an antenna are identical for both transmitting and receiving, so the same antenna that boosts the effective power of an outbound signal can also increase a receiver's sensitivity to a weak incoming signal.

An outdoor antenna must also survive in the physical environment where it is operating. High winds can shift a directional antenna away from the target where it was originally aimed; accumulated ice and snow can attenuate the signal and increase the amount of weight that the physical mounting hardware must support; and sunlight can cause a plastic enclosure to deteriorate. Therefore, many antennas are sealed inside radomes or other packages that offer additional protection.

2.4 GHz antennas exist in many shapes and sizes. An omnidirectional antenna can be a single element just a few inches long, with or without an enclosure. The antennas built into PCMCIA adapters are even shorter. The most common directional antennas are yagis (smaller versions of rooftop TV antennas), patch antennas that resemble smoke detectors, parabolic reflectors that can be up to three feet high, and large panels with extremely wide aperture angles.

Remember that an 802.11b network uses digital radio signals, so there is absolutely no advantage to using higher power or a fancy antenna or placing your antenna on a rooftop, if you can exchange adequate signals with smaller, cheaper equipment. If an antenna with a moderate amount of gain produces acceptable signals, your data won't be any better when you replace it with something bigger and more expensive. And smaller antennas are also a lot less conspicuous, which can reduce the likelihood of complaints from neighbors and local zoning agencies.

Antenna Characteristics

Wireless network devices use the same antennas for both transmitting and receiving radio signals. An antenna handles a lot more energy when it's transmitting than when it's receiving, but the performance characteristics are identical. The same antenna that increases the effective radiated output power of a transmitted signal also boosts the sensitivity of a receiver by the same amount, so an antenna connected to a Wi-Fi access point or network adapter will improve the strength of the radio signals moving in both directions across a radio link. The most important characteristics that define the performance of an antenna are *aperture angle* and *gain.*

The aperture angle of an antenna is the angle or arc within which the antenna radiates or detects energy at maximum power or sensitivity. If, for example, an antenna's aperture angle is 20 degrees, the "window" of maximum signal strength extends 10 degrees to each side of the front of the antenna. Signal strength will drop when both antennas in a radio link are not within the aperture angle of the other. Figure 10.1 shows the effect of aiming a pair of directional antennas at each other.

The built-in antennas supplied with many access points and most network adapters are not directional, so they radiate and detect signals equally in all directions. The specifications for a nondirectional antenna (also called an omnidirectional antenna) don't include an aperture angle, but if they did, the aperture angle would be 360 degrees. As the name suggests, the antennas in a point-to-point link are aimed directly at each other, so their aperture angles can be extremely narrow.

An antenna's gain is its effective output power or sensitivity relative to a standard dipole antenna. So, if you measure the strength of signals from two identical transmitters or the same signal through two separate receivers, the signal that passes through an antenna with a gain of 3 dBi will be 3 dB stronger than a signal through a reference dipole antenna. The gain of an antenna increases with the size of the antenna and as the signal is focused within a narrow aperture.

It's useful to think about antenna angles and gain as similar to focused lights. A standard light bulb radiates the same amount of light in all directions (except back to the base of the bulb). However, if you place a reflector behind one side of the light source, or if you focus the light in a particular direction, the apparent

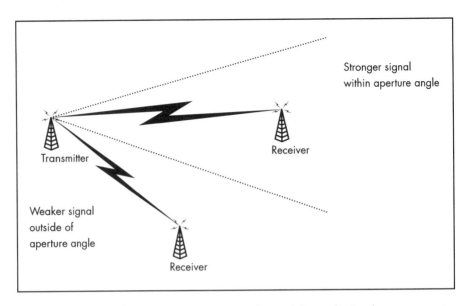

Figure 10.1: Directional antennas can increase signal strength by condensing the same amount of power into a smaller area

brightness of the light will increase within the target area, but it will look dimmer when you move away from the target area. The total amount of light radiated by the bulb is the same, but more of that light is concentrated in certain places.

Radio antennas work the same way, more or less. A nondirectional antenna will radiate equal amounts of energy in all directions, while a directional antenna can concentrate more energy in some directions than in others.

Directional antennas with tight aperture angles are useful for point-to-point links, but that's not the only way to take advantage of a directional antenna in a wireless network. When you have a potential problem with interference from other radio signals, it's often helpful to place a directional antenna with the source of interference off-axis from the aperture angle, so the receiving antenna is much less sensitive to the source of interference than to the signal you want. And when you're trying to provide network coverage to your own property while limiting the amount of spillover to your neighbors, you can place one or more directional antennas at the edge of the area you want to reach and aim the antennas inward.

An antenna with a greater surface area is more effective than a smaller antenna, but the exact size of the antenna is also extremely important. The ideal antenna for any radio frequency is cut to a length exactly equal to the wavelength of that frequency or some multiple or fraction of that wavelength. So it's important to use an antenna specifically designed for operation at 2.4 GHz (2,400 MHz) with your 802.11b network. An antenna of the correct size will send and receive Wi-Fi signals far more efficiently than an antenna with a random length.

Power

The maximum amount of power produced by an 802.11b radio transmitter is determined by the design of the radio; the people operating the network usually can't adjust it, or if they can, it's most often nothing more than a choice between "high" and "low" power. However, the output power of one of those radios is considerably less than the legal maximum, so it's often possible to increase the amount of power that reaches the antenna without breaking the law.

Since you often cannot boost the amount of power produced by the transmitter, the only way to increase the power of the signal from a radio in an access point or a network adapter is to place a device called an RF amplifier between the radio and the antenna. You can think of an RF amplifier as a black box that takes a low-power signal at its input and provides a stronger signal with exactly the same content at the output.

Some RF amplifiers are designed for use indoors, next to the access point, router, or network adapter. Others mount outdoors on the tower or mast next to the antenna. Indoor amplifiers are usually easier to install and maintain, and they're a lot easier to connect to an AC power source, but they're less efficient because a long feed cable to the antenna will absorb some of the RF power coming out of the amplifier. An amplifier in a weatherproof enclosure near the antenna will supply more power to the antenna, but it will be more difficult to reach when you have to repair or replace it. If you do use an outdoor amplifier, look for one that obtains DC power through the antenna feed cable.

HyperLink Technologies and other manufacturers offer RF amplifiers for use at 2.4 GHz. Many of these devices amplify both inbound and outbound signals. This is a useful feature because it makes it possible to install an amplifier on just one end of a link and still increase the signal strength in both directions.

Antenna Height

Radio signals at 2.4 GHz travel along a line-of-sight path, so you can increase the distance that a signal can travel by raising one or both antennas. That's why it's common practice to place radio antennas on rooftops, hilltops, and tall towers. In order to compensate for the curvature of the earth, the average height of the two antennas must increase as the signal path gets longer.

Radio "line of sight" is actually broader than the visual path between the two antennas. Radio waves travel within a cigar-shaped region called the *Fresnel zone* (pronounced fru-NEL zone) that surrounds the direct path between the transmitting and receiving antennas. For the best possible transmission, the Fresnel zone must be free of hills, trees, buildings, and other obstructions.

So the maximum distance that a wireless network signal can travel depends on the average height of the two antennas, with allowance for the curvature of the earth and the requirement for an unobstructed Fresnel zone. Table 10.1 lists one set of estimated minimum heights required for various distances at 2.4 GHz. Remember that these are estimates, so you might actually move your data over somewhat greater distances.

Table 10.1: The Relationship Between Antenna Height and Maximum Signal Path

Distance	Average Antenna Height
1 mile	13 feet
3 miles	27 feet
5 miles	35 feet
8 miles	48 feet
10 miles	57 feet
15 miles	83 feet
20 miles	115 feet

Source: HyperLink Technologies, Inc.

Note that the height of the two antennas is the average height above average terrain; if one antenna is higher than the average height, the other antenna can be closer to the ground. So if one end of a five-mile link is on a hillside or on the roof of an eight-story building, the other end of the link could be close to ground level if there are no obstructions between the two locations.

When you're trying to provide Wi-Fi network coverage to a large area, it's more efficient to place the access point's antenna as high as possible, rather than trying to raise a lot of separate client antennas.

Cable Attenuation

The cable that carries a radio signal from a radio transmitter to an antenna or from the antenna to a receiver is not a perfectly efficient transmission medium; every foot of cable absorbs a small but measurable amount of power. This means that the amount of power that reaches the antenna drops as the cable length increases.

The effect of this cable attenuation on a short cable is usually insignificant, but it can make a huge difference over a longer run. If the antenna is high on a tower or rooftop, or if you're trying to estimate the antenna gain necessary for a long point-to-point link, you must allow for cable loss when you calculate the strength of the signal reaching the antenna. The amount of loss in a particular type of cable depends on the diameter of the cable and the materials used to produce the cable. The specifications for each type of cable will include the amount of attenuation, often expressed in dB per 100 feet at different operating frequencies.

If the cable loss is rated at 6.80 dB at 2,500 MHz, you can estimate that a 20-foot cable at 2.4 GHz (2,400 MHz) will lose about 1.3 dB. If the output power from an access point or network adapter is 20 dBm, the antenna will receive only 18.7 dBm through that cable. So when you push that signal through an antenna with a gain of 6 dBi, the effective radiated power would be about 24.7 dB (20 − 1.3 + 6 = 24.7).

Every foot of feed cable increases the amount of cable loss, so you should place your access points and network adapters as close to the antenna as possible. If the antenna is mounted on a roof or the wall of a building, try to place the radio in a nearby equipment closet or other space where you have access to AC power and your Ethernet cables. It's a lot more efficient to run a longer Ethernet cable to the access point and a shorter antenna feed cable.

When you install an antenna feed cable, it's good practice to allow a little slack at each end to make it easier to connect and disconnect the cable from the antenna and the radio. But don't leave a long coil of excess cable wound up on the floor just because the premade cable is longer than you need. All that cable wastes signal with no compensating benefit.

Campus Networks

As a general rule, a campus network provides wireless access to the Internet, and sometimes to a LAN, for users in two or more buildings or in the outdoor spaces that surround those buildings. A "campus network" can exist on a college or university campus, but the same kind of planning and design can also apply to other locations. For example, a campus network might operate in an office park or an industrial park, in a public space such as a park or a shopping and entertainment center, or even in a farm or a marina. Several cities have installed campuslike networks to provide public Internet access throughout their central business districts. Another form of temporary campuslike network might exist at a special event such as a music festival, a boy- or girl-scout jamboree or a gathering of old-car enthusiasts.

The simplest campus networks occur by accident: the radio signals from the access points that provide network service to the interior of a building don't stop at the building's walls, so a user in the parking lot or the backyard can also establish wireless access to the network. A larger and more complex campus network might have additional access points in locations specifically chosen to reach network clients on the college lawn or the coffee shop across the street.

A campus network might be a complement to a set of wireless links that connect two or more buildings to the same network, but it's not the same thing; a campus network should provide broad coverage to a lot of outdoor space, while a point-to-point link simply extends a single LAN to spaces inside of several buildings. Chapter 11 of this book contains detailed information about designing and using point-to-point network links.

Setting Up a Campus Network

In general, the same rules apply to a campus network that you would use in designing a Wi-Fi network to serve a single building. Choose locations for your access points that will provide signals to as much of the area as possible, and allow for about 20 percent overlap from one footprint to each adjacent footprint. Each pair of overlapping coverage areas should use a different radio channel.

In almost every case, the access points that serve an outdoor network should have connectors for external antennas, rather than the captive antennas built into many access points designed for indoor use. Choose the antenna with the best characteristics for your particular needs, and use a cable to connect it to an access point located out of the weather.

Connecting the Access Points to a LAN and the Internet

If your access points are all located in buildings that already have network service, you can treat the access points with outdoor antennas as a simple extension of the existing network. If you don't already have a network connection at your access point, you'll have to create one.

In order to connect your campus network to a LAN or the Internet, you must bring a point of network presence to every access point. The connection can be through an Ethernet cable, a data circuit leased from the telephone company, or a point-to-point radio link.

Every access point requires a source of electric power, but it's not always necessary to run a long extension cord from the nearest AC outlet. Many access point manufacturers offer a "power over Ethernet" option that carries power for the access points through the same cable that carries the Ethernet data.

Ethernet cables are easy to connect to an access point, but they're not the best choice for links between buildings except in very specific situations. First, you must have a secure path for the cable to follow; you can't just string the cable through the trees or run it across the lawn. On a college campus, it's sometimes possible to run cables through steam or other utility tunnels, but that's not practical in most other locations. But even if you have a way to route the cable from one building to another, the maximum practical distance for a 10Base-T or 100Base-T twisted-pair cable connection is only about 100 meters. If your access point is more than 100 meters from the network hub, you'll have to add one or more repeaters to the line or replace the twisted-pair cable with a fiber-optic connection. Either way, the cost is probably greater than using a radio link.

Sometimes the ideal location for an access point is on a building that has existing Internet service, but that's not part of the LAN you want to use for your campus network. In that case, you can set up a virtual private network (VPN) link that creates a "tunnel" through the Internet back to your own network. The access point will pass data to and from your own network through the VPN, just as if it were connected through a short cable.

The third alternative is often the most practical choice. Use point-to-point wireless links between the network hub and each of your remote access points. Outdoor routers and related hardware and software designed specifically for this purpose are available from Orinoco, D-Link, and many other suppliers. You can find detailed information about point-to-point links in the next chapter of this book.

How Big Are Your Cells?

The largest possible coverage footprint for every access point is not always the best design for your wireless network. Like cellular telephone systems, the demand for access to the network should dictate the amount of bandwidth available. An area that has a lot of users, such as the reading room of a library, might support two or more overlapping access points, while an area that gets only occasional users, such as a parking lot, could get by with just one. When you design your own network, you can use the directional characteristics and gain of different antennas to find the ideal balance for each location.

Public or Private?

Access to a campus network may be restricted to members of the community that operates the network, or it may be open to any user within range of the radio signal. Or the network might be configured to allow anybody to connect to the Internet, but not to other local computers. For example, the network administrator for a college might want to provide on-campus wireless Internet access to students, faculty, and staff, but not to the general public. On the other hand, a business might want to provide unlimited access to the Internet and the corporate network for employees, but allow only visitors to connect to the Internet.

Controlling access to a campus network is no different from controlling access to any other wireless network—all the same tools are available to keep unauthorized users out of the network that you would use in an indoor network. These include the WEP encryption tools and MAC address filtering functions included in the access points, and external firewalls that can require a user to enter an account name and password before the network will allow a connection.

Using a Campus Network

As a network user, a campus network looks just like any other Wi-Fi network: the wireless network adapter in your computer detects a radio signal, and if it recognizes the SSID and other security options, it establishes a link. Some campus networks offer access only to the Internet, while others also provide local connections to a LAN or a WAN.

If your computer can't get a strong enough signal to establish a network link, it's always a good idea to try moving to a different location. Minor obstructions such as trees, reflected signals from the walls of buildings, and other structures can interfere with the two-way signal path between your computer and the nearest access point. Even a change of just a foot or two can be enough to make a huge improvement.

Networking Your Neighborhood

Someplace between the relative simplicity of a home-based wireless network and a complex campus network, you might want to think about extending your own home- or small-business network: you can share a high-speed Internet connection with nearby neighbors or allow your employees to take their laptop computers to the coffee shop next door. If you or your children like to play multiplayer games with the family next door, or if you want to go online from your Palm or Pocket PC while schmoozing with your neighbors at the annual block party, a neighborhood network might be the way to go.

Before you decide to hang an antenna on your roof, consider exactly what you want to accomplish with your neighborhood network and how you plan to maintain security in the rest of your network. If you're trying to add a particular location to your network (such as a particular neighbor's house or the cafe that has become your *de facto* branch office), use a directional antenna that will focus your signal to the specific location you want to reach. On the other hand, if you want to provide an Internet hot spot for everybody within half a block or more, you can place a high-gain nondirectional antenna at the highest point on your own building. And if you're using the same LAN for both in-house and neighborhood use, make sure a firewall keeps your own computers separate from the public portion of the network.

If your network adapter has a connector for an external antenna, you might want to either buy or build a directional antenna that you can point toward the community network's nearest access point. It's quite possible that you will discover nearby signals that were not detected by the low-gain omnidirectional antenna built into the adapter. We'll talk more about building an antenna in the next chapter.

Keeping Your ISP Happy

It seems like a perfectly logical idea: share your high-speed cable modem or DSL service with your next-door neighbor, and split the cost. Or let everybody in your apartment building or on your suburban block share a single connection.

But consider the potential aggravation factor of dealing with your Internet service provider, which might view your generous sharing of a cable or DSL account as a threat to its (real or potential) revenue stream and as a violation of its terms of service. Some major ISPs, including AT&T Broadband, SBC, and Time Warner Cable, have specific policies that do not allow customers to share connections through neighborhood networks. Many other ISPs don't care or even encourage the practice.

The ISPs are legitimately concerned that neighborhood networks might generate a lot more demand for network bandwidth than they expect. When you design and construct a communications network, you calculate the maximum capacity of your network based on predicted peak demand. If you get it right, your network can handle the demand with enough to spare for emergencies, but if the demand increases beyond your expectations, the whole system is overloaded, and you have to add more capacity.

This kind of planning applies to telephone systems, highways, and streetcar lines, as well as Internet connections. If you have enough streetcars (or bandwidth) to handle your rush-hour traffic, the system runs efficiently and the number of dimes and quarters in the fare box should cover your expenses. But when a big new factory opens at one end of the line, 500 more passengers suddenly want to use your system. Unless you add more capacity, the cars are too crowded and everybody complains.

Experience can give you a pretty accurate idea of how much demand will exist at any given moment—you might not know exactly who is online at 10:15 on a Tuesday morning, but you can predict how many streetcars or how much bandwidth you will need to handle the total demand.

In the case of an Internet account, the ISP has built enough bandwidth to handle the peak demand. If that demand doubles, though, it'll have to buy and install more equipment and find a source of revenue to pay for it. Naturally, it wants to prevent the kind of additional demands for bandwidth that can break down the whole system. Or more accurately, it wants to know about it and plan (and charge) accordingly.

So you have two choices: either ask your own ISP if it has a policy on shared connections and follow its guidelines (or find a different ISP); or go ahead and install your neighborhood access points and hope the telephone company, cable service, or other ISP doesn't find out about it.

Network Security: Everybody is Your Neighbor

The simplest configuration of a neighborhood network is a single access point with a wide coverage footprint and an unprotected connection to the Internet. Anybody with a network adapter within range of your signal can use your network to exchange data through the Internet. That includes the family next door, but it also includes the guy in the van parked on the street who's using your network to download pornography.

Unless you are intentionally creating a public Internet hot spot for everybody who comes along, you should use at least one of the security tools built into the 802.11b specification:

- Turn on WEP key encryption. It's true that a dedicated intruder can crack a WEP key in less than an hour, but it does discourage the casual drive-by user.

- Use MAC address filtering to restrict access to your network to specific network adapters. Again, it's not difficult to spoof a MAC address with the right software, but it's one more impediment to unauthorized access.

- Turn off the DHCP function that automatically assigns a numeric IP address to each client, and assign a specific address to each authorized user.

- Turn on the firewall function in your access point or router.

- Use an external server or other firewall that forces each user to supply a user name and password before it connects to the Internet.

- Use a virtual private network (VPN).

If you're using the same network to link two or more of your own computers, use a firewall to isolate that part of the network from the public access point. Also, encourage all of the legitimate users of your network to pay close attention to filesharing, so they don't allow outsiders to read or write data on their computers.

Finally, be sure to change the access point's administrative password. Do not use *admin* or any other widely used default password. An intruder who breaks into your access point can cause massive damage to your network.

11

POINT-TO-POINT LINKS AND REPEATERS

Using radio to extend a LAN is not a new idea. Equipment and software for adding remote clients to networks have been around for at least ten years. Schools, businesses, academic researchers, and Internet service providers have all used spread-spectrum wireless links to extend local networks and Internet service to places where traditional wired networks were impractical or impossible. But the cost and complexity of the process made it a job for professionals and expensive consultants.

As low-cost Wi-Fi equipment has become widely available, many users have thought about aiming an antenna at a nearby building or a hillside five or ten miles away to create a cheap, high-speed data link. Some experimenters and tinkerers with more time than money have even designed their own antennas out of tin cans, potato chip canisters, and junk from their basement workshops. They have generally discovered that Wi-Fi links can be a reliable way to move data across a lot of ground. This chapter contains information about designing and using point-to-point wireless network links.

A point-to-point wireless link can be part of a larger Wi-Fi network, it can act as a simple bridge between two wired LANS, or it can add a single distant site to an existing LAN. Point-to-point service differs from other 802.11b networks, because it moves data between two specific locations rather than broadcasting a network signal to any network client within range of the radio signal. It's also possible to use an 802.11b link as part of a wireless gateway that provides Internet access to a community or an isolated location where affordable landlines are not available.

Why extend a wireless network? Point-to-point links can serve several purposes:

- They can extend a single network to include users in more than one building. In an office park or on a college campus, a business or academic department that occupies space in more than one building can use wireless links to share LAN services among all the organization's spaces.

- They can move data across a barrier such as a highway or a river. If there's a clean line of sight, a wireless link can jump across a gap that could make it difficult or impossible to string cables from one building to another.

- They can provide LAN and high-speed Internet access to users and unattended computers in remote locations. A wireless link can extend a broadband connection to places that are not served by broadband DSL, cable-modem Internet service, or even by plain-old telephone service.

- They can establish wireless network links as an inexpensive alternative to leased lines. Private data circuits supplied by the telephone company or other common carriers normally involve a one-time installation fee and a recurring monthly payment. The annual cost of a leased line can often be many times greater than the one-time cost of buying and installing a radio link.

In a sense, a point-to-point 802.11b network link is a completely different category from a wireless LAN. Both use the same radio technology, and it's quite possible to extend a wireless LAN beyond the limits of a single building, but a point-to-point link could just as easily use some other type of radio modulation at some other frequency, rather than DSSS at 2.4 GHz, and perform the same function. You can find some pointers to alternative methods for connecting remote sites to your network later in this chapter.

Extending the LAN

A point-to-point wireless network link can be either a LAN at one end connected to a single client device at the other end or a bridge between two LANs. In other words, the endpoints of a link can be either a single computer or other device or a full network.

A wireless LAN with a remote client, like the one shown in Figure 11.1, works the same way as a network with two or more access points within a single building. The only difference is that one or more access points connected to the LAN use an outdoor antenna aimed at a client computer in a remote location. The remote computer appears to the network exactly like every other computer on the same LAN.

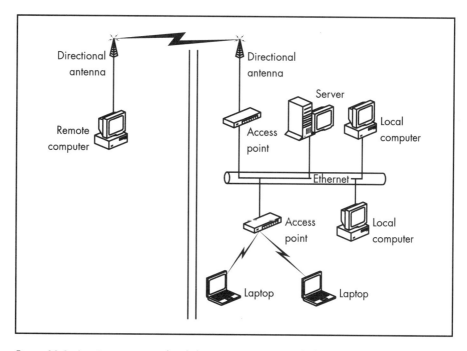

Figure 11.1: A point-to-point wireless link can connect to a single device in a remote location

A wireless network bridge, like the one shown in Figure 11.2, is a link between two segments of the same LAN. The two segments might be separated by as little as a few hundred feet or as much as several miles or more.

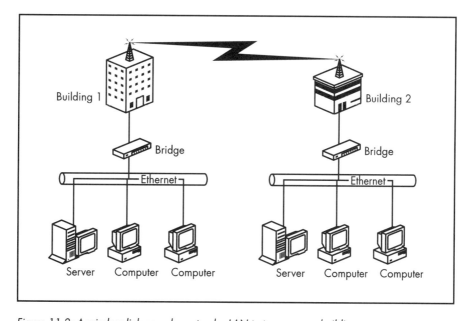

Figure 11.2: A wireless link can also extend a LAN to two or more buildings

If the distance between the endpoints is too far for a single radio link, or if there are obstructions to the line-of-sight signal path, a point-to-point link can include one or more repeaters at relay points between the origin and the destination. A relay point can be at an isolated location, such as a radio tower or a rooftop, or it can be a place with additional network clients, such as a third building between the two endpoints.

A point-to-point link can use any access point and network adapter that has connectors for external antennas. However, several manufacturers offer wireless routers that have been specifically designed for outdoor bridging applications, and these are often a better choice. Routers made by Plexus, HyperLink, Orinoco, and other manufacturers all combine access points with routers, so they make the network a lot easier to assemble.

Point-to-Point and Point-to-Multipoint

An indoor access point uses either an omnidirectional antenna that radiates equal amounts of energy in all directions from the middle of the intended coverage area or a directional antenna with a wide-aperture angle located at one edge (or a corner) of the coverage area. An access point that provides wireless service to any location within a designated area (such as an office or a house) is a *point-to-multipoint* service; it can exchange data with many network clients at the same time.

A *point-to-point* link has a different objective: it moves as much of the radiated signals as possible between two fixed locations. Radio signals move across the link in both directions, so each access point, router, or network adapter uses the same antenna for both transmitting and receiving. The goal is to focus the radio signal toward the antenna at the other end of the link, so at least one of the endpoints uses a directional antenna. If the link covers a long distance, both antennas should be directional for the strongest possible signals.

In a campus or similar area where the network connects several buildings, the network links can be "split" to distribute network service from a central location to remote sites in more than one direction. In this kind of system, the central access point uses a nondirectional antenna, and each remote site uses a directional antenna, as shown in Figure 11.3. In a system where two remote sites are in the same general direction, the best choice might be a directional antenna with a wide operating angle. A more complex system might include a combination of directional and omnidirectional antennas.

Installing a Point-to-Point Link

The first step in a point-to-point site survey is to identify a possible signal path. In theory, it ought to be possible to calculate the required height of both antennas and identify the path between them, but it almost never works out that way. There's almost always a certain amount of tweaking required before you can fire up your radios and start to move data across the network. You can perform a preliminary survey with a good map (such as a topographical map from the U.S. Geological Survey), but at some point you will want to climb up onto the roof (or look out the window) and confirm that there's a line of sight to the place you

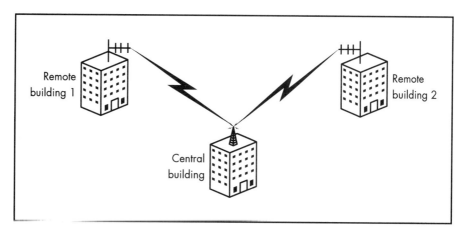

Figure 11.3: An omnidirectional antenna can distribute signals to two or more remote locations at the same time

want to put the other end of the link. If the path extends more than a couple of hundred yards, bring a pair of binoculars with you.

You can generally place an antenna on your own building without any special permits, but if you want to use the roof of a commercial building, you will probably need permission from the property owner and maybe from the local zoning board or other land use agency. This probably won't be a problem when you're mounting an inconspicuous antenna, but keep it in mind if you have to use a relatively large dish or something similar. If you're using an existing pole or tower to support the antenna, make sure you're not producing interference for other antennas nearby or receiving interference from them.

Climbing a pole or tower with a belt full of tools and securely mounting a bulky antenna in a precise position 30 or more feet in the air is not a casual afternoon project. Don't even consider it without appropriate safety equipment, including hard hats for everybody involved — a dropped wrench or bolt can be lethal. If you don't have experience with this kind of work, there's no shame in hiring somebody to do the job for you. The people who sell point-to-point antennas can tell you where to find a qualified antenna rigger in your area.

Choosing a Signal Path

The first step in installing a link is to decide exactly where it will go. If you're just extending the network across a parking lot or a highway, the path will be obvious; choose a location that avoids the big tree in front of the building. But if the link is more than about half a mile, you will probably want to lay out the path on a map first.

Topographical maps, either on paper or online will give you the best level of detail. http://www.topozone.com has maps for the entire United States; http://toporama.cits.rncan.gc.ca is the source for maps of Canada. If the exact locations for both endpoints are not immediately obvious on a map, a GPS (global positioning system) device can provide precise geographic coordinates.

Reaching the Boondocks: Long-Range Links

The distance covered by most point-to-point wireless network links can probably be measured in yards rather than miles, so installing the link is relatively easy. The other end of the link is in plain sight, so the antennas are easy to aim at each other. Signal strength is usually not a problem on a short hop, especially with directional antennas.

A longer link is more difficult, because the signal will be weaker, and it's a lot more difficult to point the antennas accurately. Figure 11.4 shows why a receiver becomes harder to find as you move farther away from the transmitter.

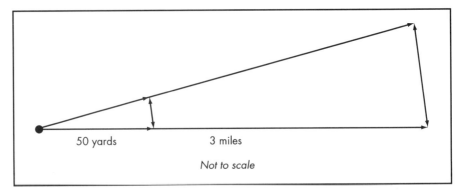

Figure 11.4: A small change in the direction an antenna is aimed can have a huge effect on a receiver several miles away

It's also more difficult to locate a particular building or other endpoint with the unaided eye when it's one of many buildings on a hillside or in a valley several miles away, so a telescope or a pair of binoculars is an essential part of your installation tool bag. Starting at the location where the network connection is already in place, look for the target site from the roof or an upper-story window. If you can find it, you can probably install a network link from here to there.

However, at least one of the antennas in a long-range link must be high enough to overcome the obstructions caused by Fresnel zone interference and the curvature of the earth. This isn't a serious problem for a one- or two-mile link — the roof of a two-story building is probably high enough to give you the clearance you need unless there are a lot of trees in the way — but if you're trying to push a signal five miles or more, the height of the antenna is a significant issue. This is the reason you often see radio towers on top of hills and tall buildings.

Aligning the Antennas

For best performance, a directional antenna must be aimed directly toward the antenna at the other end of the link. If the antennas at both endpoints are directional, they must both be pointed correctly. In most cases, the best place to locate an antenna is on the roof or a tower, or bolted to an outside wall, but sometimes it's possible to place it indoors next to a window, if there's a clean line of sight to the other end of the link. Most commercial antennas come with information regarding their *radiation pattern*— where the signal is strongest horizontally and vertically. When in doubt, be sure to refer to this documentation, as it is not immediately obvious with all antennas where the strongest signal points are. Yagi-style antennas, for example, are strongest slightly off-center, and on a long-range link this could make the difference between success and failure.

It's entirely possible to align a pair of antennas by watching the signal strength display in your Wi-Fi configuration software, but when you're working with long-range links and weak signals, a piece of test equipment called a spectrum analyzer will provide much more precise information. A spectrum analyzer is a very expensive radio receiver that displays a portion of the radio spectrum as a visual image. Because the display shows any radio signal it detects as a spike in the graphic display the spike will grow larger as the signal strength increases. Therefore, you can use the display to find the best possible positions for your antennas.

Unfortunately, spectrum analyzers that can display a 2.4 GHz signal are quite expensive devices—a new one will probably cost several thousand dollars. Your best bet is to rent or borrow one for the day or two it will take to install your antennas. If you can't find a spectrum analyzer easily, don't worry about it; the signal strength display in the Wi-Fi software will work almost as well.

Installing and aligning the antennas for a point-to-point link is not a one-person job. At a bare minimum, you will need one person to adjust the antenna's position, and another to watch the computer or spectrum analyzer to find the strongest signal. If you can place a team at each end of the link with telephones or two-way radios, it will save a lot of time and aggravation.

To aim the antennas properly, follow these steps:

1. Choose the exact location where you want to install each antenna, and securely mount the masts or poles that will hold the antenna.

2. Use the mounting hardware supplied with each antenna to attach it to the mast, pole, or other supporting structure. Point the antenna toward the other endpoint of the link, but don't tighten the mounting screws yet; you will want to adjust the antenna's position more precisely.

3. Run the feed cables from the antenna to your wireless router, access point, or network adapter. If you have access to a spectrum analyzer that can operate at 2.4 GHz, connect it to the feed cable coming from the antenna.

4. Connect the routers or access points to their respective networks, and turn on the radios at both ends. If you are using a spectrum analyzer, tune it to the frequency of the radio channel that your access point or router is using. If you don't have a spectrum analyzer, start the configuration utility on your network device. If only one end of the network link has a directional antenna, that's the one to adjust.

5. Slowly move the antenna connected to the router or the spectrum analyzer. You should see a peak in the signal strength display when this antenna is aimed directly at the other end of the link. Move the antenna left and right first, and then adjust the vertical angle. When the signal strength display or the spectrum analyzer shows the strongest signal, tighten the antenna's mounting hardware to maintain that position.

6. If the other antenna is also directional, repeat the signal peaking process. If you have a second team at the remote site, they can make the adjustments on their antenna while they talk on a radio or telephone to the people at the point of origin.

7. If it's not already connected to the network device, connect the feed line from the antenna to your router, access point, or network adapter.

At this point in the process, you should be able to exchange data between the two endpoints in both directions. If you can't get enough signal through the link to produce a usable network connection, you might have to boost the signal with an RF amplifier or replace one or both antennas with other antennas that have more gain.

Obstructions and Relays

Each antenna in a point-to-point link must have an unobstructed line of sight to the antenna at the other end of the link. If there's a building or a mountain between the origin and the destination, you'll have to find a way to get your signal over it or around it. If the signal path goes through a wooded area, try to run your site survey during the spring or summer, because a signal that passes through bare branches without any trouble can often be shut down by leaves and other foliage. A safe estimate for foliage is a loss of 3dB, or half of your signal power, per tree.

You can't bend a radio signal around an obstruction, so the only way to get past it is to use a repeater at a location that has a line of sight to both endpoints. A repeater can be a single router with space for two radios, such as the Orinoco Outdoor Router, two separate routers connected through an Ethernet network cable, or a pair of access points connected through a network hub. In order to reduce the effects of interference between the two antennas, each segment of a multi-hop network link should use a different radio channel.

As a side benefit, the same router that relays the network to a second radio can also provide network service to the building where the relay is located, or split the network and relay signals to two or more remote endpoints. So, for example, the central control point of a Wi-Fi network might be located on a valley floor, with a link to a relay point on a nearby hilltop or rooftop. From the hilltop repeater, the same network can be extended to two or more locations in as many different directions.

Alternatives to 802.11b

Long-range 802.11b links are not the only way to connect remote clients to a LAN. Other methods for extending a network are often easier or more reliable.

The main reasons to use Wi-Fi equipment in a point-to-point wireless link are that the equipment is widely available and relatively inexpensive, it doesn't require a special license, and the link can be part of an existing wireless LAN. But it's also possible to use other radios that use different (licensed or unlicensed) radio frequencies or different types of radio signals.

The IEEE's 802.11 specification (without the *b*) covers radios that use both direct-sequence spread spectrum (DSSS) and frequency-hopping spread spectrum (FHSS) modulation. In a radio environment where interference from other wireless LANs is a problem, a different technology can often cut through the noise to produce a stronger and cleaner stream of data.

Each type of radio offers a different combination of data transmission speed and signal range. For example, the Alvarion (formerly BreezeCom) PRO.11 family of wireless network products uses FHSS radios that can move data at up to 3 Mbps over a distance of up to 30 miles. A BreezeNET Workgroup Bridge connects directly to a 10Base-T Ethernet LAN.

If the 11 Mbps data speed of an 802.11b is not fast enough to meet your requirements, other devices can provide faster connections, but they generally have shorter ranges than a Wi-Fi link. 802.11a equipment has a maximum data speed around 54 Mbps at 5 GHz. C-SPEC's OverLAN HS 100 has a top speed of about 100 Mbps, but the signal range is significantly shorter than an 802.11b link.

Barry McLarnon has gathered information about dozens of wireless LAN products that use several different operating frequencies, including 915 MHz, 2.4 GHz, and 5.8 GHz. His Web site at http://hydra.carleton.ca/info/wlan.html is an excellent source of equipment reviews, articles, and links to manufacturers' sites.

This is a book about wireless networks, but sometimes it's useful to remember that the point of the exercise is a network connection and not a wireless link. If a broadband connection to the Internet already exists at the remote location, go ahead and use it. Just because a point-to-point wireless link is possible, it's not always the best approach.

For example, a virtual private network can provide all the advantages of a point-to-point wireless link, without the hassles of setting up a pair of antennas. As far as the people using the network are concerned, a single network with a VPN tunnel connecting two or more buildings looks just like a network with a radio link. Another approach that can often be effective is to run cables from one building to the next through utility tunnels.

Antennas for Network Adapters

If you're using a point-to-point link to reach a single distant network client, you will need a network adapter that accepts an external antenna. Several manufacturers, including Zoom and Orinoco, offer wireless network adapters on PC Cards with antenna connectors. The ZoomAir Model 4103, shown in Figure 11.5, comes with a detachable omnidirectional antenna that you can replace with a cable and a directional antenna.

Orinoco PCMCIA adapters include two internal antennas and a connector for an external antenna. The antenna connector is located under a tiny cover at the edge of the card, as shown in Figure 11.6. You can remove the cover with the point of a pin.

Because the Orinoco adapter uses a proprietary connector, it requires a special cable called a *pigtail* with a standard antenna cable connector at one end and a plug that matches the Orinoco connector at the other. An Orinoco-brand pigtail can cost more than the network adapter card, but pigtails that work just

Figure 11.5: The ZoomAir Model 4103 uses an external antenna

Figure 11.6: The antenna connectors on Orinoco adapters are located at the outside edge of the PC Card

as well are also available at less than a third of Orinoco's prices from several other sources, including Fleeman Anderson & Bird (http://www.fab-corp.com), HyperLink Technologies (http://www.hyperlinktech.com), and Invictus Networks (http://www.invictusnetworks.com).

Build Your Own Antenna?

Many community network enthusiasts have designed and built their own antennas out of odd hardware, plastic spacers, copper wire, empty tin cans, and potato chip canisters. Depending on the contents of your junk box and your pantry, the materials for a homemade high-gain directional antenna might cost as little as three or four dollars, not counting the price of a can of coffee, beef stew, or potato chips. If you have to go out and buy all the parts and hand tools necessary for the project, you might have to spend $20 or more.

However, when you add the value of the time necessary to assemble the antenna and tweak it for optimal performance, it's not at all clear that rolling your own would be less expensive than buying an inexpensive commercial antenna. It's not unusual to spend three to six hours or more assembling one of these "cheap" homebrew antennas. A few minutes of online searching (look for "2.4 GHz antenna") should find several sources for directional antennas under $50 that will work at least as well as the ones you can build. Keep in mind that your access point or network client adapter transmits only a fraction of a watt, so it doesn't need an antenna that can handle high power; you can get by with a relatively lightweight unit.

The most common type of directional antenna for point-to-point communication is called a "yagi," or more properly, a Yagi-Uda antenna system. It was named for the two Japanese engineers, Professor Hidetsugu Yagi and Professor Shintaro Uda of Tohuku University, who designed and constructed the first ones around 1926. A typical yagi antenna, like the one shown in Figure 11.7, has a single active element, whose length is exactly half the wavelength of the radio frequency at which the antenna will operate (at 2.4 GHz, that's about 2.35 inches). Quarter-wavelength elements will also work. Additional elements called reflectors and directors are located parallel to the active element at very specific intervals determined by the size of the active element. Reflectors are located behind the active element, while the directors are in front of it. Most of the rooftop TV aerials that were common before the days of cable and satellites were yagis.

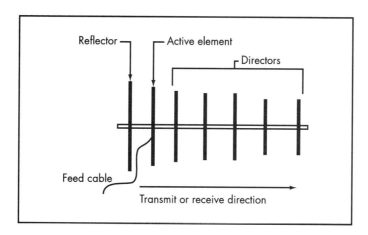

Figure 11.7: A yagi antenna has one active element, one reflector, and several directors

A yagi always has just one reflector, which is about 5 percent longer than the active element, and several directors, about 5 percent shorter than the active element (each additional director should be slightly shorter than the one behind it). As you add more elements to a yagi, the amount of gain increases. If you want to consider building a yagi of your own, take a look at Rob Flickenger's antenna built inside a Pringles Potato Chip can at http://www.oreillynet.com/cs/weblog/view/wlg/448.

Many designs for homebrew 2.4 GHz yagi antennas use one-inch washers as reflectors, directors, and active elements. These will work, but they're not ideal for two reasons: first, at 2.437 GHz (the center frequency of Channel 6) a quarter-wavelength active element should be about 1.16 inches long, so those washers are about 16 percent smaller than they ought to be for ideal performance; and second, the reflector and directors are the same size as the active element, which reduces the gain (or sensitivity) of the antenna. But considering that the whole thing was built out of about $7 worth of parts, it's close enough. If a pair of these antennas gets your signal from here to there and back again at high speed, it doesn't matter that the reflectors and directors aren't exactly the right size.

Darren Fulton's more traditional 13-element design at http://www.users. bigpond.com/Darren.fulton/yagi/13_element_yagi_antenna_for_2.htm, shown in Figure 11.8, uses antenna elements cut to length from heavy-gauge brass or copper wire, and a reflector made of sheet aluminum.

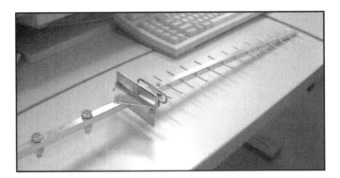

Figure 11.8: Darren Fulton's homebrew yagi antenna has a total of 13 elements

A yagi isn't the only type of directional antenna that lends itself to build-it-yourself designs. Waveguide antennas, with a radiating element inside a reflective metal cylinder or cone, use another extremely effective design. The antenna's performance depends on the size of the enclosure, the length of the radiating element, and its exact position. Greg Rehm's instructions for assembling a tin-can waveguide antenna are online at http://www.turnpoint.net/wireless/cantennahowto.html.

If you want to boost your signal gain in all directions, you will want to use an omnidirectional antenna. Tim Kyle's discone design at http://kyleti.aswwc.net/index.php?page=projects&old_project=80211b_Discone looks like a good place to start.

Based on the tests and measurements posted on the Internet for these and other homebrew antennas, it appears that they're both effective and cheap, especially if you don't include the value of your time when you calculate the cost. It's all a matter of attitude: if you thought "that sounds like a fun project" when you read about building homebrew antennas, go for it. But if spending an afternoon with a soldering iron in your hand sounds like a form of cruel and unusual punishment, remember that an inexpensive commercial antenna will do the same job just as well, with a lot less effort.

12

PUBLIC AND COMMUNITY NETWORKS

The same Wi-Fi network technology that provides wireless network access to businesses and homes can also allow users to connect their portable computers and handheld devices to the Internet from other locations, including hotels, conference centers, and airport passenger terminals. Many Internet service providers, cellular telephone companies, and independent wireless network services have established public Internet hot spots. A growing number of coffee shops, restaurants, and similar businesses are hosts to these hot spots in the hopes that they will encourage customers to spend time and money in their establishments while they read their email and browse the Internet.

People who use wireless networks at work and at home can use the same portable computers and network adapters to send and receive mail, browse the Internet, and exchange files through public wireless services. These services offer access to users who pay for one-time connections or monthly subscriptions.

When they are available, these networks can supply convenient high-speed access to the Internet and corporate networks as a relatively inexpensive alternative to dial-up connections.

Wireless Ethernet technology has also inspired a new generation of hobbyists and community organizers who are installing antennas on rooftops and hillsides where they can reach entire neighborhoods with public wireless network connections.

Up until now, we've been talking exclusively about setting up and operating your own wireless network and connecting computers to that network. This chapter will explain where and how to find public networks and how to configure your computer to use their services.

The most important difference between a private wireless network and a public network is the amount and type of access control that the network's owners and managers impose on their users. A private network located in an office, a factory, or a college campus might use some combination of passwords, WEP encryption, and a secret SSID to keep unauthorized users out. In contrast, most public networks are configured as "information utilities" that are open and accessible to anybody with a network adapter and a credit card.

Before wireless access became practical, most people who wanted to use the Internet or connect to their corporate network when they were away from their own homes or offices would use a dial-up modem and a telephone line to make the connection. This works, but it's often a big nuisance to find a public telephone with the right kind of plug, balance the computer on that little shelf in the phone booth, and find a local telephone number for your Internet service provider (ISP) that doesn't produce busy signals all the time. If you're lucky, you might connect at a big fat 56 Kbps. Wireless access to the Internet typically offers several important advantages over dial-up: it's fast, it provides an instant connection, and it uses radio signals instead of cables, so you aren't tethered to the nearest telephone outlet.

What about connecting through a cellular telephone? It can be done, but it often requires a tedious and time-consuming sequence of dialing, signing on, connecting, verifying, and so forth before you can start using the network. When you do get connected, the link is slow and subject to dropouts. Other wireless services such as CDPD (Cellular Digital Packet Data) are easier and more reliable than cell phones and modems, but the maximum speed is a relatively glacial 19.2 Kbps. Wi-Fi connections are almost instantaneous, and the data speed is significantly faster.

Most people who connect to public wireless networks use them to connect to the Internet or their employers' corporate networks. Unlike users on a private wireless LAN, people generally don't use a public network to share files with other computers on the same LAN or to send documents to a local printer. Ad hoc peer-to-peer networks and infrared links are better methods for that kind of across-the-table file transfer.

Public Networks

Public networks sell wireless Internet access by the minute or by the day, and they also often offer flat monthly rates for unlimited connection time. They are most often located in places where business travelers are likely to want fast and easy access to email and Internet services, and in restaurants and coffee shops whose owners hope to attract customers who will buy lots of coffee and pastries while browsing the Web or reading their mail. A few public wireless networks are even in coin laundries.

As wireless service has been introduced into hotels and conference centers, the people who run those tedious meetings with too many PowerPoint slides have begun to notice that some members of their audiences are paying more attention to the laptop computers open in front of them than to the speakers at the front of the room. They may be listening to Next Year's Marketing Plan with half an ear, but some of them are concentrating on the messages or the Web pages their computers are receiving through the air, and others are posting their own notes and comments about the presentation to Web logs or relaying them to friends and colleagues who are not attending the meeting. Will this force the presenters to make their speeches more interesting? Don't hold your breath. But it will permit people in the audience to use instant messaging to keep up a running commentary on the speakers (just as long as they don't laugh at the wrong times).

The public wireless network business is still in its very early stages. There are wireless signals in a handful of airports and hotels and in a couple hundred coffee shops in North America and Europe, but that's just a tiny proportion of the total number of public wireless locations that will probably be available in a few more years, especially as internal wireless adapters become standard features in new laptop computers.

At the moment, it's still necessary to have separate accounts with multiple public and community wireless services to obtain truly broad coverage. If you carry your laptop or PDA from, say, an airport served by Boingo to a coffee shop with a hereUare hot spot, you will need accounts with both services. As the Wireless Internet Service Provider (WISP) industry grows and matures, roaming among hot spots operated by more than one WISP will become common, allowing a user to use a single account to connect from a multitude of locations. WISP companies are working on roaming plans that will allow subscribers to use their accounts through the nearest public access point, even if it belongs to a different service provider.

Eventually, wireless network service should be as seamless as cellular telephone coverage; just turn on the computer, and if you're within range of a public access point, you'll be able to log on. But we're not there yet.

Setting Up a Connection to a Public Network

Like just about everything else related to wireless Ethernet, access to a public network almost always requires some fiddling with the computer's network configuration settings. If you've read (or even skimmed) the earlier chapters of this book, you probably know more about wireless network configuration than 90 percent of the people who use public wireless networks, so adding new settings for WayPort or one of the other public networks shouldn't be difficult.

Finding a Network

There are two ways to find a public wireless network: you can consult a published (or online) directory, or you can fire up your computer on site and see if any networks are within range. If your wireless network configuration utility doesn't automatically display the SSIDs of all the network signals it detects, your best bet will be to consult the directories for each of the service providers before you try to connect. But if you're using a system that will scan for nearby signals and let you choose the one you want to use, you may discover public wireless networks that aren't listed in any directory.

However, this is one of the "features" that is not consistent from one brand of wireless network adapter to another. It's possible that your configuration utility might show you a list of the networks it has detected and let you choose the one you want to join. If you're using an Apple PowerBook with an AirPort Card and AirPort software, the software displays a menu of nearby wireless networks in the Control Strip module and in the AirPort Application. The Wireless Network Settings tool in Windows XP does the same thing. In some Windows and Linux utilities, when the SSID is not specified, or if it is set as "ANY", the adapter will automatically associate itself with the first network it detects. If your adapter is set to detect unknown networks, it should find a public network whenever one is within range.

Of course, many of the networks that you will identify in your search will be private LANs rather than public networks. Some of those networks may be accessible to outside users because the owners have failed to apply the WEP encryption and other security features of the 802.11b standard, but there's a real difference between theft of service and taking advantage of a public network.

It's almost always easier to join a known network than to search for a random signal. When you set up an account with one of the public network services, you can set up an alternative configuration profile that will detect that network. Some configuration utilities automatically scan through their lists of profiles, while others require a user to manually change profiles. Either way, when your portable is within range of that service, it will immediately associate itself with the network you want to join.

Each of the active public network services has a "Where to Find Us" page on its Web site that lists all of its active locations. So when you arrive at an airport served by Boingo, or a coffee shop with a T-Mobile network, you can activate the configuration profile for that service and log on without the need to search for a service. In addition, several Web sites offer combined directories that include access points and hot spots operated by multiple service providers. These include http://www.wifinder.com and http://www.80211hotspots.com.

If you don't know which public wireless service has the network service contract at the airport where you're waiting to change planes or the convention center where you're attending meetings, you'll have to let your computer search for a signal. If you don't already have an account with that wireless service provider, don't worry; most allow new users to set up new accounts on the spot. If you're lucky, the service provider will have a roaming agreement with a service with whom you already have a subscription, so you won't have to set up a new account.

It's often possible to log on to a public network from a location outside the business that operates the access point. For example, Tully's Coffee is a Seattle-based coffee shop chain whose real-estate strategy is to open its own stores close to existing Starbucks outlets. It doesn't offer Wi-Fi access yet (it's planned for the future), but many of its customers log in through the access point at a nearby Starbucks. Tully's Chairman Tom O'Keefe told the *Seattle Times,* "It just so happens that they're sitting in our stores, drinking a wonderful cup of Tully's coffee, eating our bagel—and they're tapped into the Wi-Fi at Starbucks across the street. As you know, Wi-Fi travels."

The specific steps for finding a wireless network signal are different for different operating systems and configuration utilities, but the basic steps are always the same. Before you make changes to your computer's network settings and connection profile, make a copy of the original settings in a notebook or some other place where you can find them. You'll need to return to those settings when you get back to your own office or home network.

To search for a wireless network, follow these steps:

1. If it's not already connected, insert the wireless network adapter card into your computer's PCMCIA socket, or connect the adapter to the computer's USB port.

2. Turn on the computer if it's not already on.

3. Use the computer's TCP/IP network settings tool to instruct the computer to obtain an IP address from a DHCP server.

4. Save the changes to the network settings. Reboot the computer if necessary.

5. Open the wireless network configuration tool.

6. If you know the name of the network service you want to use, set that name as the SSID in the active connection profile. If you want to search for a network, set the SSID to "ANY" or leave the SSID blank.

7. Choose the new configuration profile as your active profile.

8. Open the wireless status tool.

If your computer is within range of a wireless network, the status tool will display the signal strength and signal quality of the signal, and, depending on the program, it may also show the name of the network.

Searching for a Network in Windows XP

In Windows XP, it's even easier to search for a network:

1. Insert your wireless adapter into the computer's PCMCIA socket or connect it to a USB port.

2. If it's not already on, turn on the computer.

3. Double-click the Network icon in the system tray (next to the time). If the wireless network adapter detects one or more nearby signals, the Wireless Network Connection Status window, shown in Figure 12.1, will open.

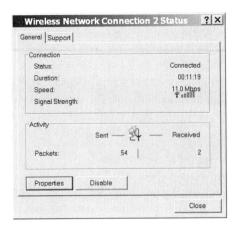

Figure 12.1: The Wireless Network Connection Status window shows the condition of the wireless link

4. Click the Properties button and select the Wireless Networks tab to open the Wireless Connection Properties window shown in Figure 12.2.

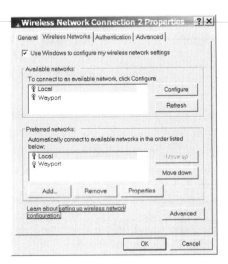

Figure 12.2: The Wireless Connection Properties window shows a list of wireless networks within range of the local computer

5. The list of available networks shows all the active networks that the wireless adapter has detected. To connect to one of these networks, select the name of the network from the list, and click the Configure button.

6. Windows automatically fills in the Network Name field. Public networks do not normally use WEP encryption, so you can ignore the Wireless Network Key section. Click Cancel to close this window.

7. Click OK in the Properties window, and click Close in the Status window.

Once you have found a network and set up a connection, open your Web browser. If the browser is set to automatically open a home page, it won't find that page, but it will open the public network service's login page. If you don't already have an account with this service, follow the on-screen instructions to create a new account. If your browser is set to start with a blank screen, it won't automatically display the login screen, but the login will appear when you try to connect to a site from your Bookmarks or Favorites list (or any other Web site, for that matter).

Wireless Network Search Tools

If your wireless configuration tool doesn't automatically scan for all available network signals, Marius Milner's Network Stumbler is a very slick Windows utility that will find them and display a list like the one in Figure 12.3 that shows everything you need to know about a detected network signal, including the MAC address, SSID, channel number, and signal strength and quality.

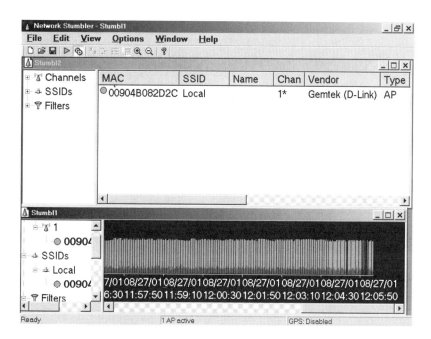

Figure 12.3: Network Stumbler finds and displays extensive details about every wireless Ethernet signal that it can find

Network Stumbler is *beggarware*, which means that it's available at no cost, but users who consider it useful are invited to send an unspecified donation to the developer. You can download Network Stumbler from http://www.netstumbler.com/download.php.

One of the major operators of wireless hot spots, Boingo Wireless, offers its own free sniffer program, shown in Figure 12.4. Boingo's software features its own

sites, but it also detects and displays hot spots operated by others. Download
Boingo software from http://www.boingo.com.

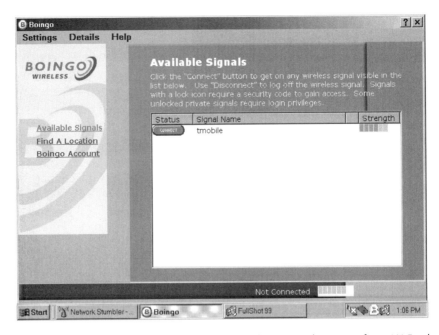

Figure 12.4: Boingo software identifies active wireless hot spots within range of your Wi-Fi adapter

Hewlett-Packard's Wireless Connection Manager is another free program
that detects and connects to Wi-Fi networks. Unfortunately, it only works with
Windows 2000 or Microsoft Pocket PC 2002, and the Compaq WL110 Wireless PC
Card, so it's useless for the majority of users. But it is free, so it's worth trying if
you have exactly the right set of hardware and software. For more information,
see the HP Web site at http://www.hp.com/solutions1/corporatebusiness/wcm.

The software page at wardriving.com (http://www.wardriving.com/code.php)
has links to many other tools for sniffing Wi-Fi signals, as well as others that provide
additional security and controls.

Sending Mail Through a Public Network

Many business LANs and Internet service providers have configured their mail
servers to let users receive their mail from anywhere on the Internet, but they
accept outbound mail only from within their own networks. This restriction prevents spammers and other unauthorized users from relaying mail through an
unprotected server, but it can also make it difficult for legitimate users to send
messages when they are away from home.

In order to overcome this problem, most public Internet services run mail
servers that accept outgoing mail from subscribers who are temporarily logged in
to their networks. If your usual server rejects messages when you are connected
through a public wireless network, try changing the name of the SMTP server in
your mail client program. The name of the SMTP server is usually mail.[*network*

name], but if that doesn't work, ask the public network's tech support center. Don't forget to change the setting back to the original server when you get back home.

Public Networks in Airports

Providing public wireless network service to airport terminals is a new and growing industry that appears simple from the consumer's point of view—just install enough access points to cover all the concourses and the airlines' lounges, connect them to a broadband Internet trunk, and wait for customers to start paying for network access. It sounds like a license to print money. Of course, it's not that simple. Now that the dot-com investment bubble has burst, money for new Internet services is a lot more difficult to find. And nothing that involves a government-owned airport authority and a facility that supports dozens of different radio services for everything from air traffic control to rental car returns and shuttle buses is ever simple.

Coordinating all those radios is not a simple job. The technical facilities managers of major airports insist on complete control over every radio transmitter that operates on their property. Somebody has to make sure the taxi dispatcher's radios in front of the passenger terminal don't interfere with the ones in the airport's fire engines or the ramp agents' walkie-talkies. The controllers in the tower have to talk to aircraft in the air and on the ground. A dozen or more airlines all need their own private company channels, and four or five separate cellular telephone companies and paging services all expect to provide service to their customers with transmitter sites in each concourse. And don't forget the satellite dish on the roof that feeds those TV monitors that play CNN at every gate, or the low-power AM radio station that broadcasts to people looking for space in the parking garage. Adding an "unlicensed" wireless Ethernet service is just one more headache for the airport's radio specialists.

Things get even more complicated when the airport signs a franchise agreement with one wireless service and an airline contract with a different company to provide wireless service to all of its VIP clubs—should the airport permit the airline to provide its own service in its rented space? Or does the airport-wide deal take precedence? Will the two services interfere with one another? Will they interfere with any other radio services? Who controls the transmitters?

It seems as if the management of every airport has come up with a slightly different set of answers to these questions, so you can't assume that the account you set up to connect in the Admirals' Club in Chicago will also work at the waiting area near Gate A-14 in Seattle. The only thing you can do to find out is fire up the computer, set the SSID to "ANY," and see if it detects a signal. If the wireless status utility tells you that it has found a signal, remember to look at the menu or window that shows the names of all the networks within range. If you have an account with one of those networks, go ahead and log on. If not, choose the network with the best signal quality and set up a new account.

If you travel through the same airports a lot, or if you belong to one of the airlines' VIP clubs, you will want to set up a prepaid account with the company that provides service to those locations. When you find yourself in an airport (or any other location) that uses a different service, you can usually sign up for a pay-as-you-go account on the spot.

For the moment, it's almost essential to download and print copies of the current "Where to Find Us" list from each public wireless service where you have an account and carry them in your computer bag. Some services don't have access points that reach the entire passenger terminal at certain airports, but they might have coverage within a limited area, such as a particular airline's concourse or a name-brand coffee shop. If you've already paid for unlimited service on Boingo, for example, you might want to use its service, even if it means carrying the computer to a different part of the airport.

When the different wireless services complete their roaming agreements, this whole process will be much easier: you will have an account with the service that you use the most, and you will use your prepaid connect time wherever you happen to be traveling. The wireless networks will take care of the cross-service billing, so you won't have to worry about it. But until those agreements go into effect, you'll need a different account every time you log in to a new service.

T-Mobile HotSpot

The cellular telephone carrier T-Mobile operates one of the largest wireless network service providers in the United States. The footprint for its network coverage covers the "business ribbon" that includes airports, airline clubs, hotels, restaurants, and conference centers. Its networks are active in many American Airlines terminals and Admirals' Clubs. T-Mobile also has a partnership deal to provide wireless coverage in more than 3,000 Starbucks coffee shops by the end of 2003. Starbucks Chairman Howard Schultz expects that this "will bring many new customers into the stores, and many will stay longer."

T-Mobile offers a range of service plans that meet the different needs of occasional users, frequent travelers, and users who plan to use the network within a single metropolitan area. You can select the plan that best meets your own needs at http://www.t-mobile.com. Starbucks offers a free one-day trial of the T-Mobile HotSpot service in their coffee shops. Check Starbucks' Web site at http://www.starbucks.com/retail/wireless.asp for the current promotion code.

Boingo

Boingo is the other of the "big two" public wireless network service providers. Boingo has wireless networks in airport terminals, hotels, convention centers, and other locations that serve business travelers. Its airport networks include Dallas–Fort Worth, Austin, Seattle, and San Jose, and it has announced plans to introduce additional service at airports in Atlanta, Chicago, Washington, and Boston. Boingo's latest directory of active locations is at http://www.boingo.com.

hereUare

hereUare is not a wireless service provider, but it offers a common account that will allow a user to connect to wireless hot spots owned and operated by several networks. A single user ID and password will work at any participating location.

Unfortunately, several of the most widely distributed wireless networks don't participate in the hereUare program, but many others do. You can download its Global Locator software that provides a searchable list of hereUare sites, with the exact location and the SSID necessary for login at each site, from http://www.hereuare.com.

Public Access to Private Networks

Many businesses and institutions, such as universities, hospitals, and libraries, that operate their own wireless LANs allow visitors to connect to the Internet through their networks. In locations where this kind of service is available, the network manager has probably prepared an instruction brochure that explains how to configure a computer to use the service. If you're visiting a company where wireless network access might exist, ask the receptionist or the person whom you are visiting for more information.

Joining a Community Network

Wireless community networks use 802.11b network technology to share high-speed Internet access within a neighborhood or an entire city. The operators of these networks place the antennas for their access points on rooftops and in other locations chosen for the widest possible coverage.

While it's true that the maximum range for a useful wireless Ethernet signal is only about 300 feet (100 meters) unless you use some kind of high-gain antenna, that's enough to provide service to maybe half a city block. And if more volunteers install additional access points on *their* rooftops, the coverage area can grow to reach even more people. Some community networks also use point-to-point links with directional antennas (often using homemade reflectors made out of tin cans and other low-cost parts, as described in Chapter 11) to extend their coverage to locations beyond the range of the local access points.

Eventually, the organizers of these networks hope to create seamless "alternative grids" that supply free or very low-cost Internet access to entire neighborhoods or whole cities and metropolitan areas. If they succeed, it ought to be possible to find a free or inexpensive wireless Internet connection from anywhere inside a network's footprint. Today, the number of active sites is still very small, so it's a matter of pure luck whether or not you're within range of a network signal.

This is still a grassroots movement that is mostly made up of enthusiastic technogeeks and network hackers, but it has the potential to offer some serious competition to the multi–billion dollar 3G (third-generation cellular) wireless networks that are supposed to be the next wave of mobile Internet connectivity. If one or more of these noncommercial networks that have been thrown together with duct tape and old Pringle's potato chips canisters ever come close to providing complete coverage of a neighborhood or even an entire city at 11 Mbps, the 3G cellular folks are going to have a lot of trouble convincing people to buy their 9,600 bps service instead. The commercial cellular and wireless network operators are watching the community network movement very carefully.

Community wireless networks are usually volunteer-run, cooperative services that operate public networks to provide Internet access to large or small areas. In some cities, including Seattle, San Francisco, and London, local community networks have attracted dozens of base stations and relay points. In Australia, public airwave networks are operating in several cities, and another group is talking about serving the entire island state of Tasmania.

Many community network groups have ambitious plans to provide service to a broad coverage area, but their actual operations often include only a handful of access points that may or may not be close to one another. At their current stage of development, community networks are more of a curiosity than a useful resource, because they don't yet have significant coverage footprints. Today, most community networks are actually little more than a small number of isolated hot spots that may share the same SSID. If and when that changes, they will become a very important part of the urban communications infrastructure.

The Personal Telco Project maintains a directory of links to active networks around the world at http://www.personaltelco.net/index.cgi/WirelessCommunities. Most of the networks in the Personal Telco Project list have online maps and node lists that show the locations of their active access points. For example, Figure 12.5 shows the access points in the PDX Wireless network in and around downtown Portland, Oregon.

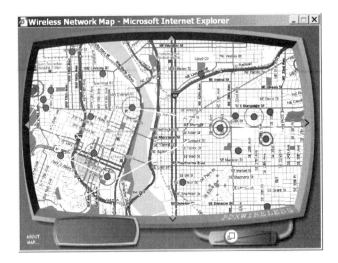

Figure 12.5: The PDX Wireless network in Portland has access points on both sides of the Willamette River

Depending on your point of view, community networks are already either a useful supplement or significant competition to commercial 802.11b networks. When T-Mobile installed a wireless hot spot at a Starbucks store in Portland's Pioneer Courthouse Square, it chose the same operating channel that a community network had been using to provide free service to the square. Of course, this arrangement created significant interference to both networks. After a couple of days' wrangling, T-Mobile shifted to a different channel.

If you can find a community network signal, you're generally welcome to use it as an Internet connection, but don't expect to get a lot of technical support or other help from the network operators. Many community networkers will help if they can, but these networks are free services; don't ask for the same kind of hand-holding you would expect from a commercial Internet service provider. If you do need help, try sending a polite email request to the network coordinator's address shown in the network directory.

The owners of some community access points have some restrictions on the use of their networks, but they're usually the kind of common-sense rules that are easy to live with: don't use the network to send unsolicited spam mailings, don't try to transfer enormous files, and so forth. The basic rule of thumb should be "Don't do anything that will interfere with the operation of the network."

If you expect to use a community wireless network link as your permanent Internet connection, it's a very good idea to let the access point owner know that you're out there. If you're close enough to use an access point all the time, the owner is probably a neighbor who will be surprised and pleased if you show up at his door some time with a batch of homemade cookies. Community networks are usually run by groups of enthusiastic volunteers; if you take advantage of their efforts, consider joining the group and contributing some labor of your own. Even if you don't have significant technical skills, there are almost always other ways to contribute your efforts.

Before you can use a community network, you'll have to find a signal and figure out how to configure your own computer's network settings. It might be productive to fire up a sniffer program like Network Stumbler, Boingo, or the wireless configuration tools in Windows XP and AirPort, but even if you find a live signal, you probably won't be able to tell whether it's a community network that welcomes your traffic or a private network that hasn't bothered to turn on network security. It's better to use the online guides that each community network has posted on the Internet. The description of each network access point should give you the information you will need to make a connection: the location, the network's SSID, whether DHCP is active, and so forth.

Security on a Public Network

Network security goes both ways — the network manager doesn't want unauthorized users messing with the network, and individual users don't want anybody to get to their personal files. When you're logged in to a public network, you should take some precautions to prevent anybody else on the network from reading your files. You should remember to turn off File Sharing before you try to connect to a public network.

Use this procedure in Windows 95, Windows 98, and Windows ME:

1. From the Control Panel, open the Network dialog box.
2. Click the File and Printer Sharing button.
3. In the File and Printer Sharing dialog box, disable the I Want to Give Others Access to My Files option.

In Windows 2000 and Windows XP, there isn't a central place to turn off file shares, so you must turn off each share separately. Follow these steps to turn off sharing:

1. Open the My Computer window.

2. The icons for all of your shared drives and folders appear with a hand "serving" the icon. To turn off sharing, right-click the icon and choose Sharing and Security from the menu.

3. Turn off the Share This Folder on the Network option.

4. Click OK to close the dialog box.

5. Repeat the process for every shared folder or file. Don't forget the Shared Documents folder.

When you get back to your own office or home network, you'll have to reverse the procedure to start sharing your files again.

What about the danger of somebody grabbing your data as it passes through the radio link? It can be done, even if you're using WEP encryption, but it's not likely unless you're a target of government snooping or industrial espionage. You have to assume that any data transmitted through a wireless network is not secure. A determined eavesdropper with the right equipment and software can copy your data packets as they move through the air.

The only way to be absolutely sure that nobody is monitoring your wireless network is to stop using it. It's even easier to monitor the cordless phone in your kitchen. In general, you can assume that a connection through a public network is no more or less secure than a link to your own network. If somebody is serious about stealing your network packets, they will probably find a way to do it . The best way to protect yourself is to minimize the amount of sensitive data sent over the network, and always use a strong encryption method such as SSH (essentially encrypted telnet) or a VPN (Virtual Private Network, used by many companies to provide secure access to the corporate network for external users) when you must send private information. This kind of security issue isn't directly related to public networks. For more details about network security (or the lack of it), read Chapter 14.

13

GUERILLA NETWORKING

Guerilla networking (also known as *wardriving*) is a polite term for stealing Internet access from unprotected wireless networks. It's probably illegal, it's certainly unethical, and it's amazingly easy in many places where the owners or managers of wireless networks haven't bothered to use WEP encryption or otherwise secured their networks. In many downtown office districts, high-tech industrial parks, and upscale residential neighborhoods, a casual visitor can often find and log on to half a dozen or more wireless networks within a couple of blocks.

If you can detect a network signal, you might be able to log on or connect through that network to the Internet. With the right software tools, you can monitor other users' data as it passes through the network and crack their WEP encryption keys. Of course, nobody who is reading this book would ever consider trying to log on to somebody else's network or eavesdrop on somebody else's network traffic without permission, so I won't go into any detail about how and where to set up a connection. If you want to try, you're on your own. A few minutes with a good Web search engine can supply a list of factory default SSIDs and WEP codes for many popular network access points and software for cracking WEP encryption. Many users, especially in home networks and small businesses, don't turn on WEP encryption because it's "too complicated" or "too much trouble." And many more never bother to change their default settings.

It's just a little harsh to say that people who don't secure their networks deserve to have outsiders break into their systems. But the strongest security tools don't do any good at all if you don't use them.

This kind of quasi-legal wireless network hacking, or wardriving, is an extension of the older hackers' practice of wardialing—using a modem to dial random telephone numbers in search of other computers with unprotected dial-in ports.

Some wireless networks, like the ones described in Chapter 12, actually welcome public access, so there's a legitimate reason for wardriving (or warwalking with a Wi-Fi enabled PDA). And even if you don't actually try to set up a connection to a network, it can be instructive (and yes, entertaining) to wander around and see what's out there.

Security on a Public Network

As manager of your own wireless network, this should raise a whole lot of questions in your mind. Questions like: "Is my network secure? Can somebody on the street connect to my network without my knowledge? How do I keep those #*@&$! out of my network?" For the answers to these and other questions about wireless network security, go immediately to Chapter 14 of this book.

At the very least, you should understand that Wi-Fi networks are not absolutely secure, and every 802.11b access point and network adapter radiate signals that can be detected by outsiders. You can take steps to restrict access to your network, but you can't keep the existence of the network a secret from a serious snoop.

Sniffer Tools

A sniffer tool is a program that uses a wireless network adapter to scan for active networks and displays the characteristics of each network. I've described them in earlier chapters, but they're also essential for finding Wi-Fi signals that are not otherwise obvious.

The most widely used sniffer for Windows is Network Stumbler for Windows (http://www.netstumbler.com); if you're using Linux, Kismet is the most common choice (http://www.kismetwireless.net). But they're not the only choices. The wireless configuration and control software in Windows XP, the programs supplied with several brands of network adapters (including Orinoco and HP-Compaq), and the Boingo Wireless tool (available from http://www.boingo.com) can all provide similar information.

The process of using any of these tools is pretty much the same: fire up your computer with a wireless adapter installed and a sniffer running to detect and display nearby signals. Use the information supplied by the sniffer tool to configure your adapter to make a connection.

Searching for a Signal

If you're planning to spend a lot of time driving around searching for networks with your laptop (it's not particularly practical to do this on foot, except in an urban center), you might want to consider assembling a special wardriving kit that includes the best tools for the job: a network adapter that accepts an external antenna (such as an Orinoco or a Zoom), a cable that allows you to power your laptop computer from the car's cigarette lighter, and an antenna with more gain than the one inside the adapter.

If you don't know exactly where nearby Wi-Fi signals originate, your best choice is an omnidirectional antenna mounted on the roof of your car. Orinoco, HyperLink, and other manufacturers make off-the-shelf 2.4 GHz mobile antennas that will do the job well, but if you don't want to spend money on a permanent installation, it might be possible to jury-rig something with a pigtail adapter, some clip leads, and maybe an antenna from a 2.4 GHz cordless phone, or even a coat hanger or other rigid wire. It won't be perfect, but for a cheap and dirty temporary lash-up, it will do the job. Many plans for omnidirectional antennas exist on the Internet; a quick search should locate them quickly.

You can also try one of the homebrew directional antennas built inside a tin can or a Pringles potato chip canister, but a directional antenna is not the best tool for finding unknown access points. You'll have to physically wave the antenna toward each building you pass in order to search for possible signals. Obviously, this is not a good idea when you don't want to attract a lot of attention.

One more thing about wardriving: keep your eyes on the road. Don't try to watch your computer while you're driving. Either take a friend along to operate the computer while you drive, or park the car before you try to capture radio signals. Running down a stray pedestrian or colliding with another vehicle can ruin your whole day.

Searching Without a Sniffer—Warchalking

It's not yet clear whether warchalking is a new standard for identifying accessible Wi-Fi signals or some kind of summer fad that will disappear with the falling leaves. Either way, it's an interesting phenomenon. As a high-tech extension of the traditional hobos' marks left on gateposts that would advise others who followed what to expect (for example, there were symbols for "kind lady lives here" or "food here if you work"), warchalking symbols are supposed to identify locations where a Wi-Fi network signal is present and instruct people who know the code how to connect to that network.

Originally proposed by the English Web designer Matt Jones in the summer of 2002, his warchalking symbols (shown in Figure 13.1) quickly became known around the world. The code is simple. A closed circle indicates a closed network; two back-to-back half-circles identify an accessible ("open") network; and a circle with a W inside is a network with WEP encryption. The network's SSID appears above the symbol, and the bandwidth shows up underneath it.

Warchalking has all the elements of a great news feature story—exotic technogeeks using unusual images to support their obscure hobby—so dozens

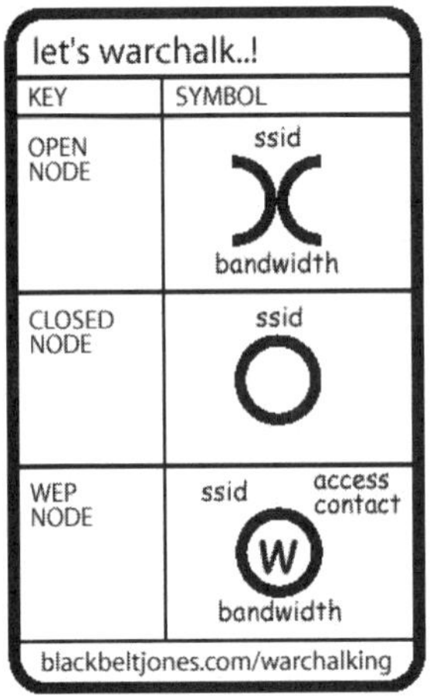

KEY	SYMBOL
OPEN NODE	ssid ✕ bandwidth
CLOSED NODE	ssid ◯
WEP NODE	ssid / access contact Ⓦ bandwidth

let's warchalk..!

blackbeltjones.com/warchalking

Figure 13.1: Matt Jones's original warchalking symbols

of newspapers and broadcasters around the world reported on this strange new activity. But in practice, it's too soon to know whether warchalking marks will actually become common after the initial novelty wears off. The owners of most private networks don't want outsiders to know that their networks exist, and the operators of public networks generally place a plain-text announcement in their shop windows or inside their own spaces. Except for the community networkers, most people who operate Wi-Fi access points don't want to encourage outsiders to use them.

However, if you want to play the game, it's easy enough to do. Just carry a piece of chalk along with your wardriving kit (playground chalk from a school supplies place is best), and make an inconspicuous mark on a wall or sidewalk when you find a wireless network signal. Include the network's SSID and bandwidth if you know them, and go on your way. Don't use paint or any other permanent marker — if the owner of the property wants to obliterate the mark, they should be able to do so without a major cleanup.

If you discover one of these symbols already in place, that's a good indication that you've found a good place to try making a wireless connection. But don't expect to find a lot of warchalking marks — there are probably more journalists reporting on this phenomenon than actual users. If you *do* discover one of these symbols as you wander around downtown San Jose or central London, you can impress your friends by pointing to it and telling them what it means.

In general, guerilla networking, or wardriving, or whatever you want to call it is one of those activities, like monitoring your neighbors' cordless telephone conversations, that is sort of fun, but not exactly within the limits of polite conduct. Yeah, you can argue that anybody who's dumb enough to operate an unprotected wireless network deserves to have other people use it or that the bandwidth is right out there for the taking, but that's not likely to convince the owner of the network (or the nice policeman who comes knocking on your car door while you're online) that your intentions are entirely honorable and not doing anybody any harm. And they're probably correct.

If you treat wardriving as a nonintrusive hobby, like those people who take their radio scanners to a railroad freight yard and listen to conversations between train dispatchers and individual locomotive engineers, or those birdwatchers who keep a book that lists every species they've ever seen, then it's probably quite harmless. But when you cross the line and actually establish an unauthorized connection, you should understand exactly what you're doing — stealing bandwidth — and be ready to accept the consequences.

Okay, end of sermon. In the next chapter, we'll look at guerilla networking from the other side: we will talk about wireless network security and keeping the people who read this chapter *out* of your network.

14

WIRELESS NETWORK SECURITY

Wireless networks are not secure. Let me repeat that: Wireless networks are not secure. They are safe enough for many users most of the time, but it's just not possible to make a Wi-Fi network absolutely private.

The simple truth is that a wireless network uses radio signals with a well-defined set of characteristics, so somebody who wants to dedicate enough time and effort to monitoring those signals can probably find a way to intercept and read the data contained in them. If you send confidential information through a wireless link, an eavesdropper can copy it. Credit card numbers, account passwords, and other personal information are all vulnerable.

Encryption and other security methods can make data a little more difficult to steal, but they don't provide complete protection against a really dedicated snoop. As any policeman will tell you, locks are great for keeping out honest people, but serious thieves know how to get past them. An entire catalog of tools for cracking WEP encryption is easy to find on the Internet.

To make things even more dangerous, many network managers and home wireless users leave the doors and windows to their networks wide open to intruders by failing to use encryption and the other security features that are built into every 802.11b access point and network node. "Drive-by logins" to unprotected private networks are possible in many urban and suburban business districts and in a surprising number of residential neighborhoods. In the spring of 2001, the

San Francisco Chronicle reported that a network security expert with a directional antenna mounted on the roof of a van in downtown San Francisco could log on to an average of half a dozen wireless networks *per block*. The number is probably larger today. A year later, a group of Microsoft employees who ran an "unofficial test" found more than 200 unprotected open-access points in a suburban neighborhood outside Seattle. And Tully's Coffee shops report that they're seeing many of their customers logging into Wi-Fi networks — through access points at Starbucks stores across the street.

Do the math: Your access point has a range of 150 feet or more in all directions, so the signal probably extends beyond your own property lines (or the walls of your apartment). A network device in the building next door or across the street can probably detect your network. And so can a laptop or PDA inside a car parked on the street. If you don't take some precautions to prevent it, the operator of that device can log in to your LAN, steal files from your servers, and tie up your Internet connection with streaming videos or multiplayer games.

It's important to understand that we're talking about two different kinds of security threats to a wireless network. The first is the danger of an outsider connecting to your network without your knowledge or permission; the second is the possibility that a dedicated eavesdropper can steal data as you send and receive it. Each represents a different potential problem, and each requires a different approach to prevention and protection. While it's certainly true that none of the tools currently available can provide complete protection, they can make life more difficult for most casual intruders. And since they're out there, you might as well use them.

Wireless networks are a trade-off between security and convenience. The obvious benefits of a wireless network connection — fast and easy access to the network from a portable computer or an isolated location — come at a cost. For most users, that cost does not outweigh the convenience of wireless operation. But just as you lock the doors of your car when you park it on the street, you should take similar steps to protect your network and your data.

Protecting Your Network and Your Data

As the operator of a wireless network, what can you do to keep outsiders out? You have two basic choices: you can accept the fact that 802.11b networks are not completely secure, but use the built-in network security features to slow down would-be intruders; or you can forget about the built-in tools and use a firewall to isolate the wireless network instead.

It's clear that the security features built into the 802.11b protocols are not adequate to protect 100 percent of the wireless data 100 percent of the time. If you read the articles about wireless security in trade magazines and follow the discussions in online forums, it would be easy to believe that Wi-Fi networks leak like the proverbial sieve. But that probably overstates the real threat to your own network. Remember that most of the people close enough to eavesdrop on your messages or hack into your network are not just sitting and waiting for you to start to transmit data. And to be brutally honest, most of the data that passes through your network is really boring stuff. But the encryption tools are available in every Wi-Fi network, so you really ought to use them.

The more serious threat is not that people will eavesdrop on your messages as they pass through the network, but that they will create their own connection to your network and either read files stored on other computers on the network or use your broadband connection to the Internet without your knowledge or permission.

It does make sense to take steps to maintain control of your network. If you choose to implement 802.11b security, here are some specific steps to take:

- If possible, place your access point in the middle of the building rather than close to a window. This will reduce the distance that your network signals will extend beyond your own walls.

- Use the WEP (Wired Equivalent Privacy) encryption function included in all 802.11b network nodes. Given enough time and the right equipment, WEP keys are not difficult to crack, but encrypted packets are still more difficult to read than data transmitted without encryption. There's more information about WEP encryption later in this chapter.

- Change your WEP keys often. It takes time to sniff WEP encryption keys out of a data stream, and every time the keys change, the miscreants trying to steal your data are forced to start again from scratch. Once or twice a month is not too often to change keys.

- Don't store your WEP keys on the network where they are used. This seems obvious, but in a widespread network, it might be tempting to distribute them on a private Web page or in a text file. Don't do it.

- Don't use email to distribute WEP keys. If an intruder has stolen account names and passwords, the thief will receive the messages with your new codes before your legitimate users get them.

- Add another layer of encryption, such as Kerberos, SSH, or a VPN on top of the WEP encryption built into the wireless network.

- Don't use your access point's default SSID. Those defaults are well known to network crackers.

- Change the SSID to something that doesn't identify your business or your location. If an intruder detects something called BigCorpNet and they look around to see the BigCorp headquarters across the street, they'll home right in on your network. Same thing for a home network; don't call it Perkins if that's the name painted on the side of your mailbox out front.

- Don't use an SSID that makes your network sound like it contains some kind of fascinating content—use a boring name like, oh, "network," or even a string of gibberish, such as W24rnQ.

- Change your access point's IP address and password. The factory default passwords for most access point configuration tools are easy to find (and they are often the same from one manufacturer to another—hint: don't use "admin"), so they're not even good enough to keep out your own users, let alone unknown intruders who want to use your network for their own benefit.

- If it's an option, turn off the "broadcast SSID" feature in your access point, which accepts connections from clients without the correct SSID. This won't guarantee your network will stay hidden, but it might help.

- If possible, turn on the access control feature in your access point. Access control limits network connections to network clients with specified MAC addresses. The access point will refuse to associate with any adapter whose address is not on the list. This may not be practical if you want to allow visitors to use your network, but it's a useful tool in a home or small business network where you know all of your potential users. Like the "broadcast SSID" option, this isn't a guarantee, but it can't hurt.

- Test your network's security by trying to find your network from outside your own building. Take a laptop computer running a sniffer program, such as Network Stumbler or your network adapter's status utility, and start walking away from the building. If you can detect your network from a block away, so can an intruder. Remember that intruders may be using high-gain directional antennas that can extend this distance.

- Treat the network as if it was wide open to public access. Make sure everybody using the network understands that they're using a nonsecure system.

- Limit file shares to the files that you really want to share; don't share entire drives. Use password protection on every share.

- Use the same security tools that you would use on a wired network. At best, the wireless portion of your LAN is no more secure than the wired part, so you should take all the same precautions. In most cases, the wireless portion of your network is much less secure than the wired.

- Consider using a virtual private network (VPN) for added security.

Some computer security officials take a different approach to wireless security. They accept as a fact the idea that an 802.11b network is not secure, so they don't even try to use the built-in security features. For example, the network security group at NASA's Advanced Supercomputing Division in California has recognized that "the network itself provides no reliable authentication and no security from eavesdropping," and "802.11b security features…only consume resources without delivering any real security." Therefore, it has disabled all the 802.11b security features and uses its own Wireless Firewall Gateway (WFG) instead. The WFG is a router located between the wireless portion and the rest of their network, so all network traffic to and from wireless devices (including access to the Internet) must pass through the gateway.

As a side benefit, this approach to security keeps the administrative overhead in each packet to a minimum, because they don't include authentication or encryption. This reduces the number of bits in each packet, which increases the effective data speed through the network.

Other wireless network operators use VPNs to control access through their wireless gateways. A VPN adds another layer of end-to-end security at the IP layer (rather than the Physical layer where 802.11b encryption occurs) before a user can do anything on the network.

Network security goes both ways — the network manager doesn't want unauthorized users messing with the network, and individual users don't want anybody to get to their personal files. When you're logged in to a public network, you should take some precautions to prevent anybody else on the network from reading your files.

To turn off File Sharing before you try to connect to a public network, use this procedure in Windows 95, Windows 98, and Windows ME:

1. From the Control Panel, open the Network dialog box.

2. Click the File and Printer Sharing button.

3. In the File and Printer Sharing dialog box, disable the I Want to Give Others Access to My Files option.

In Windows 2000 and Windows XP, there isn't a central place to turn off file shares, so you must turn off each share separately. Follow these steps to turn off sharing:

1. Open the My Computer window.

2. The icons for all of your shared drives and folders appear with a hand "serving" the icon. To turn off sharing, right-click the icon and choose Sharing and Security from the menu.

3. Turn off the Share This Folder on the Network option.

4. Click OK to close the dialog box.

5. Repeat the process for every shared folder or file. Don't forget the Shared Documents folder.

When you get back to your own office or home network, you'll have to reverse the procedure to start sharing your files again.

Another, quite different security problem is the danger of an eavesdropper monitoring the data that moves over a radio link and stealing confidential information on the fly. This is not as common as a snooper gaining access to the network and reading files, but it's possible. Encryption and other security tools might make the data more difficult to decipher, but it's best to treat a Wi-Fi network like a cellular telephone: don't ever send a message or a file that contains confidential information.

802.11b Security Tools

The security tools in the 802.11b specifications aren't perfect, but they're better than nothing. Even if you choose not to use them, it's essential to understand what they are and how they work, if only to turn them off.

Network Name (SSID)

As you learned in Chapter 1, every wireless network has a name. In a network with just one access point, the name is the Basic Service Set ID (BSSID). When the network has more than one access point, the name becomes the Extended Service Set ID (ESSID). The generic designation for all network names is the SSID, which is the term you will see most often in wireless access point and client configuration utility programs.

When you configure the access points for a network, you must specify the SSID for that network. Every access point and network client in a network must use the same SSID. On computers running Windows, the SSID of the wireless adapter should also be the name of the Workgroup.

When a network client detects two or more access points with the same SSID, it assumes that they are all part of the same network (even if the access points are operating on different radio channels), and it associates with the access point that provides the strongest or cleanest signal. If that signal deteriorates due to interference or fading, the client will try to shift to another access point on what it thinks is the same network.

If two different networks with overlapping signals have the same name, a client will assume that they're both parts of a single network, and it might try to perform a handoff from one network to the other. From the user's point of view, this misdirected handoff will look as if the network has completely dropped its connection. Therefore, every wireless network that could possibly overlap with another network must have a unique SSID.

The exceptions to the unique SSID rule are public and community networks that provide access only to the Internet, but not to other computers or other devices on a LAN. Those networks often have a common SSID, so subscribers can detect and connect to them from more than one location.

Some access points, including Apple AirPort Base Stations and similar Orinoco systems include a feature that offers a choice between "open" and "closed" access. When the access point is set to Open Access, it will accept a connection from a client whose SSID is set to "ANY", as well as from devices configured to talk to the access point's own SSID. When the access point is set to Closed Access (Apple calls this a "hidden network"), it only accepts connections whose SSID matches the one in the access point. This is a good way to keep some intruders out of your network, but it works only if every node in the network uses an Orinoco adapter (the Apple AirPort Card is a private-label version of the Orinoco adapter). If an adapter made by some other manufacturer tries to connect to a closed access point, the access point will reject it, even if the SSID matches.

A network's SSID provides a very limited form of access control, because it's necessary to specify the SSID when you set up a wireless connection. The SSID option in an access point is always a text field that will accept any name you care to assign, but many network configuration programs (including the wireless network tools in Windows XP and those supplied with several major brands of network adapters) automatically detect and display the SSIDs of every active network within their signal range. So it's not always necessary to know the SSID of a network before you try to connect; sometimes the configuration utility (or a network monitor or sniffer program like Network Stumbler) will show you the names of every nearby network in a list or a menu. For example, Figure 14.1 shows the result of a Network Stumbler scan at Seattle-Tacoma Airport, where WayPort served the passenger terminal, and MobileStar provided coverage in the American Airlines VIP club. (MobileStar was absorbed by another service shortly after I ran that survey, so the names of the networks have changed, but the service remains in place.)

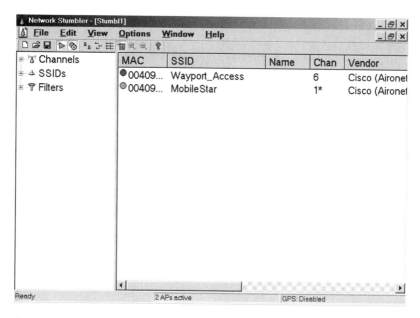

Figure 14.1: Network Stumbler and many configuration utilities display the SSIDs of every nearby wireless network

Every access point comes with a default SSID setting, and these defaults are well known and documented within the community of network snoops (see for example, http://www.wi2600.org/mediawhore/nf0/wireless/ssid_defaults). Obviously, the defaults should never be used in any network.

Many access points come with an option to hide the SSID, often called a "Closed Network" or "Cloaked Network." This option will help prevent some sniffers from detecting your network name, but every time a new client connects to your network or an existing client gets a weak signal the SSID is transmitted, and software like Kismet can detect it. Cloaking your SSID may slow down the casual observer, but it offers no real protection.

WEP Encryption

WEP encryption is an option in every 802.11b system, so it's important to know how it works, even if you choose not to use it. As the name suggests, the original intent of the Wired Equivalent Privacy (WEP) protocol was to provide a level of security on wireless networks that was comparable to the security of a wired network. That was the goal, but there is very strong evidence that a network that depends on WEP encryption is almost as vulnerable to intrusion as a network with no protection at all. It will help keep out the casual snoops, but it's not particularly effective against a dedicated intruder.

WEP encryption is intended to serve three functions: it prevents unauthorized access to the network, it performs an integrity check on each packet, and it protects the data from eavesdroppers. WEP uses a secret encryption key to encode data packets before a network client or an access point transmits them, and it uses the same key to decode the packets after they have been received.

When a client tries to exchange data with a network using a different key, the result is garbled and ignored. Therefore, the WEP settings must be exactly the same on every access point and client adapter in the network. This sounds simple enough, but it gets confusing because manufacturers use different methods to identify the size and format of a WEP key. The functions don't change from one brand to another, but identical settings don't always have identical descriptions.

How Many Bits in Your WEP Key?

First, a WEP key can have either 64 bits or 128 bits; 128-bit keys are more difficult to crack, but they also increase the amount of time needed to transmit each packet.

The confusion among different manufacturers' implementations arises because a 40-bit WEP key is the same as a 64-bit WEP key, and a 104-bit key is the same as a 128-bit key. The standard 64-bit WEP key is a string that includes an internally generated 24-bit initialization vector and a 40-bit secret key assigned by the network manager. Some manufacturers' specifications and configuration programs call this "64-bit encryption," but others describe it as "40-bit encryption." Either way, the encryption scheme is the same, so an adapter that uses 40-bit encryption is fully compatible with an access point or adapter that uses 64-bit encryption.

Many network adapters and access points also include a "strong encryption" option that uses a 128-bit key (which is actually a 104-bit secret key with the 24-bit initialization vector). Strong encryption is downward-compatible with 64-bit encryption, but it's not automatic, so all of the devices on a mixed network of 128-bit and 64-bit devices will operate at 64 bits. If your access point and all of your adapters accept 128-bit encryption, use a 128-bit key. But if you want your network to be compatible with adapters and access points that only recognize 64-bit encryption, set the entire network to use 64-bit keys.

Is Your Key ASCII or Hex?

The length of the key is not the only confusing thing about setting WEP encryption. Some programs request the key as a string of ASCII characters, but many others want the key in hexadecimal numbers. Still others can generate the key from an optional passphrase.

Each ASCII character has 8 bits, so a 40-bit (or 64-bit) WEP key contains 5 characters, and a 104-bit (or 128-bit) key has 13 characters. In hex, each character uses 4 bits, so a 40-bit key has 10 hex characters, and a 128-bit key has 26 characters.

In Figure 14.2, which shows the Wireless Setting screen for a D-Link access point, the 40-bit Shared Key Security field uses hex characters, so it has space for ten characters. The D-Link program runs all ten characters together in a single string, but some others split them into five sets of two digits, or two sets of five.

The key looks the same to the computer either way, but it's easier to copy the string when it's broken apart.

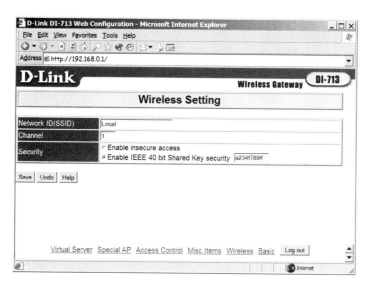

Figure 14.2: The configuration utility for a D-Link access point accepts WEP keys in hex format

Many client utilities, such as the Wireless Network Properties dialog box in Windows XP (shown in Figure 14.3), offer a choice of either hex or ASCII, so you can use the format that matches the one specified in your access point.

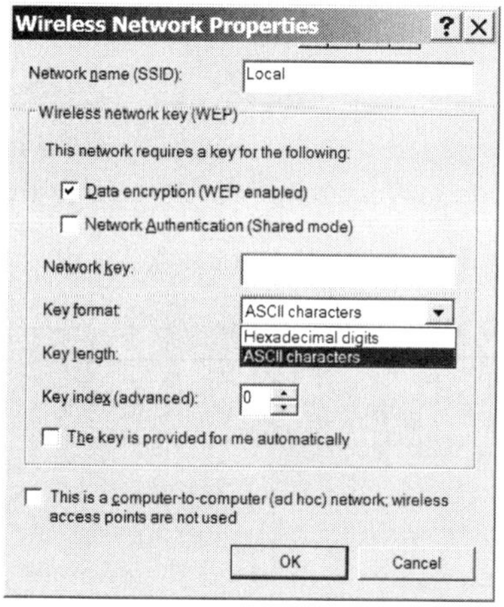

Figure 14.3: The Windows XP Wireless Network Properties tool offers a choice of WEP key formats

A passphrase is a string of text that the adapters and access points automatically convert to a string of hex characters. Because humans can generally remember actual words or phrases more easily than hex gibberish, a passphrase can be easier to distribute than a hex string. However, a passphrase is only useful when all the adapters and access points in a network come from the same manufacturer.

What Are the Options?

Like just about everything else in an 802.11b configuration utility, the names of the WEP options are not consistent from one program to the next. Some use a straightforward set of options such as "enable WEP encryption," but others use technical language taken from the formal 802.11 specification. *Open system* authentication is another way of saying "WEP encryption is disabled."

Some access points also offer an optional shared key authentication option that uses WEP encryption when a network client has the key, but unencrypted data with other network nodes.

Mixing Hex and ASCII Keys

Setting up a mixed network becomes more complicated when some network nodes use hex only and others require ASCII keys. If that's the situation in your network, you will want to follow these rules for setting the WEP keys:

- Convert all your ASCII keys to hex. If a configuration program demands an ASCII key, enter the characters 0x (zero followed by a lowercase letter *x*), followed by the hex string. If you're using Apple's AirPort software, you'll have to enter a dollar sign ($) at the beginning of a hex key instead of the 0x.

- Make sure all your encryption keys have exactly the right number of characters.

- If all else fails, read the security sections of the manuals for your network adapters and access points. It's possible that one or more of the devices in your network have some obscure proprietary feature that you don't know about.

Changing WEP Keys

Many access points and network client adapters can hold four different 64-bit WEP keys, but only one is active at a time, as shown in Figure 14.4. The other keys are spares, which can permit the network manager to update the network's security on short notice. Adapters and access points that support 128-bit encryption hold only one 128-bit WEP key at a time.

In a network that takes WEP encryption seriously, the WEP keys should change on a regular schedule. Once a month is adequate for a network that does not carry mission-critical data, but a more essential network might need a new key as often as once or twice a week. Don't forget to keep an offline log of your current WEP keys in a safe location.

In a home or small business network, you will probably change all the WEP keys yourself. If that's not practical, the network manager or security specialist should distribute new WEP keys by paper memos rather than email. For an added layer of safety in networks that use 64-bit keys, instruct your users to change two keys at a time (not the current default keys). Send a separate memo advising users which key will become the new default and when the change will occur.

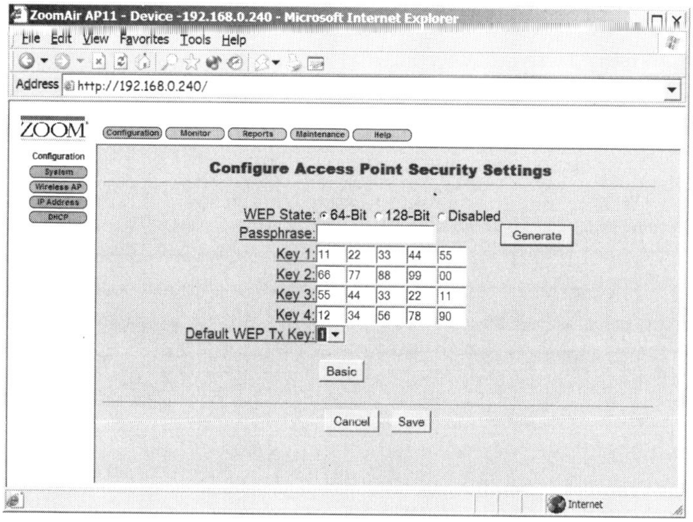

Figure 14.4: To change to a different WEP key, change the default. Real keys should be less obvious than the ones in this sample.

So a typical weekly memo might say

```
Please enter the following new 64-bit WEP keys:
Key 1:   XX XX XX XX XX
Key 4: YY YY YY YY YY
```

Another memo a week later would provide the codes for Key 2 and Key 3.

A separate memo might say, "Our network will shift to Key 3 at midnight Tuesday. Please change the default key in your network adapter." Choose a time for the shift when as few people as possible are likely to be using the wireless network, because any link that is active when the key changes at the access point will probably drop its connection and won't be able to restore it until the key changes on the client adapter. Users can load the new keys in advance, as alternates to the currently active key, and change them with just a few mouse clicks when the new key becomes effective.

Is WEP Secure Enough to Use?

Several academic computer scientists have published reports about WEP encryption that argue against trusting it to protect confidential data. They all point to serious flaws in the cryptographic theory and practice that were used to define the WEP encryption algorithms. These experts are unanimous in their recommendations: anyone who uses an 802.11 wireless network should not rely on WEP for security; they should employ other methods to protect their networks.

A group at the University of California at Berkeley has identified numerous flaws in the WEP algorithm that make it vulnerable to at least four different kinds of attacks:

- Passive attacks that use statistical analysis to decrypt data
- Active attacks that construct encrypted packets that mislead the access point into accepting false commands
- Attacks that analyze encrypted packets to construct a dictionary that can then be used to automatically decrypt data in real time
- Attacks that alter packet headers to divert data to a destination controlled by the attacker

The Berkeley report concludes with an unequivocal statement: "Wired Equivalent Privacy (WEP) isn't. The protocol's problems are a result of misunderstanding of some cryptographic primitives and therefore combining them in insecure ways."

Researchers at Rice University and at AT&T Labs have published their own description of their attack against WEP-encrypted networks (http://www.cs.rice.edu/~astubble/wep) that led them to a similar opinion: "802.11 WEP is totally insecure." They were able to order and receive the necessary hardware, set up a test bed, design their attack tool, and successfully capture a 128-bit WEP key in less than a week.

Both the Berkeley and the AT&T Labs reports are written by and for technical experts with a background in cryptography. Their conclusions are clear, but their methods do assume that an intruder has some serious technical knowledge. However, tools for less sophisticated code-breakers are also easy to find. Both AirSnort (http://airsnort.shmoo.com) and WEPCrack (http://sourceforge.net/projects/wepcrack) are Linux programs that monitor wireless network signals and exploit the weaknesses in the WEP algorithm to extract the encryption key.

The developers of AirSnort claim that their program can successfully crack most networks in about two weeks or less. Their technique monitors network signals without interfering with them, so it's not possible for a network manager to detect an attack in progress. They released the program to force the issue; if it's easy to crack WEP encryption, the standards-setting groups will have to either find a way to make it more secure or replace it with something that is much more difficult to crack.

Bottom line: Go ahead and encrypt your network data. Encrypted data is more secure than plain-text transmission, and it takes time to crack a WEP key, so WEP does add another (admittedly weak) layer of security, especially if you change keys frequently. WEP encryption may not do much to protect you against serious attackers, but it will probably keep out both the casual network eavesdropper who stumbles onto your network from across the street and the drive-by network snoop. It's a lot easier to break into an unencrypted network (and there are plenty of them out there), so a cracker who detects your encrypted signal will probably move on to a target with less protection.

Help Is on the Way

Obviously a security scheme that has holes big enough to drive a very large digital truck through is almost as bad as no security at all. The successful attacks on WEP encryption and freely available tools for exploiting the protocol's security problems have members of the Wi-Fi Alliance seriously concerned about protecting their franchise as the *de facto* standard for wireless networking. They've been using words like "crisis" to describe the attention these problems have been receiving. They want a fix before the bad publicity about security cracks overpowers the growing demand for wireless Ethernet equipment that they've been carefully building and encouraging.

The new standards that address these security problems will be called 802.11i. The IEEE's 802.11 standards committee started to discuss the problem several months before it became widely recognized. A committee called Task Group i (TGi) is hard at work on a new and improved security specification that will (it hopes) address all of the known flaws in the WEP encryption standards. The group promised that the new security tools will work automatically and will be compatible with older hardware that doesn't use the new tools. The task group has a Web site at http://grouper.ieee.org/groups/802/11/Reports, where you can find information about its meetings and read some of its technical documents.

The Wi-Fi Alliance wants its members to start using the TGi fix as soon as possible, so they can defuse the situation before it turns into a commercial disaster. As soon as the engineers are satisfied that they have a solution, the manufacturers of access points and network adapters will all incorporate the new security methods into their products, and the Alliance will add it to the Wi-Fi certification test suite. Software and firmware updates will make existing 802.11b products compatible with the new 802.11i protocols.

Access Control

Most access points include an option that permits the network manager to restrict access to a specific list of client adapters. If a network device whose MAC address does not appear on the list of authorized users tries to connect, the access point will not accept the request to associate with the network. This can be an effective way to keep intruders from connecting to a wireless LAN, but it does force the network administrator to keep a complete list of users' adapters and their MAC addresses. Every time a new user wants to join the network, and every time an established user swaps adapters, somebody must add one more MAC address to the list. This is probably manageable in a home or small office network, but it could be a major undertaking for a larger corporate or campus-wide system.

Every access point configuration utility uses a different format for its access lists. The manual and online documentation supplied with your access point should provide detailed instructions for creating and maintaining an access-control list.

The 802.11b standard does not specify a maximum size for an access point's access-control list, so the numbers are all over the map. Some access points limit the list to a few dozen entries, but others, such as the Proxim Harmony AP Controller, will support as many as 10,000 separate addresses. Still others accept an unlimited number. If you plan to use a list of addresses to control access to your network, make sure your access point will work with a large enough list to support all of your users, with enough expansion space for future growth. As a rule of thumb, the access point should accept at least twice as many MAC addresses as the number of users on your network today.

MAC authentication cannot protect against all attackers, because changing the MAC address on most wireless cards is trivial — all an attacker needs to do is watch the traffic on your network long enough to find a valid user and clone their MAC address. However, like WEP, it can be a reasonably effective means of slowing down the casual intruder.

Authentication: The 802.1x Standard

Because of the security gaps in the WEP encryption specification, many wireless network equipment manufacturers and software developers have adopted yet another IEEE standard, 802.1x, to add another layer of security to their networks. The 802.1x standard defines a structure that can support several additional forms of authentication, including certificates, smart cards, and one-time passwords, all of which offer more protection than the access control built into 802.11. In wireless 802.11 networks, a technique called the Robust Security Network builds upon the 802.1x framework to restrict access to a network to authorized devices.

Most end users need to know two things about 802.1x: first, it's built into some (but not all) 802.11b hardware and software, including the wireless configuration utility supplied with Windows XP and many recent access point products, so it can provide one more potential layer of security; and second, it still has serious flaws that a dedicated network cracker can exploit to break into a wireless network. The ugly technical details are in an analysis prepared by two researchers at the University of Maryland, available online at http://www.cs.umd.edu/~waa/1x.pdf.

It seems as if a pattern is emerging, doesn't it? Engineers from interested hardware and software companies gather under the flag of an IEEE task force to develop yet another new set of network security tools to make their products safe from hackers, crackers, eavesdroppers, and other nasties, and a few months later, an independent researcher at some university or government agency discovers that the new tools have their own serious problems that expose the "protected" data to break-ins and leaks. In the meantime, the poor end users of the world are running as fast as they can to keep up, but their wireless networks still aren't completely secure.

What to do? Is a secure wireless network an unreachable ideal? If you look at wireless security as a cat-and-mouse game, it's pretty clear that the mice (the snoopers and network crackers) are winning. But those mice need some sophisticated knowledge and equipment to work around the existing encryption and authentication tools. Think of it like the front door to your house: If you leave the door wide open, anybody can walk in and steal your stuff, but when you lock the door and latch all the windows, it will be much more difficult for a burglar to enter. An expert can pick the lock, but that takes a lot of time and trouble.

Firewalls

If you accept the idea that WEP encryption and 802.1x do not provide adequate protection for a wireless LAN, the next logical step is to find another way to keep intruders out of your network. You need a firewall.

A firewall is a proxy server that filters all the data that passes through it on the way to or from a network, based on a set of rules established by the network manager. For example, a firewall might reject data from an unknown source or files that match a particular source (such as a virus). Or it might pass all data moving from the LAN *to* the Internet, but allow only certain types of data *from* the Internet. The most common use of a firewall in a LAN is at the gateway to the Internet, as shown in Figure 14.5. The firewall monitors all inbound and outbound data between the local network on one side, and the Internet on the other. This kind of firewall is intended to protect the computers on the LAN from unauthorized access from the Internet.

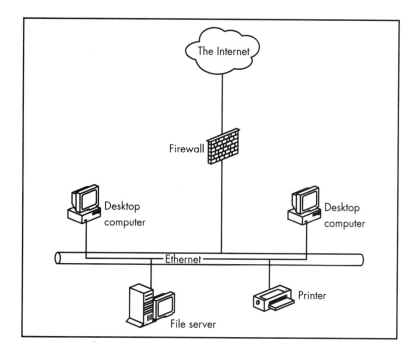

Figure 14.5: A network firewall isolates a LAN from the Internet

In a wireless network, a firewall can also be placed at the gateway between the wireless access points and the wired network. This firewall isolates the wireless portion of the network from the wired LAN, so intruders who have connected their computers to the network without permission can't use the wireless connection to reach the Internet or the wired part of the LAN. Figure 14.6 shows the location of a firewall in a wireless network.

Keep Wireless Intruders at Bay

Most people who try to tap into a wireless network don't care about the other computers on the local network; they're looking for free high-speed access to the Internet. If they can't use your network to download files or connect to their favorite Web pages, they'll probably move on to find some other unprotected wireless hot spot. That doesn't mean you should store confidential data in file shares on unprotected computers, but if you can limit or restrict access to the Internet, you will make your wireless network a lot less attractive to intruders.

A firewall in a wireless network can perform several functions: it acts as a router between the wireless network and a wired LAN or a direct connection to

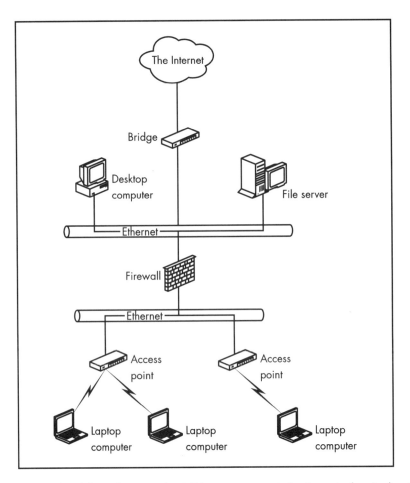

Figure 14.6: A firewall in a wireless LAN acts as a protected gateway to the wired portion of the same network

the Internet, and it blocks all traffic moving from the wireless side to the wired network that doesn't come from an authenticated user, but it does not interfere with commands, messages, and file transfers from trusted users. A legitimate user can connect to network nodes on the wired part of a mixed LAN or to the Internet, but an intruder would be cut off at the firewall.

Because authorized users and intruders are both on the unprotected side of the firewall, it does not isolate wireless nodes from one another. An intruder can still gain access to another computer on the same wireless network and read shared files, so it's a good idea to turn off File Sharing in any computer connected to a wireless network.

A firewall for a wireless network should use some kind of authentication to allow legitimate users through the gateway but reject everybody else. If the access control based on MAC addresses built into 802.11b systems and the added authentication in 802.1x are not adequate, then an outboard firewall should require each user to enter a login and password before they can connect to the Internet.

If your wireless network includes computers running more than one operating system, your firewall must use a login tool that works on any platform. The easiest way to accomplish this is with a Web-based authentication server, such as the one included in the Apache Web server (http://httpd.apache.org).

The NASA NAS Center uses Apache on a dedicated server to create a Web site that instructs users to enter an account name and password. The server uses a Perl/CGI script to compare the login and password to a database; if they are correct, it instructs the server to accept commands and data from the user's IP address. If the username is not in the database or the password is incorrect, the Apache server displays an "Invalid Username and Password" Web page.

The Apache Web server is available as a Unix application that can run on an old, slow computer with an early Pentium or even a 486 CPU, so it's often possible to recycle an old junker that is no longer in daily service and use it as a firewall. Both the Apache application and a Unix operating system are available as open source software, so you should be able to build an Apache firewall at extremely low cost.

If you prefer to use Windows rather than Unix, you have several options. You can use the Windows NT/ 2000 version of Apache, or you can use a commercial utility such as Sygate's Wireless Enforcer (http://www.sygate.com/products/sse/sse_swe_security.htm). Wireless Enforcer works with other elements of the Sygate Secure Enterprise Suite to assign and verify a unique fingerprint for each authorized user. If intruders try to connect to an access point without a proper fingerprint, the network will lock them out.

Isolate Your Network from the Internet

Attacks on a wireless LAN don't all come through the air. A wireless network also requires the same kind of firewall protection against attacks from the Internet as every other network. Many access points include configurable firewall features, but if yours does not, the network should include one or more of these firewalls:

- A firewall program on each computer
- A separate router or a dedicated computer acting as a network firewall
- An integrated security suite such as the Sygate suite described in the previous section

Client firewall programs provide another line of defense against attacks through the Internet from outside your own network. Some of these attacks come from miscreants who are looking for a way to read your files and other resources that you don't want the entire world to see. Others may want to use your computer as a relay point for spam or for attempts to break into some other computer halfway around the world, in order to make the real source more difficult to identify. Still others spread viruses or use Really Unpleasant programs that take over control of a PC and display threatening messages. Also, an unprotected system with a lot of unused storage space can be an attractive target for hackers who want to distribute pirated software, music, or video files (you don't think they store that stuff on their own computers, do you?).

The number of such idiots out on the Internet is surprisingly large; if you install a firewall that notifies you when an outside computer tries to connect to your network, you will probably see several break-in attempts every day.

Access Points with Firewalls

The easiest firewall to use with a wireless network is one that's built into an access point. Some combine the functions of a wireless access point with a broadband router and an Ethernet switch, so they support both wired and wireless network clients.

As you know, a network router provides translation services between the numeric IP address that identifies the LAN to the Internet and the internal IP addresses that identify individual computers within the local network. The firewall normally blocks all incoming requests for data to network hosts, but this creates problems when you want to use one or more of the computers on the local network as fileservers. To solve this problem, the firewall includes a virtual server that redirects certain types of requests to the appropriate computer inside the firewall.

Each request for a connection to a server includes a specific port number that identifies the type of server. For example, Web servers operate on port 80, and FTP servers use port 21, so those port numbers are part of the request for access. To accept requests for access to a server, you must instruct the firewall's network address translation (NAT) function to forward those requests to a specific computer within the LAN. In Figure 14.7, the virtual server is configured to use the computer with the local IP address 192.168.0.177 as a Web server and 192.168.0.164 as an FTP fileserver. Table 14.1 lists the most common service port numbers.

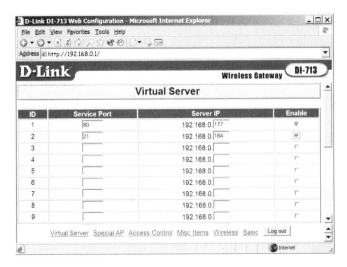

Figure 14.7: The D-Link access point directs requests for access to fileservers to specific computers within the network

Table 14.1: Common TCP/IP Service Port Numbers

Port Number	Internet Service
20	FTP-data (FTP default data)
21	FTP (file transfer)
23	Telnet
25	SMTP (outgoing mail)
37	Time
53	DNS (Domain Name System)
70	Gopher
79	Finger
80	HTTP (Web server)
88	Kerberos
110	POP3 (incoming mail)
119	NNTP (network news)
1863	Microsoft MSN Messenger
5190	AOL Instant Messenger
7070	RealAudio

Hundreds of other port numbers have been assigned, but you will never see most of them in actual use. The official list of port assignments is at http://www.iana.org/assignments/port-numbers.

NAT translation assumes that the IP addresses of each virtual server don't change from one request to the next. A Web server on 192.168.0.23 today won't migrate to 192.168.0.47 next week. That's generally not a problem on a wired network, but in a wireless setting where network clients join and depart the network all the time, the DHCP server automatically assigns the next available address to each new client. If one of those clients is the home of one of the network's service ports, the NAT probably won't find it. This is not a common problem, because most networks don't use portable computers as servers, but it can happen. The solution is either to turn off the DHCP server and assign a permanent IP address to each client or to forward the service port to a computer than has a wired connection to the network.

Firewall Software

A wireless gateway firewall at the interface between the access point and the wired part of your LAN will keep intruders from using your network to reach the Internet, and a firewall at the Internet connection will turn away attempts to connect to your network *from* the Internet, but there's still one more form of protection necessary in a wireless network. If somebody gains access to your wireless LAN without permission, you want to keep them out of the other legitimate computers on the same network. That means you need a client firewall program on each network node.

Client firewalls perform the same functions at a computer's network interface that a LAN or enterprise firewall performs for the entire network; it detects attempts to connect to TCP service ports and rejects them unless they match one or more of the firewall program's configuration settings.

Several good firewall products are available as shareware, and others are free to noncommercial users, so it's easy to try them on your own system and choose the one you like best.

Here are some Windows programs:

- ZoneAlarm (http://www.zonelabs.com/store/content/home.jsp)
- Tiny Personal Firewall (http://www.tinysoftware.com/pwall.php)
- Sygate Personal Firewall (http://www.sygate.com/products/shield_ov.htm)
- Norton Desktop Firewall (http://enterprisesecurity.symantec.com)
- Norton Personal Firewall (http://www.symantec.com)
- GFI LANguard (http://www.languard.com)

Unix and Linux users also have plenty of firewall options. Most of them were written for use on stand-alone firewall computers that are commonly used as network gateways, but they could be equally appropriate as protection for individual network clients.

In Linux, the firewall is part of the kernel—either ipchains or iptables. Both are well documented at http://linuxdoc.org/HOWTO/IPCHAINS-HOWTO.html and http://www.netfilter.org/unreliable-guides/packet-filtering-HOWTO/, respectively. IP Filter is a software package that provides firewall services to FreeBSD and NetBSD systems. The official IP Filter Web site is http://coombs.anu.edu.au/~avalon, and there's an excellent how-to document at http://www.obfuscation.org/ipf/ipf-howto.txt. The program can deny or permit any packet from passing through the firewall, and it can filter by netmask or host address, establish service-port restrictions, and provide NAT translation services.

NetBSD/i386 Firewall is another free Unix firewall. It will operate on any PC with a 486 or later CPU and as little as 8MB of memory. The NetBSD/i386 Firewall Project home page is at http://www.dubbele.com.

PortSentry is a port scan detection tool that is integrated into several widely used Linux distributions, including Red Hat, Caldera, Debian, and Turbo Linux. It's available for download from http://www.psionic.com/products/portsentry.html

Virtual Private Networks

VPNs can add one more layer of useful security by isolating the connection between network nodes from other network traffic. A VPN is an encrypted transmission channel that connects two network endpoints through a "data tunnel." Many network security experts recommend a VPN as an effective way to protect a wireless network from eavesdroppers and unauthorized users. You can find more detailed information about setting up and using a VPN in the next chapter.

Physical Security

Up until now, we've been talking about keeping electronic intruders out of your wireless network. It's easy enough to gain access to a network using off-the-shelf equipment that hasn't already been configured for that network; it's even easier when the intruder has stolen a computer from an authorized user.

Losing a laptop computer to a thief is bad enough. Letting the thief use a stolen computer to log on to a network is even worse. As a network operator, you should remind your users that their portables are attractive targets for thieves and offer some guidelines for protecting them. And, as a user yourself, you should remember the same set of rules.

The first rule is simple: don't forget that you're carrying a computer. It seems obvious, but London taxi drivers found about 2,900 laptops (and 62,000 mobile phones!) left in their cabs in a six-month period. Uncounted others have been abandoned in airplanes, hotel rooms, commuter trains, and conference centers. It doesn't take a thief to separate a computer from its owner if the owner just walks away.

Don't advertise the fact that you're carrying a computer. Those nylon bags that say "IBM" or "COMPAQ" on the side in great big letters may be fashionable, but they're not as safe as an ordinary briefcase or a conservative carrier bag.

Next, keep the computer in your hands or on your shoulder whenever it's not locked in a closet or storage locker. Look away for a minute, and a skilled thief can make it disappear. Airport terminals, railway stations, and hotel lobbies are common places for quick snatch-and-grabs. If you have to use the computer in a public space, use a bicycle chain or a steel cable to secure it to an immovable object.

Don't leave an unsecured laptop computer in an office overnight.

Watch out for airport scanners. Ask the security people to inspect it by hand, or make sure you're able to retrieve the computer as soon as it comes off the conveyor belt. Two people working together can do a fine job of delaying you and grabbing the computer before you can get to it. If somebody does try to steal your computer from a security check, make some noise and get help from the guards.

Make sure your computers and loose components like PC Cards have property labels inside and out. Engrave your name or company name and telephone number on network interface cards and other removable parts. A company called Security Tracking of Office Property (http://www.stoptheft.com) offers registered security plate labels with a cyanoacrylate adhesive that requires something like 800 pounds of pressure to remove and an indelible chemical tattoo marked "Stolen Property" that appears if somebody does remove the label.

If you can convince your users to use alarm devices on their computers, they might improve the chances of recovering them. TrackIT (http://www.trackit-corp.com) is a two-piece alarm that uses a key-chain transmitter with a miniature receiver that stays in the computer bag. When the transmitter is more than 40 feet from the receiver, the receiver sounds a 110 dB siren, which usually encourages the thief to drop the stolen bag.

And finally, keep a list of models and serial numbers separately from the devices themselves. You'll need that information for your insurance claim.

When you discover that one of the computers that connects to your wireless network has been lost or stolen, it's essential to protect the rest of the network. If possible, change the network's SSID, passwords, and WEP keys as soon as you can. If your network uses a list of MAC addresses to control access, remove the stolen device's MAC address from the list of authorized connections.

Sharing Your Network with the World

If you use your wireless network to provide public Internet access to your neighborhood or campus, or if you want to allow customers and other visitors to connect to your wireless net, you won't want to use WEP encryption or other security tools to limit access to known users, but you should still give some thought to security. Just because you want to give people a direct connection to the Internet, that doesn't mean that you want to let them poke around the other computers in your network—it's necessary to isolate the wireless access points from the rest of the network.

If all of the local nodes on your LAN are connected through wires, the best approach is to place a firewall between the wireless access point and the wired LAN that only allows the access point (and the computers connected to it through wireless links) to communicate with the Internet, but not with any local nodes on the wired LAN, as shown in Figure 14.8.

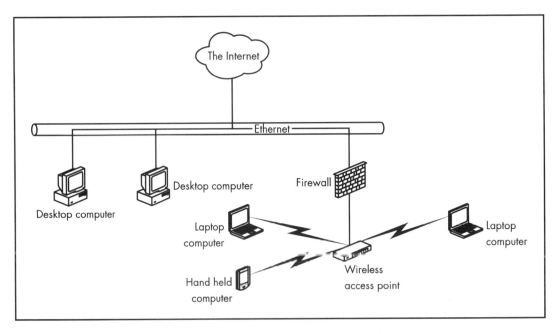

Figure 14.8: The firewall isolates the wireless segment from the rest of the network

However, if one or more of your in-house computers use wireless connections, you need to protect them from access by outsiders who are using the public portion of your network. There are a couple of ways to do that: Figure 14.9 shows a wireless network with a software firewall in each in-house computer, and Figure 14.10 shows a system that uses two separate wireless networks with different SSIDs, both connected to the same Internet hookup. In general, the basic rule is to use one or more firewalls to isolate the public portion of your network from the computers that you don't want open to everybody in the world.

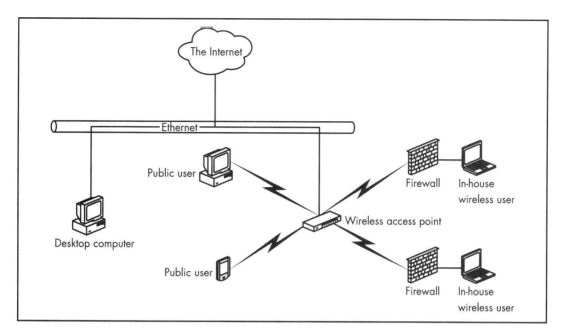

Figure 14.9: Every in-house wireless computer includes a software firewall

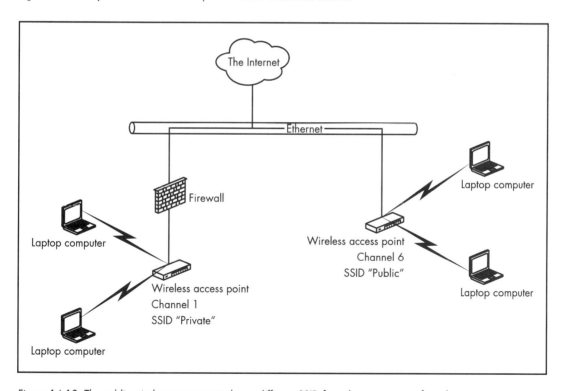

Figure 14.10: The public wireless access point has a different SSID from the access point for in-house users

15

VIRTUAL PRIVATE NETWORKS

The security tools in the 802.11 specification are not good enough to protect data transmitted through a wireless network. So what's the alternative? A virtual private network (VPN) can add another effective form of security to data that moves from a wireless network client to a host that can be located anywhere with a network connection.

A VPN uses a "data tunnel" to connect two points on a network through an encrypted channel. The endpoints can be a single network client and a network server, a pair of client computers or other devices, or the gateways to a pair of LANs. Data that passes through a public network, such as the Internet, is completely isolated from other network traffic. It uses login and password authentication to restrict access to authorized users; it encrypts the data to make it unintelligible to intruders who intercept the data; and it uses data authentication to maintain the integrity of each data packet and to ensure that all data originates with legitimate network clients. A VPN is not just another layer of encryption; it isolates the end-to-end data path from other network users, so unauthorized users can't get to it. VPN functions occur at the IP, or network, layer of the ISO model. Therefore, they can operate on top of the 802.11b protocols, which operate at the Physical layer. VPNs can also pass data across a network connection that includes more than one physical medium (for example, a wireless link that passes data onward to a wired Ethernet network). In other words, a VPN is an end-to-end service; it doesn't matter whether it's using a wireless link, an Ethernet cable, a plain ordinary telephone line, or some combination of those and other transmission media. The VPN is a tunnel that extends from one network endpoint to the other, regardless of what media are carrying the data. This adds another level of security to (or provides an alternative to) WEP encryption, which applies only to the wireless portion of the network.

In a traditional VPN, a remote user can log on to a distant LAN and obtain all the same network services that are available to local clients. VPNs are commonly used to extend corporate networks to branch offices and to connect users to the LAN from home or from off-site locations such as a client's or customer's office.

A client device connected through a VPN server presents the same appearance to the rest of the (VPN-protected) network as a client device in the same room or building. The only difference is that the data from the VPN passes through a VPN driver and a public network instead of moving directly from the network adapter to the LAN. Figure 15.1 shows a typical VPN connection to a remote network.

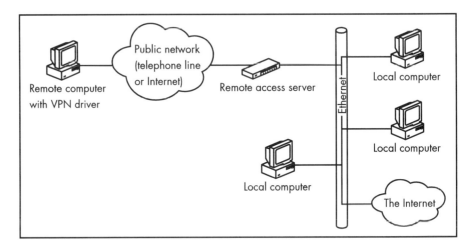

Figure 15.1: A remote network can connect to a LAN through a virtual private network

All of the security benefits of a regular wired VPN also apply to a short-range VPN that tunnels through a wireless link and to a longer-range VPN that starts on a wireless network and relays the data to a remote server. These are two different uses for a VPN: a local VPN may only extend across the wireless portion of a network between the client devices and the access point, and an extended network can carry VPN-encoded data beyond the access points to a VPN server through a public network such as the Internet or a dial-up telephone connection.

An extended network is a traditional VPN (one that passes through a public network such as the Internet) that happens to originate from a wireless network client. The same VPN can also support connections that don't include a wireless segment, along with logins from public wireless services at airports or coffee shops. This is the conventional way to use a VPN.

Local, short-range VPNs are more interesting to people operating wireless networks, because they add another layer of security to wireless links. Because the data moving between wireless clients and the network access point is encrypted (using an algorithm that is more secure than WEP encryption), it is unintelligible to any third party who might be monitoring the radio signal. Also, because the VPN server at the access point won't accept data links from wireless clients that are not using the correct VPN drivers and passwords, an intruder can't break into the network by associating a rogue client with the access point.

The goal of a wireless VPN is to protect the wireless link between the clients and the access point and to lock out unauthorized users. Therefore, the isolated and encrypted data may move only across a single room rather than hundreds or thousands of miles. Of course, the access point might also relay VPN-encoded data onward through the Internet to a network host in another location.

Figure 15.2 shows a wireless connection to a VPN. The VPN server is located between the wireless access point and the host LAN, so all of the packets that move through the wireless portion of the network are encrypted. For clarity, the diagram shows the VPN server as a separate component, but in practice the most practical way to add VPN security to a wireless LAN is to use a router or gateway that incorporates VPN support. VPN-enabled routers are available from several vendors, including Alvarion, Colubris, and Nexland.

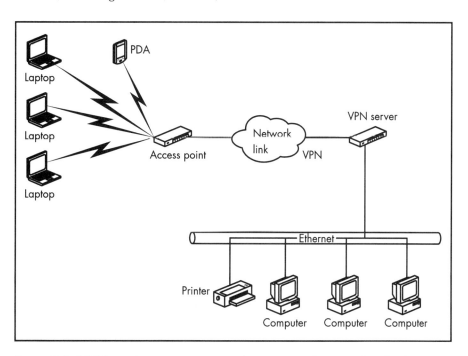

Figure 15.2: A VPN provides a secure connection between a wireless network and an Internet gateway or a LAN

VPN Methods

A VPN moves data through one or more intermediate networks to a destination on another network. The VPN's tunneling client encapsulates the existing data packets or frames by adding a new header with the routing information that instructs them how to reach the endpoint of the VPN. The transmission path through the intermediate networks is called a *tunnel*. At the other end of the tunnel, the VPN server removes the tunneling header and forwards the data to the destination specified by the next layer of headers. The exact form of the tunnel doesn't make any difference to the data, because the data treats the tunnel as a point-to-point connection.

The tunneling headers can take several forms. The methods used most widely in VPNs are Point-to-Point Tunneling Protocol (PPTP), Layer Two Tunneling Protocol (L2TP), and IP Security (IPSec) mode. PPTP and L2TP can move data through IP, IPX, and NetBEUI networks; IPSec is limited to IP networks. Both the client and the server must use the same protocol.

In PPTP and L2TP, the client and server must configure the tunnel for each transmission before they begin to exchange data. The configuration parameters include the route through the intermediate network and the encryption and compression specifications. When the transmission is complete, the client and server terminate the connection and close the tunnel.

In an IPSec network link, the client and server must establish the tunnel through the intermediate networks in a separate transaction before they begin to exchange data.

Each of these protocols offers specific advantages and disadvantages, but they're all good enough to create a secure link between a wireless network client and an access point. The differences among the three are technical rather than practical. You can find an excellent explanation of the internal operation of all three protocols in Microsoft's white paper entitled *Virtual Private Networking in Windows 2000: An Overview*, which is available online at http://www.microsoft.com/windows2000/docs/VPNoverview.doc.

VPN Servers

A VPN server can be part of a Unix or a Windows server or built into a stand-alone network router or gateway. If your network already uses a separate computer as a dedicated server, you can use that computer as the VPN server. However, a separate piece of hardware might be a better choice if your network does not already have a full-blown network server.

Dozens of VPN equipment makers offer routers, gateways, and other products that support one or more VPN protocols. Each of these products has a different feature set, so it's essential to test the specific combination of client and server that you intend to use on your own network before you commit to them. The Virtual Private Network Consortium (VPNC) is moving toward a set of interoperability tests and certification standards (much like the Wi-Fi standards for 802.11b equipment). The VPNC Web site, http://www.vpnc.org, lists the products that have passed the interoperability tests, and it also provides links to sources of information about a long list of VPN products.

Configuring a Windows Server for a Wireless VPN

If you're committed to using a Windows server, PPTP is probably the easiest protocol to use because it originated as a Microsoft specification. It provides extensive support for PPTP in many versions of Windows, so it's relatively easy to configure PPTP clients and servers without the need for third-party software. Windows 2000 and Windows XP also support L2TP, so that's another acceptable choice.

A computer used as a PPTP server must run one of Microsoft's server operating systems: Windows NT Server 4.0, Windows 2000 Server, or Windows XP Server. The server also requires two network interface cards: one connected to the wired LAN or the Internet gateway and the other connected to the wireless network. The interface card connected to the wireless port normally connects directly to the wireless access point's Ethernet port.

The exact process of installing PPTP on a Windows server is slightly different in each version of Windows, but the general steps are the same. For specific information about configuring a particular operating system, consult the online Help screens, Microsoft's Resource Kit, and other online documentation for your operating system. The following sections describe the configuration steps in general terms.

Configuring the Connection to the Wired Network

The link to the LAN or other network is a dedicated connection through a network adapter. The network connection profile for this connection must include the IP address and subnet mask assigned to this connection and the default gateway address assigned to the network gateway.

Configuring the VPN Connection

The VPN connection is usually an Ethernet link to one or more access points. The connection profile on the server for the VPN connection must include the IP address and subnet mask assigned to this port and the addresses of the DNS and WINS name servers used by this network.

Configuring the Remote Access Server as a Router

The server must use either static routes or routing protocols that make each wireless client reachable from the wired network.

Enabling and Configuring the Server for PPTP or L2TP Clients

Windows uses Remote Access Service (RAS) and Point-to-Point Protocol (PPP) to establish VPN connections. The Routing and Remote Access service enables RAS, and a VPN connection requires these RAS configuration options:

Authentication Method	Encrypted PPTP connections use the MS-CHAP or EAP-TLS authentication methods.
Authentication Provider	Either Windows 2000 security or an external RADIUS server can verify network clients.
IP Routing	IP Routing and IP-based remote access must be active. If the wired network acts as a DHCP server for the wireless clients, DHCP must be active.

Configuring PPTP or L2TP Ports

Set each PPTP or L2TP port to accept remote access.

Configuring Network Filters

Input and output filters keep the remote access server from sending and receiving data that does not originate at a VPN client. These filters will reject data sent to or from unauthorized users, so those intruders will not be able to obtain an Internet connection (or a connection to the wired LAN) through the wireless network.

Configuring Remote Access Policies

The remote access permission for each wireless client must be set to allow access to the RAS server. The port type must be set to the correct VPN protocol (for example, PPTP or L2TP) and the profile for each connection must include the type of encryption in use. In Windows, these are the three encryption strength options:

- Basic: Uses a 40-bit encryption key
- Strong: Uses a 56-bit encryption key
- Strongest: Uses a 128-bit encryption key

VPN Servers for Unix

PoPToP is a PPTP server for Linux, OpenBSD, FreeBSD, and other Unix variations. Setup and other how-to information and a download of the current release are available from http://poptop.lineo.com.

All of the BSD variations (including FreeBSD, NetBSD, OpenBSD, and Mac OS X) include an IPSec VPN client and server as part of the release package.

Linux FreeS/WAN is the most popular implementation of IPSec for Linux. Go to http://www.freeswan.org for downloads, documentation, and access to the community of FreeS/WAN users.

If you are using a Linux firewall, you may want to consider VPN Masquerade as an alternative to an add-on program like PoPToP. Linux uses the IP Masquerade function in the Linux kernel to share a single connection to the Internet among multiple clients. VPN Masquerade is the section of IP Masquerade that supports PPTP and IPSec clients. The how-to for Linux VPN Masquerade is at http://www.linuxdoc.org/HOWTO/VPN-Masquerade-HOWTO.html.

Network Hardware with Built-in VPN Support

A dedicated computer running Linux or one of the BSD versions of Unix can be an inexpensive VPN server; or if you're using a Windows server for other purposes, it can also provide VPN support at little or no additional cost. However, a full-size network server is often a big and complicated solution for a relatively simple problem. It's not always the best choice. Many switches, routers, gateways, and firewall devices also include VPN support. Cisco, 3Com, Intel, and many other manufacturers make VPN products that are often a great deal easier to install and maintain than a separate computer.

In a wireless network, the VPN server does not need all the same bells and whistles as a server in a larger corporate network. As Figure 15.3 shows, a router located between the wireless access point and the wired portion of an enterprise network can easily double as a VPN server. In a home network, the VPN server can operate between the access point and a DSL or cable modem.

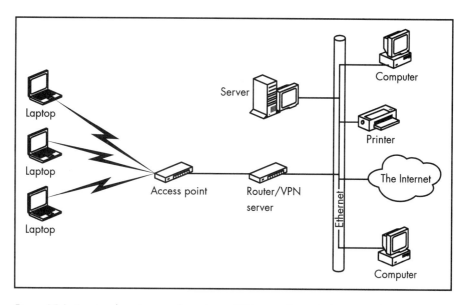

Figure 15.3: A network router can also act as a VPN server for a wireless network

Stand-alone VPN client hardware that sits between the computer and the network is also available, but it's not as practical in a wireless network because the wireless network adapter is almost always plugged directly into the computer itself.

VPN Client Software

A wireless client connects to a VPN server through its wireless Ethernet link to the network access point, which the operating system sees as a LAN connection. In order to set up a VPN tunnel through that connection, it's necessary to install the tunneling protocol as a network service.

Configuring Windows for VPN

Windows includes support for virtual private networks in most versions, but it's not part of the default installation. So, the first step in setting up a VPN client is to install the protocol. In consumer versions of Windows, follow these steps:

1. From the Control Panel, select Add/Remove Programs.
2. Open the Windows Setup tab in the Add/Remove Program Properties window.
3. Select Communications in the Components list, and click the Details button. The Communications window shown in Figure 15.4 will open.

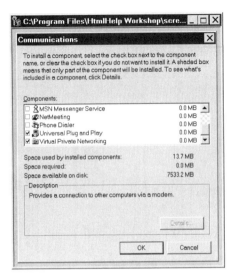

Figure 15.4: Select Virtual Private Networking in the list of Communications components to install the VPN protocol

4. Scroll down the list of components to find Virtual Private Networking. Check the box next to this item.

5. Click the OK buttons in the Communications window and the Add/Remove Programs window.

6. Reboot when the computer tells you to do so.

   In Windows NT and Windows 2000, follow these steps:

1. From the Control Panel, select the Network option.

2. In the Protocols tab, click the Add button. The Select Network Protocol dialog box will open.

3. Select Point to Point Tunneling Protocol from the list of Network Protocols and click OK. Windows will load the PPTP files.

4. When the PPTP Configuration window appears, select the number of VPN devices you want to support on this client. In most cases, one device is sufficient for a wireless client.

5. Click the OK buttons in all the open windows.

6. Restart the computer to make the VPN client active.

7. To add the VPN client as a Remote Access Service port, open the Control Panel and select Network again. Choose the Services tab and select the Remote Access Service option.

8. Click the Properties button to open the RAS Properties dialog box.

9. Click the Add button to open an Add RAS Device window.

10. If VPN1-RASPPTPM is not visible, open the drop down list of devices, select VPN1-RASPPTPM, and click OK.

11. Select the VPN port and click the Configure button. Choose the option that specifies the wireless network port and click OK.

Finally, you must create a connection profile that makes the connection to the VPN server:

1. From the Control Panel or the My Computer window, open Dial-Up Networking.

2. Double-click the Make New Connection icon. The Make New Connection Wizard will start.

3. In the first screen of the wizard, shown in Figure 15.5, enter a name for your VPN server in the Type a Name field.

Figure 15.5: Choose the Microsoft VPN Adapter option to create a VPN connection profile

4. Open the Select a Device menu and choose the VPN Adapter option. Click Next to move to the next screen in the wizard.

5. Enter the IP address of the VPN server in the Host Name or IP Address field. Click Next. The wizard will confirm that it has created a new connection profile.

6. Click Finish to close the wizard. You should see an icon for the new connection profile in the Dial-Up Networking window.

7. If you plan to use the wireless VPN connection frequently, create a shortcut to the new connection profile. Windows will automatically place the shortcut on your desktop.

In Windows XP, a wizard makes the whole process a lot simpler:

1. From the Control Panel, open Network Connections.

2. Double-click the New Connection Wizard icon.

3. When the Network Connection Type window shown in Figure 15.6 opens, choose the Connect to the Network at My Workplace option.

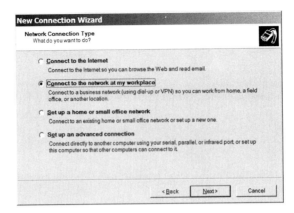

Figure 15.6: The option for creating a VPN link specifies connecting to a workplace network, but it also applies to a wireless VPN

4. In the Network Connection window (shown in Figure 15.7), choose the Virtual Private Network Connection option and click Next.

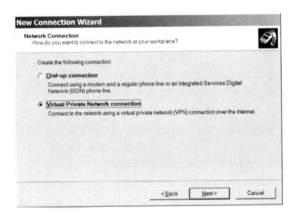

Figure 15.7: Select the Virtual Private Network Connection option to create a VPN connection

5. In the Connection Name window, type a name for the wireless VPN connection. This name will appear on desktop shortcuts to this connection. Click Next.

6. In the Public Network window (shown in Figure 15.8), choose the Do Not Dial option, because you don't need to connect through a telephone line. Click Next.

7. In the VPN Server Selection window shown in Figure 15.9, type the IP address of the VPN server.

8. Click Next and then click Finish to complete the wizard.

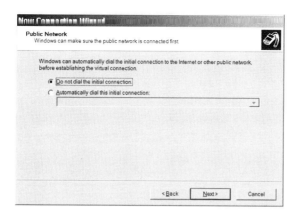

Figure 15.8: In a wireless network, the VPN does not require a dial-up connection

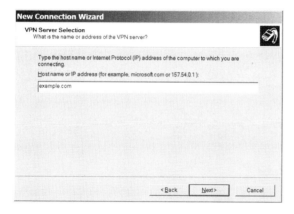

Figure 15.9: The Host Name IP address identifies the VPN server at the other end of the wireless link

The Microsoft L2TP/IPSec VPN Client

Microsoft includes a client for L2TP connections with IPSec in Windows 2000 and Windows XP. A similar client program for Windows 98, Windows Me, and Windows NT Workstation 4.0 is available for free download from Microsoft. To find the program, go to Microsoft's Windows 2000 Tools and Utilities Web page (http://www.microsoft.com/windows2000/downloads/tools/default.asp)and choose the appropriate link.

Making the Connection in Windows

Once the VPN connection profile is in place, it's easy to connect a Windows client to the host LAN or the Internet through the wireless VPN link: just double-click the icon for the connection profile. Windows will ask for a login and password and then make the connection.

If your wireless connection is the method you use most often to connect to the Internet, you can make it the default connection, which will open whenever you run a network application such as a Web browser or email client program. To make the VPN profile the default, follow these steps:

1. Open the Internet Properties window from the Control Panel.
2. Select the Connections tab.
3. In the Dial-Up Settings section, select the VPN connection profile from the list and click the Set Default button.
4. Click the Settings button. In the Dial-Up Settings section, type your login and password on the VPN server.
5. Choose the Dial Whenever a Network Connection Is Not Present option.

Windows XP Options

Windows XP offers many VPN options that were not available in earlier versions of Windows. To set these options, follow these steps:

1. Open the Network Connections window from the Control Panel. If you have a shortcut to your VPN connection on the desktop, you can skip this step.
2. Double-click the VPN icon. A Connect window like the one in Figure 15.10 will open.

Figure 15.10: Use the Connect window to configure a VPN in Windows XP

3. Click the Properties button. The Properties window for your VPN client will open. Figure 15.11 shows the General tab of the Properties window.
4. The IP address of the VPN server should already be visible in the Host Name field. The Dial Another Connection First option should be disabled. Click the Networking tab to see the options shown in Figure 15.12.
5. Choose the type of VPN server your network will use from the Type of VPN menu. If you don't know the VPN type, choose the Automatic option.

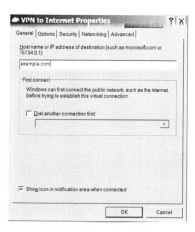

Figure 15.11: The General tab controls the destination of a VPN connection

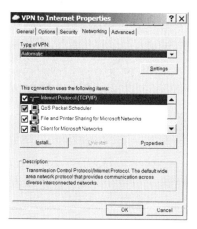

Figure 15.12: The Networking tab controls the VPN's network configuration options

6. Select Internet Protocol (TCP/IP) from the list of connection items, and click the Properties button to change the network settings, including whether you will use a DHCP server or manual settings for IP address and DNS.

7. Click the Advanced tab to display the window shown in Figure 15.13. If your network is not already protected by a firewall, turn on the Internet Connection Firewall option. This will protect the wireless client from attacks coming through the Internet.

The Options and Security tabs in the Properties window control connection options that normally don't change from the default settings. Network managers who want to change the security settings should instruct their users how to configure these options to comply with the network's specific requirements.

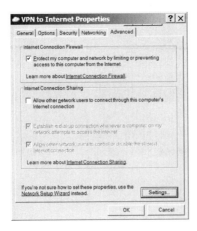

Figure 15.13: The Advanced tab controls the use of a firewall on the VPN

VPN Clients for Unix

Using a VPN client on a computer running Unix is more complicated than running VPN from a Windows machine because the client is not integrated into the kernel. Therefore, you must find a client program that works with the version of Unix *and* the VPN protocol you are trying to use. No single program offers a universal VPN client, and some combinations, such as PPTP on BSD Unix versions, don't seem to exist at all.

PPTP-linux

PPTP-linux is a Linux client that connects to PPTP servers. The developers of the program have encouraged users to create ports to other versions of Unix, but their own activities are concentrated on Linux.

The unofficial home page for the PPTP-linux client project is at http://www.scooter.cx/alpha/pptp.html.

IPSec Clients

Linux users can choose from several IPSec implantations:

- FreeS/WAN (http://www.freeswan.org)
- pipsecd (http://perso.enst.fr/~beyssac/pipsec)
- NIST Cerberus (http://www.antd.nist.gov/cerberus)

IPSec is included in the OpenBSD distribution. You can find a tutorial that explains how to use it at http://www.x-itec.de/projects/tuts/ipsec-howto.txt.

The IPSec implementation for FreeBSD is at http://www.r4k.net/ipsec.

For information about NetBSD IPSec, take a look at http://www.netbsd.org/Documentation/network/ipsec.

Using a Wireless VPN

When you design a VPN to protect the data on your network as it passes through the wireless link, it's important to understand exactly where the endpoints of the VPN tunnel are located. If the VPN tunnels only through the wireless link, as shown in Figure 15.14, the network will look exactly the same as it does without a VPN. However, if it extends beyond the wireless access points to pass through a wide area network (such as the Internet), like the one in Figure 15.15, the wireless network client can appear to be part of a LAN in another building, or halfway across the continent.

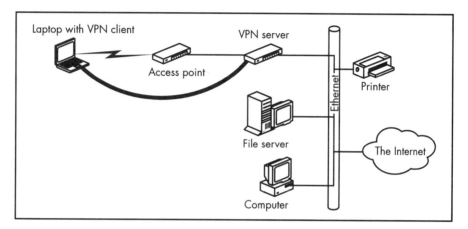

Figure 15.14: A wireless VPN with the server at the access point protects data through the wireless link, but it does not extend the network

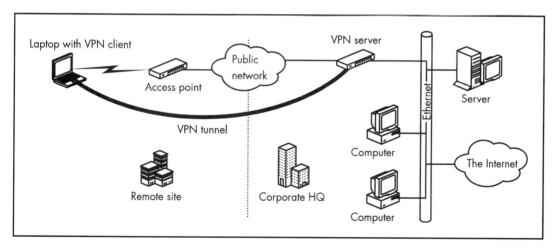

Figure 15.15: A VPN can include both the wireless link and an inter-city connection through the Internet to a corporate network

So how far should your wireless VPN extend? It depends on what you want the network to accomplish. If your wireless network is in place to support laptops and other portable computers in your office, factory, or campus, it makes sense to place the server between the network of access points and the connection to your corporate LAN. This will protect your wireless users' data and keep unauthorized users off the network, but it won't affect the other users whose computers connect to the LAN through cables.

At home or in a small business network, the access points probably connect to an Internet gateway router that provides Internet access to all the computers in the office or the house. If the access point and the gateway are separate devices, you can place the VPN server between the two. But if the access point and gateway are combined in the same box, you'll have to either use VPN clients on all your computers, including the desktop machines that are hard-wired to the gateway, and place the client between the gateway and the Internet modem as shown in Figure 15.16, or ignore the wired Ethernet ports on the gateway and add a new hub or switch between the VPN server and the Internet modem, as shown in Figure 15.17.

Making the Connection

If you use the wireless LAN with VPN protection most of the time, you should make the VPN profile your default connection. Whenever you run a network application, the computer will try to connect through the VPN unless you open a different connection (such as a dial-up telephone line) first.

To set a connection profile as the default in Windows, open the Dial-Up Networking window (in Windows XP, use the Network Connections window). Right-click the icon for the profile you want to choose, and select the Set as Default option from the menu.

To connect to a VPN that isn't your default, double-click the icon for the VPN's connection profile. You will see a login window like the one in Figure 15.18. Enter your name and password, and click the Connect button. If the VPN server recognizes your account, it will set up the connection.

Bypassing the VPN

Even though you normally use a VPN to protect your wireless data, you may sometimes want to send data in the clear, without using the VPN. For example, you might use a VPN at your own office or at home, but when you use the same computer at an airport or a coffee shop, or some other location that isn't protected by a VPN, you can use the same computer and network adapter to connect directly.

In addition, the configuration programs that control the network's operating channel, SSID, and other options are Web-based utilities that originate on the access point. Because the access point is inside the VPN tunnel, it is not possible to send commands to the access point through the VPN.

It's important to remember that you can use a VPN when you need it and bypass it when you want to make a direct connection.

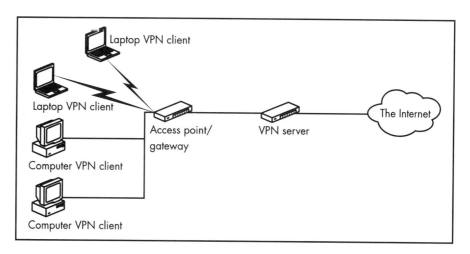

Figure 15.16: In a small LAN, you can use VPN clients on every computer

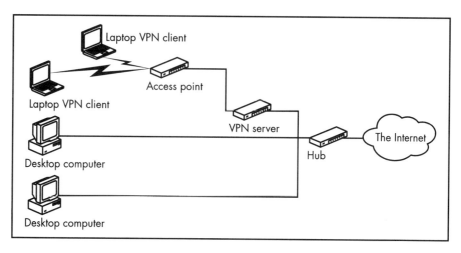

Figure 15.17: In this network, the VPN only protects the wireless links

Figure 15.18: A VPN connection normally requires a login name and password

Using a VPN Through a Public Network

When you connect your laptop to your corporate LAN through a public network at an airport or in a conference center, you can connect through their network to the Internet and onward to your corporate VPN server. Because you will have to log on to the public network before you initiate the VPN connection, you should create a separate "VPN via Public Network" connection profile in addition to the one you use from your own office. The profile should point to your corporate VPN server, but it should not be your default connection.

To connect through a public network on a computer running Windows, follow these steps:

1. Turn on the computer with the wireless network adapter in place.

2. Use your wireless configuration utility to select the public network you want to use.

3. Start Internet Explorer, Netscape Navigator, or some other Web browser. You will see the public network's login screen.

4. Enter your account name and password. The public network will acknowledge your login.

5. Minimize the browser window and open the Dial-Up Networking window.

6. Double-click the icon for your VPN via Public Network profile. The computer will connect through the Internet to your corporate LAN.

7. Enter the login and password for your corporate network.

16

TIPS AND TROUBLESHOOTING

When everything in your wireless network is working properly, you won't even know that it's there. Just fire up the wireless network adapter, and go online.

Like everything else related to computers, it works just fine when everything is set up correctly, but the essential setting is often hidden under three layers of windows, screens, and dialog boxes. If some obscure configuration option is wrong, the network connection won't work properly, if at all.

This chapter contains descriptions of common problems and instructions for fixing them.

My Computer Doesn't Detect My Network Adapter

Windows should automatically detect a PCMCIA or USB adapter when you connect the adapter to the computer or when you turn on the computer with the adapter already connected. If you're using a PC Card, you should hear a "boo-deep" sound when the PCMCIA controller detects it, and the system tray (next to the time) should show a PC Card icon like the one in Figure 16.1.

If Windows does not automatically enable your network adapter, it probably can't find the right driver, either for your PCMCIA socket or for the adapter itself. The Device Manager (shown in Figure 16.2) will display an icon with a yellow exclamation point or a red X for any device that is currently not working properly.

Right-click the listing with the exclamation point or X, and choose Properties from the menu to restore the device or reinstall the driver.

If there is no listing at all for the PCMCIA socket or the network adapter, install a driver from the disk supplied with the adapter, or download a new driver from the manufacturer's Web site.

If your Macintosh doesn't detect the AirPort adapter, try reloading the AirPort software.

In Linux, the PC Card requires PCMCIA services and Wireless Extensions. In Unix, you must install the specific driver for your network adapter.

Figure 16.1: The PC Card icon appears when a device in the computer's PCMCIA slot is active

Figure 16.2: The Device Manager identifies devices that are not working properly

The Wireless Configuration Program Won't Run

Many wireless network configuration programs were written for a specific type of network adapter. These programs search for the matching adapter when they start, and if they can't find the adapter, they automatically shut down. Therefore, a configuration program from one company probably won't work with an adapter from another company. The exceptions are adapters and configuration programs that were repackaged with more than one brand name, such as Cisco and Xircom or Orinoco and Apple, and configuration programs supplied with Windows and other operating systems.

Therefore, the solution to this problem is to install the configuration and control software that was written for the adapter you're trying to use. If you don't have the CD that was supplied with the adapter, you can probably download the program you need from the manufacturer's Web site.

The Wireless Control Program Tries to Run, Even If I'm Not Using My Adapter

Some wireless configuration and control programs automatically try to load every time you start your computer. The software supplied with D-Link adapters is particularly obnoxious about this, and others might also do the same thing. Running the wireless programs at start-up is fine for a desktop computer that uses them to connect to a LAN all the time, but it makes less sense on a laptop computer that often operates without a wireless network connection.

To remove the autostart function in Windows, follow these steps:

1. From the Start menu in Windows, choose Run.
2. Type **msconfig** in the Open field, and click OK.
3. Select the Startup tab to display a list of programs that automatically run every time you start Windows.
4. Find the entry in the list for the wireless configuration program and remove the checkmark from the box on the same line.
5. Most Windows systems have several other unnecessary programs that start automatically. While you have the program open, look for other programs that you don't need, and disable them.
6. Click OK and restart your computer when Windows asks you to do so.

If you have removed several programs from the Startup list, you will probably notice that Windows starts a lot faster than it did before.

Even though the configuration program no longer runs every time you run Windows, you can start the program when you need it. You will probably see a shortcut to one or more wireless programs on your desktop or in the Program menu.

My Computer Won't Associate with the Local Network

If you can't find the network, check these items:

- Confirm that the wireless network adapter PC Card is firmly inserted into the PCMCIA socket.
- Confirm that the cable between the USB adapter and the computer is plugged in at both ends.
- Open the wireless configuration program and confirm that the SSID matches the SSID of the access point for the network you want to use.
- If you are using an access point, confirm that your network adapter is configured as an infrastructure network; if you are trying to link directly to another wireless adapter, confirm that both systems are configured for an ad hoc network.
- Confirm that the network's WEP encryption settings match the settings for the adapter.

- Confirm that the IP address setting is correct. If the access point or some other DHCP server automatically assigns IP addresses, confirm that the computer's TCP/IP settings are set to obtain an address automatically.

- Confirm that the preamble length setting for your wireless adapter is the same as the setting for the access point. Some configuration programs call this the "Short Radio Headers" option.

- Confirm that the network manager has included the MAC address of your network adapter in the list of devices that are permitted to join the network. Don't trust the MAC address printed on the adapter's label; it doesn't always match the address actually assigned to the adapter. Use the adapter's configuration utility to find the real MAC address. Don't confuse the MAC address of the adapter with the address of the access point to which it is connected.

My Computer Connects to the Wrong Network

In an environment where signals from more than one wireless network are within range of the radio in a network adapter, the adapter will detect all of them. If the SSID option is set to join "ANY" network, the client will associate with the strongest local signal; if the configuration program includes a list of two or more SSIDs, it will search for SSIDs in the order specified by the list.

To configure your computer to join a specific network, change the SSID setting in the wireless configuration program and the name of the workgroup. Both the SSID and the workgroup should match the SSID of the access point you want to use.

To change the workgroup name in Windows 98 and Windows ME, follow these steps:

1. Open the Network window from the Control Panel.
2. Select the Identification tab.
3. Change the name in the Workgroup field.

To change the workgroup name in Windows 2000 and Windows XP, follow these steps:

1. Open the System window from the Control Panel.
2. Choose the Computer Name tab.
3. Click the Change button.
4. Change the name in the Workgroup field.

Most wireless adapters normally automatically scan through all available radio channels to search for usable network signals. However, some configuration options allow a user to lock the adapter onto a single channel. If that channel carries some other network, it's possible that the adapter could try to associate with it, so it's a good idea to check the configuration options and make sure the adapter is looking at the correct channel.

I Can See the Local Network, but I Can't Connect to the Internet

Most LANs use a gateway server to convert the internal IP addresses used within the LAN to a separate IP address that identifies this network to the Internet. In order to establish an Internet connection, your computer's TCP/IP network configuration settings must specify the addresses of the gateway and one or more DNS servers.

I Can See the Internet, but I Can't See Other Computers on My LAN

Client firewall programs like the one included in Norton Internet Security normally block inbound attempts to view files and directories. This prevents unauthorized access to your computer, but it also blocks other computers on the LAN unless you specifically allow access from those computers (using their IP addresses). The firewall controls should include a function where you can identify "trusted computers" or "allow local access" (it's different for each firewall program); consult the firewall program's documentation for specific instructions.

If the firewall isn't blocking access, it's possible that the computer you're trying to reach is not configured properly, that the access point doesn't recognize that computer's MAC address, or that the other computer has turned off File Sharing.

The Signal Strength Is Weak or Signal Quality Is Low

Assuming there's an access point within range of your computer, a weak signal is probably caused by some kind of obstruction between your network adapter and the access point. To improve the signal quality and signal strength, try moving the adapter (and the computer if the adapter is on a PC Card) to a different location. The wavelength of radio signals at 2.4 GHz is extremely short (they're called "microwaves" for a reason!), so moving the adapter even a short distance can be enough to make a noticeable difference.

If you're using a USB adapter, you can be more flexible about its location. Try placing it on top of a bookcase or in some other location with a clean shot to the access point. And try turning the adapter (or the external antenna) sideways, so it's on its side rather than upright; this might bring the polarity of the adapter's antenna closer to the polarity of the antenna in the access point.

I Can't Find a Public Network

Before your computer can connect to a public wireless network, your network adapter must associate itself with that network's access point. If the adapter doesn't automatically join the network, check these configuration settings:

1. Make sure the configuration utility is set to recognize the public network's SSID.
2. Confirm that the TCP/IP settings are configured to accept an IP address from a DHCP server.

3. Run your Web browser before you try to use some other Internet client program such as a mail reader. Most commercial public networks display a login screen through the browser, and they won't make any other connection until you identify yourself to them (and start their billing clock).

I Don't Know If I'm Within Range of a Network

Some wireless utilities detect and display the SSIDs of all nearby network signals, so you can often check for a signal by simply plugging in an adapter and running the status program.

For more detailed information about nearby networks, including their SSIDs, try using Network Stumbler (available from http://www.netstumbler.com) to identify all the signals that your network adapter can find. Network Stumbler is a Windows program that doesn't work with every brand of adapter, but if yours is compatible, it can be a valuable tool. For information about similar programs for other operating systems, try the links at http://www.wardriving.com/code.php.

The Network Is Slow

Any time a single network segment slows down, the overall performance of the network will suffer. This means a slow file transfer or download could be caused by an overloaded server or too many people trying to use the network at one time. Within the wireless segment of the network, slow performance could be caused by high demand for access to the network or interference from other wireless networks and other radio services operating on the same frequency. Signal fading and multipath interference can also cause the wireless network data speed to drop.

To reduce interference, try to shift the access point to a different channel at least six steps away from the original channel. For example, if you're currently using Channel 2, try shifting the access point to Channel 7. This requires access to the access point, so it's normally something that only a network administrator can do.

If the wireless network is overloaded because too many users are online at the same time, add more access points that use different channels.

If the data transfer speed between the access point and a single network client is slow, try changing the network adapter's speed from "automatic" to 5.5 MHz, or even 2 MHz. This seems counterintuitive—how can you improve transfer speed by reducing it?—but it can work because a transmitter using a high-speed link will resend each packet until the receiver acknowledges that it has received a clean copy. If the signal is extremely weak, or the environment is noisy, that could require multiple tries for each packet, which means it will take several times as long to move on to the next packet. When you reduce the transmission speed, each packet is easier to understand, so the network might not have to keep repeating them.

Can I Improve Performance with an External Antenna?

As a rule of thumb, an external antenna will improve the signal strength of a wireless network signal by about 15 percent or more, because it can be placed in a position free of obstructions to the signal path. The external antenna can be attached to either the access point (in which case it will increase signal strength to every network client) or to a wireless network adapter. If you can place external antennas on both ends of the link, the total improvement will be about 32.5 percent.

This assumes that the captive antenna and the external antenna have exactly the same characteristics. If the external antenna is directional, or if it has more gain than the captive antenna, the performance improvement could be even greater. On the other hand, many network adapters and access points use two captive antennas in a "diversity" system that constantly compares the signals from each antenna and selects the stronger one. In a noisy environment, a diversity antenna system might be more effective than a single antenna.

What Else Can I Do to Improve Performance?

Energy radiated from a transmitting antenna is often *polarized* in either the horizontal or the vertical plane, so a receiving antenna will detect a stronger signal from an antenna with the same polarity. In other words, if the transmitter uses a vertical antenna, the receiving antenna will detect a stronger signal if it is also vertical. If the transmitting antenna is horizontal, the receiving antenna should also be horizontal.

At short range, polarity won't make a significant difference to the performance of a wireless Ethernet link. Even if the two antennas have different polarity, they will still exchange signals that are strong enough to keep the data moving at full speed. However, when you are trying to squeeze every possible data bit out of a weak or noisy signal, you will see some improvement when both antennas are polarized the same way.

The captive antennas built into most PC Card adapters are difficult or impossible to move without turning the whole computer on its side, but many access points have antennas mounted on swivels, so it's easy to move the antennas from a vertical to a horizontal position.

When I Move to a Different Access Point, the Adapter Loses the Connection

Wireless adapters are supposed to detect all nearby access points and automatically shift their association to an access point with a clean, strong signal. However, the transfers don't always work properly. Sometimes, an adapter will just drop the network connection when the signal from the nearest access point fades out. If that happens, try shutting down the wireless link and restarting it (unplug your wireless card and plug it back in), or try rebooting your computer.

Where Can I Find a Copy of the 802.11b Standards?

IEEE standards are written by engineers for other engineers, so they don't make particularly exciting reading. However, they are the defining documents for wireless

Ethernet networks, so you might want to take a look at them. They're available online from http://standards.ieee.org/reading/ieee/std/lanman.

How Can I Find Out Who Made My Network Adapter?

In spite of the labels on the packages, many wireless network adapters and access points are private-label versions of some other company's products. It's often much easier for a company to add wireless products to its catalogs by buying them from somebody else rather than creating and building its own designs.

Some companies that sell private-label versions of adapters and access points might tell you who made them, but many salespeople will insist that they make everything themselves, and even if they don't, they stand by the warranty, so why should you care?

As a user or network manager, the name of the original equipment manufacturer (OEM) should not make any difference to you, as long as the devices carry Wi-Fi certification. If it has passed the Wi-Fi tests, you can assume that it will work reasonably well with the other equipment in your network.

Sometimes, though, it helps to know what's inside that sealed PC Card package. If you're using the adapter with a computer running Unix or Linux, the manufacturer's tech support people might not know where to find the right drivers and configuration tools for their devices; but when you know whose components are inside, you can find the drivers on your own. As a network manager, it can be useful to know which adapters are identical to the ones you're already using, so you can keep a few spares on hand that will work with the existing drivers in your users' computers.

So how do you find the name of the original manufacturer? You'll have to do your own detective work. Every piece of electronic equipment sold in the United States that can emit radio energy must carry a registration number issued by the Federal Communications Commission (FCC). This applies to radio transmitters, such as wireless network devices, and to most other computer components because they emit radio energy as a side effect of whatever function they're supposed to perform.

There is an FCC ID number on just about every wireless network device. For example, Figure 16.3 shows the label on a ZoomAir PC Card adapter. The FCC ID number is BDNWLANPCCARD11.

The FCC maintains a searchable database at http://www.fcc.gov/oet/fccid that lists every ID number, with links to copies of all the technical exhibits that the manufacturer supplied with their application for registration. Most of this information is boring technical stuff, but if you look around the exhibits, you can often find something that identifies the original manufacturer.

In this case, it's easy; the description of one of the test reports says "card is identical to Intersil card." This is the information you need to install the card on your Unix system; Intersil cards use the wi driver.

The FCC database is also a great tool for people like me who have a junk box full of old computer circuit cards that seemed important enough to save but don't have labels that explain what they were good for. The database maps each card to a listing with a description of the card and maybe even a copy of the user's

Figure 16.3: Every wireless network device has an FCC ID number on its label

manual. With a make and model number, it's usually possible to find a manufacturer's Web site that provides even more details.

Is the Software That Came with My Network Adapter or Access Point Up-to-Date?

The software supplied with wireless network adapters exists in two forms: programs that run on the computer connected to the adapter, and internal firmware that controls the adapter itself. All the software that runs on an access point is firmware.

The manufacturers of wireless networking hardware (and most other computer-related products) often issue new versions of the software that supports their products. Updated software might include fixes for bugs that were discovered after the product shipped, support for new operating systems, and additional features and functions such as improved encryption. It's always useful to check the manufacturer's Web site to see what might be available.

Installing new configuration and status programs is easy; just load the new software over the older version. In most cases, the manufacturer supplies the software in an executable file that automatically deletes earlier versions and runs a complete installation routine. It's always a good idea to read the README file or other instructions that are provided as part of the download package.

Updating firmware is more complicated. The manufacturer always includes detailed instructions, which you should follow as closely as possible. Before you update the firmware in an access point, remember to warn all your users that the network will be offline for maintenance.

How Can I Reduce the Drain on My Computer's Battery?

A radio transmitter converts electric power into radio signals, so the battery in a portable computer with a wireless adapter will run down much faster than the same computer without the adapter. Fortunately, there are a few things you can do to keep the power drain down to an absolute minimum.

First, disconnect the adapter when you're not using it. If you're on an airplane or a train or anywhere else where you're outside the range of a wireless signal, or if you're using the computer for some purpose that doesn't require network access, remove the PC Card adapter from its socket, or unplug the USB cable. If your computer has an internal wireless adapter, turn it off.

This is good advice for any plug-in device on a PC Card. If you're not using it, remove it. Modems, Ethernet adapters, and storage cards all consume power whenever they're plugged into the computer, so your battery will keep going longer if the socket is empty.

When you use your wireless network adapter, you can reduce power consumption by using the Power Saving Protocol that's part of the 802.11 specification. Someplace in the adapter's configuration utility, there's a set of power management options that can instruct the adapter to enter a power-saving mode:

- CAM (Constantly Awake Mode) consumes the most power and provides the fastest response. In this mode, the adapter is on all the time. It receives all incoming messages as soon as the access point gets them.

- PSP (Power Saving Protocol) mode consumes less power, but it also provides slower response. In PSP mode, the adapter instructs the access point to hold messages for this network node in a buffer, and it enters a low-power sleep mode. At regular time intervals (several times each minute), the adapter wakes up and polls the access point for messages. Because there's a delay between the time the access point receives each message and the time it sends the message on to the sleeping adapter, data and messages will take longer to move through the network.

Can I Use My Access Point as a Network Bridge?

An access point is a bridge between a wireless network and a wired LAN. If a single access point is not adequate to reach the entire area to be served by the wireless network, connecting additional access points to the wired LAN can extend the coverage area. A "wireless bridge," in which the wireless link connects two LANs together is a more specialized function.

Many access points offer wireless bridging as an option, but it's not part of the basic feature set. If you plan to use an access point as a bridge between networks, check the specifications before you buy it. Your best bet is to buy a separate wireless bridge rather than trying to jury-rig a generic wireless adapter.

I've Heard That Radio Signals from Cellular Phones Might Be Dangerous. What About Wireless Ethernet?

Some people believe the jury is still out on the safety of cellular telephones. Others are convinced that they're a serious health threat. Scientists and engineers have performed studies and published papers that claim to prove that extended use of a cell phone can — or can't possibly — cause cancer, make milk go sour, or have some other terrible effect. Human exposure to electromagnetic fields at the frequencies used by cell phones and wireless network adapters is within the levels that most organizations who have studied the matter consider to be safe. The dissenters believe that those levels are too high.

Even if you think cell phones are potentially dangerous, it's likely that the radios in wireless adapters are safer, for several reasons. First, when a cellular telephone is transmitting, it's just an inch or two from the user's brain, but a wireless adapter is probably a foot or more away (even though they're called "laptops," most people use them on a table rather than on their laps). The effect of non-ionizing radiation (a fancy name for radio waves) decreases at a rate proportional to the square of the distance, so a transmitter located two inches from your brain will have about 36 times more effect on your body than a radio located a foot away, if both radio signals are equally strong at the antenna.

Second, the radio in a cell phone is 20 times more powerful than the radio in a wireless adapter (0.60 watts vs. 0.03 watts), so the intensity of the signal is more than 700 times stronger.

And finally, the effect of radio frequency radiation on organic matter is cumulative — the longer the body is exposed to radiation, the greater the effect. Most cell phones transmit a continuous signal as long as the connection is active, but wireless LANs are bursty services that are only active when they are actually transmitting data. This means that the total amount of transmission time for a wireless adapter is just a fraction of the time that a cell phone is active.

Therefore, the total amount of radiation your body receives from a wireless network adapter is just a tiny fraction of the amount you receive from a cell phone. There are plenty of other, more serious threats to your health and safety.

But is a Wi-Fi signal absolutely safe? It's too soon to know what the cumulative effect over 20 or 30 years will be, so nobody can make that kind of absolute statement. But all the evidence says that they probably won't do you any serious harm.

INDEX

I

W

X

Y

Z

Z-Com adapters, *125*
ZoneAlarm, 210
zoning ordinances, 41
ZoomAir access point, 58
ZoomAir adapters, *125*
ZoomAir Model 4103, 167, *168*

STEAL THIS COMPUTER BOOK 3
What They Won't Tell You About The Internet

by WALLACE WANG

This offbeat, non-technical book looks at what hackers do, how they do it, and how readers can protect themselves. The third edition of this bestseller adopts the same informative, irreverent, and entertaining style that made the first two editions a huge success. Thoroughly updated, this edition also covers rootkits, spyware, web bugs, identity theft, hacktivism, wireless hacking (wardriving), biometrics, and firewalls.

"If this book had a soundtrack, it'd be Lou Reed's Walk on the Wild Side."
— InfoWorld

2003, 464 PP, $24.95 ($37.95 CDN)
ISBN 1-59327-000-3

THE ART OF INTERACTIVE DESIGN
A Euphonious and Illuminating Guide to Building Successful Software

by CHRIS CRAWFORD

Renowned author Chris Crawford demonstrates what interactivity is, why it's important, and how to design interactive software, games, and websites that work. Crawford's mellifluous style makes for fascinating and idea-inspiring reading that encourages you to think about design in new ways.

2002, 352 PP., $29.95 ($44.95 CDN)
ISBN 1-886411-84-0

THE LINUX COOKBOOK
Tips and Techniques for Everyday Use

by MICHAEL STUTZ

Over 1,500 step-by-step Linux "recipes" cover hundreds of day-to-day issues, including printing; managing files; editing and formatting text; working with digital audio; creating and manipulating graphics; and connecting to the Internet.

2001, 402 PP., $29.95 ($44.95 CDN)
ISBN 1-886411-48-4

THE BOOK OF OVERCLOCKING

Tweak Your PC to Unleash Its Power

by SCOTT WAINNER AND ROBERT RICHMOND

If you don't mind voiding the manufacturer's warranty on your CPU, overclocking is for you. Learn how not to fry your system while souping up everything from the Pentium II to the latest Athlon XP and Pentium 4. Sections on cooling, troubleshooting, and benchmarking make sure you get the most out of your machine.

2002, 304 PP., $29.95 ($44.95 CDN)
ISBN 1-886411-76-X

THE SOUND BLASTER LIVE!™ BOOK

A Complete Guide to the World's Most Popular Sound Card

by LARS AHLZEN AND CLARENCE SONG

Configure your hardware; watch DVDs in surround sound; record and organize digital audio MP3s; and use sequencers, MIDI, and SoundFonts to compose music. The CD-ROM includes music and audio examples, sample sound clips, SoundFonts, and audio software.

2002, 504 PP., $49.95 ($74.95 CDN)
ISBN 1-886411-73-5

PHONE:

1 (800) 420-7240 OR
(415) 863-9900
MONDAY THROUGH FRIDAY,
9 A.M. TO 5 P.M. (PST)

FAX:

(415) 863-9950
24 HOURS A DAY,
7 DAYS A WEEK

EMAIL:

SALES@NOSTARCH.COM

WEB:

HTTP://WWW.NOSTARCH.COM

MAIL:

NO STARCH PRESS
555 DE HARO STREET, SUITE 250
SAN FRANCISCO, CA 94107
USA

Distributed in the U.S. by Publishers Group West

UPDATES

Visit **http://www.nostarch.com/?wifi** for updates, errata, and other information.